MAN ENOUGH

Fathers, Sons, and the Search for Masculinity

Frank S. Pittman III, M.D.

D0167769

A Perigee Book

A Perigee Book
Published by The Berkley Publishing Group
A member of Penguin Putnam Inc.
375 Hudson Street
New York, NY 10014

The Penguin Putnam Inc. World Wide Web site address is
http://www.penguinputnam.com

Library of Congress Cataloging-in-Publication Data
Pittman, Frank S., 1935–
   Man enough : fathers, sons, and the search for
masculinity / Frank S. Pittman III.
       p.   cm.
   Originally published: New York : G. P. Putnam's Sons,
© 1993.
   "A Perigee book."
   Includes bibliographical references (pp. 296–301) and
index.
   ISBN 0-399-51883-5
   1. Masculinity (Psychology)   2. Men—
Psychology.   I. Title.[BF692.5.P58   1994]   94-11093
155.3'32—dc20   CIP

Printed in the United States of America
                7   8   9   10

dedicated to:

FRANK SMITH PITTMAN
10/3/1886–3/30/1946

FRANK SMITH PITTMAN, JR.
10/4/1908–9/27/1982

FRANK SMITH PITTMAN IV
10/6/1962–

and

LT. FRANK PITTMAN RUTTER, USN
8/18/1959–6/20/1985

ACKNOWLEDGMENTS

I've not been alone in my life as a man. I don't know how Betsy, my beloved, magnificent wife of thirty-two years, has lived with me as I've struggled with my masculinity and then obsessed over this book about it. I'm a lucky man, and I hope a day never goes by in which I don't remind her that I know it.

Two of our strong and nurturing grown children, Frank and Ginger, have been living with us for the past year or two while going to graduate school, and that has been heavenly. Our equally heavenly older daughter, Tina Pittman Wagers, is a family therapist in Boulder, Colorado. She has been a collaborator on other work, and a frequent consultant on this book. My wizardly son-in-law, Ken Wagers, has been the technical consultant on my frequently baffling computer

My niece, Virginia Rutter, as Director of Media Relations of the American Association for Marriage and Family Therapy, is professionally dedicated to explaining and promulgating family therapy ideas in the media. She is like a daughter to me, is one of my best friends, and has been my trusted reader and permanent feminist critic.

I've consulted often with the other men in my family: Jim Brawner, Jr., my inspiring eighty-nine-year-old father-in-law; Jim Brawner III, my loving, steadying brother-in-law; Ned Fox, my sister Joanna's wise and amused new husband. My stalwart band of nephews round out as fine a male chorus as any man could want: Paul Rutter, Harrison Rutter, Mike Valentine, Jimmy Brawner IV, Jim Namnoum, John Semple.

They're great playmates, too. And while I was writing this book, two new guys arrived in the family, Spencer Namnoum and Drew Semple. And there are more yet to come.

I've used every one of my friends, colleagues, and patients to help me understand the obsession of masculinity, and all of them are likely to find themselves somewhere in these pages.

The Men's Institute of the American Family Therapy Association has been a secure sanctuary for me. They were there with a manly shoulder to cry on during the hard times when it was not politically correct in my field to be concerned with the plight of men.

And I especially want to acknowledge the guys at the club with whom I work out. I want to thank them all for their openness with me. I love those guys. I feel far closer to each of them since we've been through this together. But then, since I've lived this life as a man, and written about it, I feel close to everybody.

I haven't even had to write alone. I've been lucky to have great editors. Rich Simon has edited my movie column in *The Family Therapy Networker* for the past ten years—it's been a stimulating collaboration and *Blutbrüdershaft*. And, over the years, he has pushed me to reveal entirely too much of myself in various longer *Networker* articles about men and masculinity. Stephanie von Hirschberg elicited my *New Woman* advice column for men, has made me simplify and direct my messages, and has helped me reach a totally new audience. She has respected my man's voice in a woman's magazine.

But this book really owes its life to its editor, Laura Yorke, who had read my other writings and was determined that I would write about life as a man. She has kept me coherent and structured and fired up every step of the way.

CONTENTS

INTRODUCTION

Men Without Models

Men weren't really the enemy—they were fellow victims suffering from an outmoded masculine mystique that made them feel unnecessarily inadequate when there were no bears to kill.
—Betty Friedan, quoted in
The Christian Science Monitor

I once treated Gym, a powerful businessman who came to see me because he felt like a failure. Gym had recently donated money to his old school to endow an athletic building in the name of his dead father, a famous athlete who had run off with another woman when Gym was a kid, and whom Gym rarely saw after that.

Gym's father had told him that a "real" man was never satisfied with second place, so Gym struggled aggressively at sports, despite his small size and many injuries. But his father never came to his games. Gym's father told him that a "real" man never let any other man see him sweat. Gym was always the boss. No other man had ever seen him vulnerable or unsure of himself.

Gym's father had told him that "real" men don't let their wives control them. Gym, like his father, had been married three times and had been unfaithful to all three wives, but he felt only lonely, guilty and foolish. Gym had even become the sort of father his father had been, and had humiliated his children when they didn't excel, but they had rebelled and become an embarrassment.

Now Gym had built this monument to his father's name, and he still didn't feel that he had become the man his father would respect as a son. He wanted to find some peace in life and couldn't until his father dubbed him a MAN. For a lifetime he had been hungry for a father, and he was trying to hire me as a father to tell him that he was indeed man enough.

Gym feels alone with his fragile, overblown masculinity. He can't get close to a man, he can't love a woman, he can't relax. What he does not know is that other men feel much the same way.

While I work in my practice with men who are rich and miserable, I also consult with an enlightening and controversial project through Atlanta's municipal court. Judge Clinton Deveaux has worked with family therapist Susan Adams to provide family therapy instead of fines or incarceration for young first offenders. Judge Deveaux and Ms. Adams work with these confused kids and their dedicated, overwhelmed mothers, and find that the bulk of young men and boys who get into trouble are suffering severe deficiencies of fathering. A father might show up to make a macho display in punishing a boy or getting him out of trouble, but there isn't likely to be any fatherly nurturing. All over the society, as family life crumbles and fathers desert their sons, the violence rate soars.

Not surprisingly, family therapy, which encourages responsibility rather than protecting people from consequences, is usually startlingly effective in dealing with these beleaguered families, and the recidivism rate drops dramatically. But just as expectably, the renegade fathers who feel called upon to act like dads may run in terror from the job, or fight back viciously. They didn't get enough fathering themselves to pass any on. Their lives are dedicated to making themselves feel man enough, and they fear having to give any of their hard-won masculinity back, even to their own sons.

A few men without models turn out to be tycoons, but most turn out to be streetfighters, and there is not a whole lot of difference. Neither may be fit for family life. Men fight for turf and wrestle for control over people and things, whether through war, armed robbery, or corporate takeovers. They are trying to feel like men, but no matter what they do, they never seem to feel "man enough."

The Masculine Mystique

But what is masculinity? Simply, it is what we expect of men. It's those qualities and activities that men think will make them men, that will distinguish them from women, i.e., "balls." Masculinity poet Robert Bly speaks of male strength as "fierceness." When masculinity is overripe, it becomes "machismo," a word that may derive from the Greek word for "battle" or the Spanish word "machete." Clearly, masculinity is not always a kind and gentle concept.

Masculinity is a cultural concept. We like to think of masculinity as natural, and there are slight measurable differences between the statistically average boy and the statistically average girl, but the differences are not enough to base a gender on. Norman Mailer, in *Cannibals and Christians,* points out that "masculinity is not something given to you, something you're born with, but something you gain. . . . And you gain it by winning small battles with honor."

Masculinity is "an artificial state, a challenge to be overcome, a prize to be won by fierce struggle." So says David Gilmore in *Manhood in the Making,* after he examined the ways in which boys become men in various cultures. Gilmore tries to define what it takes to be a man, what the puberty rituals attempt to instill in boys. He says, "To be a man in most of the societies we have looked at, one must impregnate women, protect dependents from danger, and provision kith and kin . . . Manhood is a kind of male procreation; its heroic quality lies in its self-direction and discipline, its absolute self-reliance." Gilmore tells us that the Fox tribe of Iowa considers being a real man "The Big Impossible." No man who sets out to achieve total masculinity can ever be man enough.

Masculinity is supposed to be about protection of the family, but the pursuit of this Big Impossible can lead men to escape domesticity and the power of women. Men can't always do what a man's gotta do to *feel like* a man and still do what a man's gotta do to *be* a man.

Masculinity varies from time to time and place to place. But it doesn't exist just in the mind of a single guy: it is shared with the other guys. It is a code of conduct that requires men to maintain masculine postures and attitudes (however they are defined) at all times and in all places. Masculinity includes the symbols, uniforms, chants, and plays that make this the boys' team rather than the girls' team. It is a fulltime job.

Masculinity is a group activity. As a guy develops and practices his masculinity, he is accompanied and critiqued by an invisible male chorus of all the other guys, who hiss or cheer as he attempts to approximate the masculine ideal, who push him to sacrifice more of his humanity for the sake of his masculinity, and who ridicule him when he holds back. The chorus is made up of all the guy's comrades and rivals, his buddies and bosses, his male ancestors and his male cultural heroes—and above all, his father, who may have been a real person in his life, or may have existed only as the myth of the man who got away.

Masculinity is different for each generation. My male chorus is different from my father's or my son's or my nephews'. My son can hear my voice, as I hear my father's, but there are other voices there, too. Many of our voices come from our culture. My father was born at the same time as John Wayne and Jimmy Stewart, while Teddy Roosevelt was in the White House. I was born under FDR, the same year as Woody Allen and Elvis Presley. I grew up in small towns in Alabama and Georgia, coming of age when Harry Truman was president, John Wayne was on the big screen, and my father was somewhere in the Pacific being masculine, fiercely battling the Japanese. Many of the voices in my chorus are shared with the other boys who came of age in those days. My son, born under Jack Kennedy, dates from the same year as Tom Cruise. The models of masculinity have changed through the years, but few of us can drown out the incessant chant of our macho choir. And for most of us, it is ordering us to pump ever more intense levels of masculinity, however masculinity is defined.

Masculinity is supposed to be passed on from father to son. Women, no matter how wonderful, no matter how loving, can't teach it to us. If we don't have fathers, we should have grandfathers, uncles, stepfathers to raise us from boys into men. If we don't have men in our family, then our need for mentors begins early. If the males we know are the other teenaged boys or the macho heroes from the movies, we may get a distorted, exaggerated concept of masculinity.

Masculinity becomes a problem when men, and women, venerate and exaggerate all that is masculine, i.e., the *masculine mystique.* Civilization, for some millennia now, has been a predominantly male affair, and men deserve most of the credit and most of the blame for what we have done to ourselves, to one another, and to the world, as we strive to tame nature and leave our mark on all we survey. The men who are messing up their lives, their families, and their world in their quest to feel man enough are not exercising true masculinity, but a grotesque exaggeration of what they think a man is. When we see men overdoing their masculinity, we can assume that they haven't been raised by men, that they have taken cultural stereotypes literally, and that they are scared they aren't being manly enough. They are in the throes of the *masculine mystique.*

Why do men love their masculinity so much? Because men have been trained to sacrifice their lives for their masculinity, and men always know they are far less masculine than they think they should be. Women, though, have the power to give a man his masculinity or take it away, so women become both terrifyingly important and terrifyingly dangerous to men. It's all quite crazy, but this, too, is a part of the *masculine mystique.*

In order for men, women, and society to come to grips with the toxic levels of masculinity we continually witness, we need to undertand how men become men: not only how they develop their masculinity, but also how they can get carried away with the *masculine mystique.*

A Roomful of Men

Recently I was in a men's group. A group of male ther-apists whom I'd never met, but who have become increasingly sensitive to these issues, spent a day together trying to define masculinity and to compare our struggles with it. We knew that what we have in common is not any sort of male power such as the feminist literature attributes to us. Nor is it our heterosexuality—the gay men and celibate men in the group go through the same things. It is not even the presence of the penis (a friend of mine lost his to cancer, and is no less a man) or the Y chromosome (I've seen genetic females raised as males, and they share the same experience, while genetic males raised as females go through life with the comparable but quite dif-ferent struggle with the demands of being a woman).

What we men share is the experience of having been raised by women in a culture that stopped our fathers from being close enough to us to teach us how to be men, in a world in which men were discouraged from talking about our masculinity and questioning its roots and its mystique, in a world that glorified masculinity and gave us impossibly una-chievable myths of masculine heroics, but no domestic models to teach us how to do it. So we grew up constantly faking our masculinity, and never knowing quite how much masculinity would be enough. We've all been, to varying degrees, male impersonators—awed by the splendor of the masculine mys-tique and ashamed of the meager masculinity we found in ourselves.

Whenever I talk about masculinity, I think of my nephew, Frank Pittman Rutter, who was like a son to me. He was a navy top gun and flight instructor who was killed when his plane went up in a puff of smoke over Meridan, Mississippi.

He radioed that he couldn't control the plane, but he stayed in it and went down, heroically, "like a man."

As I try to understand this masculine mystique for which men are trained to sacrifice their lives, I'm really asking myself why Pitt had to die.

We're all struggling with the same forces, and when we come together and share the universality of this struggle, we can feel whole and connected, perhaps for the first time, and our isolation ends.

As always in these groups, our stories sound alike, and as always we quickly get past talking about our confusion with women and then we grow closer as we talk about fatherhood. Most of us have felt barriers between ourselves and our fathers and had thought that going it alone was part of what it meant to be a man. We tried to get close to our children when we became fathers, and yet the business of practicing masculinity kept getting in the way. We men have begun to talk about that.

In this group there was one man who was devoting himself to his children, who were dying of a congenital disorder. He knew they would never grow up, he knew he was not working toward their future but his, for his own development as a man and as a human being. He wanted to get as much out of fathering as he could while there was time, but his friends could not understand how he could devote his life to something so hopelessly impractical.

An older man had taken in his grown son, who had made a mess of his life and now wasn't working or functioning, just lying around pouting about his imperfect parenting. The father, choking on tears, realized his protections were doing more harm than good. He knew he must kick his son out. It devastated him to give up on the healing power of his paternal love. We could all see that this was an act of paternal love, too.

Another man was trying, with his male partner, to adopt a child, and the adoption people required that one of the two men give up his career to be a full-time parent. He quit working to wait for a child he would raise, and he realized he was having to give up most of what made him feel like a man in order to become a father. But he also knew that the ultimate experience of masculinity would come from being a father.

There was one man who had broken off relations with his family and, with his new wife, had decided not to have children, but to devote his life to finding and developing himself. He was his own pampered child. Of course, he had nothing to give to the group either.

Without the experience of learning to be a man and a father by hanging around with one of them, boys who want to become men have to guess at what men are like. Boys without fathers might know why their fathers aren't around, and if fathers are off at war, or at work, or at the ball game, or chasing women, boys can then assume that what men do is fight or work or play games with balls or sexy women. Or boys can assume that men, being "the opposite sex" from the women they do know, must be whatever women are not. Whatever the amateur male guesses about the nature of men who have no role in the family, it is not likely to prepare him well for his role as a family man.

There is a masculine shame in men who haven't fully felt the love and approval of their fathers. In Pat Conroy's epic *Prince of Tides*, Tom Wingo (Nick Nolte) as a boy was brutalized by his father, failed to rescue his mother from an awful marriage, couldn't prevent the rape of his mother, his sister, and himself, and had to be rescued by his older brother. Tom fakes it through life, working as a football coach, marrying and raising children but hiding from his mother and always feeling shame that he wasn't really a man. When the heroic older brother is killed, Tom shrinks from life until a therapist (Barbra Streisand) pulls forth the secret shame and frees him to become a "man," which in Conroy's sense is the rescuer and protector.

Tom has to rescue and protect his therapist from her awful husband before he feels man enough to go back home to his wife and children and life and work. *The Prince of Tides* exposes the secret shame men feel when they have not been anointed by their fathers, when they don't find heroism inside themselves, when they can't reveal to one another how inadequate they feel, and when they are dependent upon women who don't understand their secret inadequacies.

Men without models don't know what is behind their shame, loneliness, and despair, their desperate search for love, for affirmation, and for structure, their frantic tendency to compete over just about anything with just about anybody. And even if they do know, as I did, that the pain is caused by the missing father, they don't know what they can do to ease the pain.

Clearly, they could recover somewhat by turning to other men for love and support, but their culturally demanded homophobia might stand in the way—we've been told it is "queer" for men to need the love of other men. An even more productive way for these fatherless men to recapture the lost father-child bond would be to throw themselves headfirst into raising their own children. If they don't have children of their own, there are plenty of underfathered children and adults available to receive their efforts at nurturing.

This book is not only about the plight of men who didn't

get the fathering they needed to make them comfortable with their masculinity, but is also about the healing power for men in rediscovering the forgotten profession of fatherhood.

Man Enough: Fathers and Sons and the Search for Masculinity has been painful and enlightening for me to write, and it has taken a while. I've been obsessed with it since Pitt's death in 1985. For the last few years, masculinity has dominated my conversation with my friends and family, the therapy I have done with my patients, the workshops I have given around the country and abroad.

The struggle to be a man that is presented here is not a clinical oddity: it is the norm. It is, of course, my own struggle as much as it is any man's, so much of the book is my often embarrassing autobiography.

The men in this book come not only from my family and my life, but from the lives of the men I have seen in my practice over the past thirty years, men under the sway of the *masculine mystique,* men who try to be "man enough" to win the love of women and the acceptance of men, and even a measure of heroism in the world, but who overdo their approximation of masculinity in a way that can become pathological. I have disguised the names and identities of the men who have been my patients and have even merged their stories, but I have gone ahead and used the real names of my family and some of my friends who did not mind being identified in the book.

I learn much from the movies about what is going on in the society, and specifically, what are the cultural norms for masculinity. In its effort to achieve universal popularity, cinema has become an important cultural artifact, our modern pipeline into the collective unconscious of myth.

Like everybody else who writes about men and masculinity, I talk much about mythology in this book. In my practice,

I have been a pragmatist and hard-nosed, no-nonsense realist. I never felt particularly influenced by Carl Jung, who spurred psychology's interest in the "collective unconscious." When I talk about mythology, I don't mean anything mystical: I mean only a story that connects with something inside us, a story that has a deep meaning for many people. Myths don't have to be old or fantastic or untrue: religion, literature, comic strips, TV, and especially movies present myths that enter our culture. Men's language has not been sufficient to explain masculinity, but men's myths have been able to communicate the meanings of men's lives. The meaning that is lost in the words can be found in the stories.

For the past two years, I've written a monthly advice column for men in *New Woman* magazine. A few of these stories have been told before in my "Not For Men Only" column.

Section I of this book is *The Obsession of Masculinity*. It begins with Chapter One on "Masculinity: The Secret Passion of Men," i.e., men's love affair with their masculinity, and how that messes up their lives. I describe some of the men in my practice, and how much they sacrifice to the *masculine mystique*. Chapters Two, Three, and Four are about three common varities of *masculopathy*, the pathological masculinity that I see in my practice, in the world, and sometimes in myself: "Philanderers," "Contenders," and "Controllers."

Section II is *Becoming a Man*. It is an effort to understand how masculinity develops. Chapter Five describes what it is like for a boy "Growing Up Male," and how a boy's masculinity is affected by his relationships with his mother, his father, his buddies, his changing body, his attempted sexual partners, his mate. I then describe, from my own experience, some of the problems a boy has growing up without enough fathering in that increasingly common predicament of having little or no intimate domestic model of masculinity.

Chapter Six, "Father Hunger," is an examination of the changing relationships between fathers and sons in our world, as patriarchy wanes and fathers grow increasingly confused about their function in family life. It looks at the history of patriarchy, the functions of fathers in patriarchal families, and the roles of fathers now. It also looks at our changing mythology about fathers.

Chapter Seven, "Mother Love," looks at mothers and sons, and at how the loss of fathers in family life makes men so frightened of women that they might bash their mothers, betray their wives, neglect their daughters, and run from commitment to any of them.

Chapter Eight, "The Brotherhood of Boys," explains the roots of male bonding, the importance of the other guys in the lives of men, and how a man's buddies bolster and direct his masculine strivings, and keep him from overloading his relationship with his mate.

Chapter Nine looks at our "Myths of Heroes," our bigger-than-life models of masculinity that can inspire boys and men to overcome their narcissism and make a contribution to their world. When fathers lose their importance as models in the lives of their sons, heroes may take their place, but may seem so dauntingly powerful they may overwhelm rather than inspire. Changing images of heroes in the movies over the past half century reflect our changing models of masculinity.

But man's truly heroic gesture is the self-achieved submission of his masculinity, submitting it to the relationships with his teammates, with his partner, and especially with his children—subjects which encompass the last section of the book.

Section III is my best advice on *Being a Man*, i.e., how a man can move past the puberty ritual of *proving* masculinity into the real life of *practicing* masculinity.

Chapter Ten looks at "A Man Among Men," and at how our masculine competitiveness training and homophobia separate us even from the other guys who could understand the crippling costs of our masculinity. The chapter reveals how a man can become a "man among men"; how a man comes to feel safe and secure in intimacy with his fellows. It offers models for masculinity that center on teamwork and emulation, striving *with* the other guys rather than striving *against* them.

Chapter Eleven examines "Mating With a Woman." It explores how masculinity training becomes a barrier to intimacy, equality, and monogamy with a woman. This chapter offers models of masculinity based on letting go of the fear of women and the need for male supremacy that is the hallmark of male shame. The chapter encourages the manly goal of equality and intimacy with a female partner, and explains how an equal relationship with a woman can make him feel man enough.

And Chapter Twelve looks at "Life As Father," and the culmination of masculinity, as he passes on to children what he has learned from being a man among men and an equal partner to a woman. The chapter reveals what a man gets from being a father, how he gets to raise himself as he raises his sons and daughters and whoever else he is lucky enough to raise, how he gets to understand and forgive his parents as he becomes one, and why fathering is a practically indispensable part of becoming a man.

I

THE OBSESSION OF MASCULINITY

ONE

Masculinity: The Secret Passion of Men

What a piece of work is man! how noble in reason! how infinite in faculty! in form and moving how express and admirable! in action how like an angel! in apprehension how like a god! the beauty of the world! the paragon of animals! And yet, to me, what is this quintessence of dust?
—Shakespeare: *Hamlet*

Macho does not prove mucho.

—Zsa Zsa Gabor

If I were to fully experience the masculine mystique, I would have to risk my life, "like a man." The opportunity to do so arose recently. I was teaching in New Zealand and took part in the up-to-date version of a puberty ritual from the New Hebrides. I bungee jumped, throwing myself 143 feet off a bridge into a raging river with a rubber band around my ankles. As I risked my life to prove my masculinity to whatever doubters lingered in my male chorus, as I suffered through this terrifying, undignified, and not completely comfortable exercise in adolescent idiocy, I knew this was nuts, but once I was on the bridge I was too frightened of humiliation to turn back. On my way down, watching my laughing wife take pictures of me, I felt very foolish and very sad that it was necessary for me to go through this, and I imagined a little headline on the obituary page saying: "Elderly Psychiatrist Succumbs to Puberty Ritual." As I crawled out of the canyon, I wondered which side of puberty I was on now. I felt both more of a boy and more of a man.

The great passion in a man's life may not be for women or men or wealth or toys or fame, or even for his children, but for his masculinity, and at any point in his life he may be tempted to throw over the things for which he regularly lays down his life for the sake of that masculinity. He may keep this passion secret from women, and he may even deny it to himself, but the other boys know it about themselves and the wiser ones know it about the rest of us as well.

Men go through life struggling with what they believe to be the demands of their masculinity. They try to be what they think a man would be, and they may make a tolerable approximation of masculinity. They may compare themselves to the myths of masculine heroes, and find themselves lacking, and give up on the struggle to be masculine. They may run from masculinity and become feminine instead, or just go through life as a boy, terrified of becoming a man. Or they may exaggerate whatever they think men are or should be.

Their hypermasculine display may become so excessive that they become monsters of machismo, unable to function at home, or at work, or even on the streets, frantically proving their masculinity and never letting it relax. The men who most strongly exhibit these syndromes seem to be unfamiliar with noncompetitive comradeships with other men in which both can display their vulnerability, and cooperative equal relationships between men and women in which both feel a full range of emotions and can talk about them. Perhaps these men had fathers that ran away, in one way or another, leaving their sons with a boy's myths of masculinity, and a belief that men become men by escaping Mama.

Masculinity on the Hoof

Like all men, I've been studying masculinity for a lifetime. But in the last few years, I've even been studying masculinity in motion. Under the tyranny of my triathlete son and my distance-running daughters, I finally stopped my three-pack-a-day cigarette habit and began to work out for the first time in my life.

I went to the exercise room in the basement of a club to which I belonged. There I found machines with which to wrestle, but I also found a repository of raw masculinity: high school wrestlers and college football players, middle-aged Republican millionaires and ex-jocks, who work as malpractice lawyers and orthopedic surgeons, Cadillac dealers and real estate developers, men with hair on their chests and on their backs, perhaps even on the soles of their feet and the palms of their hands—men who talk about sports and money and hunting and war, and compete with one another, and complain about women. These are not the sort of men who usually come to the offices of family therapists (they'd be more likely to drop off their wives or kids to get them fixed). These men live in a very real, concrete world; these are the winners of the various social and athletic contests that had scared me so in high school and college. They represent the purest examples of masculinity the society has to offer, i.e., good, strong, healthy, uncomplicatedly masculine men.

To my surprise, I did not find much pathologically exaggerated masculinity in the older guys: they don't need to be masculine impersonators; they are MEN. They good-naturedly put themselves down, complaining about their weakness even as they throw the barbells up and down like a yo-yo and about their poverty even as they trade in last year's Mercedes for the new one in the color their wife liked better, and even the best hung of them talk about their little peckers and their sexual insufficiencies. At every turn these guys figure out what is the masculine thing to do, and then they do it.

As they work out, there are intergenerational battles over the radio. The older guys prefer country music, with sad songs about men who've made a mess of their lives, but their bulky little pisscutter sons want heavy metal music loud enough to make grown men feel homicidal. Unpleasant sounds seem masculine to these kids. These men in the making strut around and scream encouragement to one another as they try to hurry through an excessive weight routine. When the average age drops much below thirty, it begins to feel like a scene from *Conan the Barbarian.*

I did not think I would fit in—as soon as I was alone in the weight room, I'd switch the radio to the classical station and work out to Mozart. I was careful not to compete with the men as I slowly tried to win their confidence. As I look back, almost a decade later, I find it strange how out of place I felt then. Now I feel totally at home and consider these guys among my closest friends. I don't have hair on my back yet, but to my surprise and delight, I'm getting enough muscles so that with my clothes off, I almost look like one of the guys.

When no one else is listening, some of the men might ask me about the world of feelings and relationships, and might tell me, directly or indirectly, of themselves—not just the older ones, with whom I have shared most of life's experiences, but even the younger guys who have myths of masculinity but no real experiences of testing out their beliefs.

At first I studied them with sympathetic but amused detachment; then I began to see their vulnerability and even their isolation and loneliness. I tried to feel superior, telling myself that I wasn't stuck in such a compulsively masculine posture. But as I studied the gender ideals that distort and pervert people of both genders, I came to see that I was one of the guys—more intellectual, more flexible about matters of gender, more self-conscious, perhaps, but not really different.

I've confessed to my workout buddies that I've been writing a book about men and masculinity, and I've been asking them lately to tell me what masculinity is. An enormous and extremely bright college football player joshed me by saying, "Masculinity is weighing about 235, benching maybe 475, and being able to go anywhere on the field you want to go." One of the even younger guys took him literally and said, "Masculinity is being able to control your turf. It's not size, it's aggressiveness." A younger boy, rather short but working out desperately, said, "Masculinity is being big." I asked, "Why big?" He said, "Because girls want guys that are big, at least the girls with good bodies do." I asked a fourth boy whether he agreed that masculinity was size, strength, and aggressiveness, and he didn't think so. He said, "I've known homosexuals who were big and strong and could beat your ass." The other boys agreed that only heterosexuals could be real men, but then they weren't too sure, and they were sorry that such an unpleasant topic had been brought up.

A wiry golfer thought masculinity was "having whatever clout it takes to get to the top of the tee-off list on the weekends." Several of the men thought that masculinity was "going the distance, like Rocky, whether you win or not." Several others spoke of "doing what you got to do without whining about it."

A pair of the wiser men began to debate. One had said that "masculinity is whatever you have to do to *look* like a man," while the other thought that "masculinity is whatever you have to do to *feel* like a man."

A former professional fooball player and trainer, a powerful man about my age but twice my size, said, "Masculinity is playing pro ball for sixteen years without a face guard." My Uncle Harry, who had won medals for his surgical stamina during World War II, had told me that "masculinity is operating for thirty-six straight hours under fire."

The strongest man in the club said he felt most like a man after he endured years of rigid discipline at Virginia Military Institute, but he continues to have nightmares about it. As he said this, I was admiring his masculinity, but for a quite different reason: after he lost his beloved eighteen-year-old son in an auto accident a few years back, he kept going, and just surrounded himself with young weight lifters who would emulate his strength and discipline. He is a mentor to hordes of imperfectly fathered boys, who follow his exercise and fitness routines.

The conversation soon got out of hand after someone asserted that a real man is someone who can eat quiche if he wants to, and several of the guys debated about what "real men" ate, and we all came up with memories of how we got a sense of our masculinity by drinking beer with shots of bourbon in it, and eating sausages so hot they raised blisters from entry point to exit. We talked of sitting at bars in our youths with the other guys eating pickled pig's knuckles, hard-boiled eggs, and other "men's food," i.e., salt and pepper floating in cholesterol. Even eating, for men, requires taking risks to show the other boys how tough we are.

As men grow older, their sense of masculinity changes, and preoccupation with physical strength gives way to preoccupation with emotional control and strength of character. One man, who had recently reconciled with his wife and suddenly felt very much in love with her, said, "Masculinity is doing what it takes to put a smile on a woman's face." He was the only grown man who even mentioned women. Most men have a far stronger passion for their masculinity than for their women, or even for their sexuality, but they try to keep that a secret.

Feminism and Masculinity

Carol Gilligan, Harvard psychosociologist and author of the crucial book on gender differences, *In a Different Voice*, speaks of the myth of Psyche, the beautiful princess who became the namesake for the human soul. Psyche had been forced to marry Cupid, who visited her only by night. Never having seen him, she came to think he was a hideous monster that she must kill, but she held up a light to him while he was sleeping and realized that he was a beautiful, vulnerable boy.

I'm not suggesting that all men are beautiful, vulnerable boys, but we all started out that way. What happened to us? How did we become the monsters of feminist nightmares? The answer, of course, is that we underwent a careful and deliberate process of gender training, sometimes brutal, always dehumanizing, cutting away large chunks of ourselves. Little girls went through something similarly crippling. If the gender training was successful, we each ended up being a half person.

Feminism has made me rethink what I thought I knew about gender. I used to think I was the very model of a liberated male, a fierce fighter for gender equality, and a man who had overcome the gender biases of our culture. When women would come into my office and complain about men, I had no idea that what they were saying applied to me, too. Then feminists in my field and in my family began to criticize me for not recognizing all the ways in which I was thinking just like a man, and failing to recognize ways in which women were getting a raw deal. I studied the feminist literature, and, as I did, I became firmly aware of two things. The first was that traditional gender training had limited women and had forced them into narrow, restrictive, and uncomfortable positions in life.

There are women who enjoy being girls and there are women who are angry about the limitations and unfairness of their gender roles. Some women are so angry about what they see as unequal power differentials between men and women that they deny having any power at all: they may assume men have taken their power and must give it back. Consequently, they emotionally mutilate any man they encounter, to get back at him for being so powerful.

Most women realize their femininity is an act they go into to control men without scaring them. They have to hide part of themselves behind the girlish performance. The feminine act is a position of considerable power but limited mobility.

The second thing I learned from the feminist literature was that traditional gender training was just about as limiting and crippling to men.

Men have been specialized and trained to sacrifice their emotions and even their lives for what they have been told is their duty as men. Men have been given few choices: men work. (In Edward Albee's play, A Delicate Balance, a woman explains to her daughter that men's "concerns are so simple, money and death, making ends meet until they meet the end.") Unlike women, most men have not questioned traditional gender arrangements. They have never thought about masculinity, other than to fear theirs is insufficient.

The majority of men I see in therapy feel they have less power than they are supposed to, are eager to please, and are helpless in the face of those emotions they have been stripped of. They may be baffled at the notion that they have more power than they should. Though few women realize it—and feminist literature doesn't convey this—men are both terrified and in awe of them. Men will shield themselves, violently at times, against the devastating power of female dissatisfaction with them. Displays of excessive masculinity are evidences that a man is afraid, threatened; that he does not feel as powerful as he believes he should be. Men who escape women, or seduce them, or silence them, or even beat and murder them are doing so not because they sadistically enjoy hurting a woman—a feminist stereotype of men's motives—but because they feel weak, burdened with a sense of imperfect masculinity.

Masculine Impersonators

How much masculinity is enough? How much masculinity is too much? In families in which there are both fathers and mothers, or at least both adult male and adult female members, children learn about gender from the interplay between the men and the women. When fathers are gone for whatever reason, little boys don't get to learn from watching real men leading a real life with real women. In adolescence, when boys are required by their peers to make a pronounced macho display, those without domesticated fathers may not realize that adolescent machismo is merely a rite of passage and not a way of life. Boys without models are likely to overdo the masculinity, like a masculine impersonator.

Carol Gilligan, in *In a Different Voice,* explained that the problem arises when women alone do the bulk of the child-raising, rather than dividing it between men and women, or doing it together. A mother raises her daughter in the expectation that the daughter's life will be much like her own, and that the daughter will remain in contact with the mother for advice and supervision in life as the needs arise. But a mother raises her son for a quite different life, one she does not and cannot fully know.

The mother must teach her son how to respect and follow the rules. She must teach him how to compete successfully with the other boys. And she must teach him how to find a woman to take care of him and finish the job she began of training him how to live in a family. But no matter how good a job a woman does in teaching a boy how to be a man, he knows that she is not the real thing, and so he tends to exaggerate the differences between men and women that she embodies.

If the boy becomes overprogrammed in the art of seduction, he may become a *philanderer,* reassuring himself that he is a man by escaping the woman at home and seducing the women away from home, thus winning double victories over the "opposite" sex. If he practices competition too compulsively, he may become a *contender,* seeing life as a contest with the other boys, in which only the winner of the most contests gets to be considered a man. And if he becomes too rule bound, he may become a *controller,* assuming it is his job to act like the boss and keep those around him under his control. All three varieties of masculopathy, pathologically overdeveloped masculinity, occur when the father is not around, not involved enough, and not sure enough of his own masculinity to tell the boy he's doing it all quite well enough and can cool down the masculine display. Each of the three syndromes of masculopathy cripples the boy in his efforts to mate, to live comfortably in a family, or even to live in peace and comfort with the world around him.

As we strive to be man enough, the world does not really penalize us for failing to live up to the masculine mystique, but for anxiously overdoing it.

Men Struggling to Be Men

> *Ever since man emerged from the dominance of nature, masculinity has been the most fragile and problematic of psychic states.*   — Camille Paglia, *Sexual Personae*

Each day in my office I see men in pain as they struggle against the restrictive bonds of their masculine mystique. Some of the men I see are masculopathic, in one or more of the three syndromes, but others are just trying to be the men they think they are expected to be, and in doing so make a mess of their lives and the lives of those around them. Their battle is not with their wives, not even with their mothers, as much as it is with their fathers—even if they haven't seen their fathers in years, or ever. These men seem locked into a struggle to somehow finally get their fathers to anoint them, and declare them men enough.

For example, here's a typical day in my practice:
8:00 A.M. Arch is a large, handsome man who grew up poor and fatherless in the black ghetto of Detroit. His father had been a semiprofessional baseball player, but had been brain damaged by a wild pitch, lingered on as an invalid for some years, and finally died. Arch's mother worked as a nurse, and

left Arch to grow up on his own. He was a good basketball player, and was athletic enough to get scholarships to college. He married young, to a strong, competent woman much like his mother. She was a physical therapist, making enough money to support them and their three children.

For years, Arch didn't make as much money as he spent on his trendy designer clothes and flashy cars. His wife tolerated such irresponsibility because she really loved his romantic nature. Arch was always around and he was fun. He also provided much of the childcare. She, too, had grown up without a father and she wanted her children to have one, whatever his deficiencies.

Still, Arch felt under pressure from somewhere inside himself to make money, so he took a job traveling. It paid fairly well, but he was on the road most of the time. When he came home, he felt the money he made was appreciated, but he didn't feel a part of the family anymore. He thought he might feel more important to his family if he brought in even more money, so when he was offered a job traveling to South America, he took it. He felt like he was man enough when he was out making money, but when he came home his family would complain that he was away too often. Arch didn't feel man enough when he was being fussed at. He could not tolerate conflict very well, and began to avoid coming home all together. He took up with other women, women who didn't know him very well and were impressed with him. He would spend money on them and tell them he was single. They weren't mad at him all the time like his wife was. As his wife learned more about Arch's secret life, she became less tolerant of him and the conflict became worse.

Recently, she presented him with an ultimatum. Either he must stop traveling and find a way to live at home with his family, or she will divorce him and take all his money. Either way he loses the money that gives him his sense of being a successful man. We met yesterday for him to decide what he wants to do. He is depressed, but he doesn't let anyone know how he feels. He spent the hour trying to charm me into liking him, despite the fact that he knows I think he's letting down everybody, especially himself. He still can't decide what to do, and the more pressure his wife puts him under, the deeper he sinks into depression. There is no way for him to be everything he thinks he should be as a man, and be everything his family thinks he should be, too.

9:00 A.M. Bart grew up in the country in a poor family. He had to leave school at fifteen when he "knocked up" the girl on the next farm and had to get married. He wasn't much good at school anyway, so his family decided it didn't matter. His father could barely read and write, but had ended up owning his own farm and preaching at his own church.

Bart's father always knew what was right, and did it. He had little tolerance for Bart's moral lapse, so even after Bart married the girl, his father would not relax his indignation. Bart ran away to the city and supported himself and his pregnant wife as a homosexual prostitute. He liked his work—his customers were nice to him, and before that he'd never had the experience of a man being nice to him. He sweetly and innocently offered his new wife's father a sexual favor for Christmas. That created an uproar. His wife's family broke up the marriage and would not let him see his baby daughter.

Bart married again, and tried to find other ways to support himself. In time, I found him in a public mental health clinic, reunited him with his daughter, and arranged with Vocational Rehabilitation for him to go to practical nursing school. He did well as a nurse, but recently, twenty-odd years after I first worked with Bart, he had had a heart attack, and was forced to stop working and go on disability. His wife brought him to see me because he was depressed. He just didn't feel good about himself unless he was doing something to get the approval of other men. I hadn't seen Bart in twelve or fifteen years, but he brought me a present—some old Mozart records he'd found at a garage sale. Bart knew how to please any man except his father. Unfortunately, his father was now dead, and Bart was going to have to handle this without him. He decided to try volunteer work at the Old Soldier's Home.

10:00 A.M. Since his parents' divorce and his father's remarriage, Chip had lived with his mother in Maine. His mother did not get her life together very quickly after her husband walked out on her, and her ex-husband still saw her as a bad influence on their only child. He had thought Chip was becoming rude and undisciplined, so he had sent him to military school in the ninth grade. To everyone's surprise, Chip loved it. He started working out, and over the past three years had built a weight-lifter's body, had become a powerful athlete, and a commanding military leader. He was splendidly disciplined all year long, and adored by his mother and all his grandparents, but his summers with his father and stepmother went badly. His father was an anxious little man who kept looking for traces in the boy of his mother. He would find things to criticize, and even to punish. Chip would get surly, and finally even openly hostile to both his father and his young stepmother. Chip's father thought maybe I could get him under control. When I saw the three of them together, the father explained that he had divorced his wife because he thought she was so unstable she made him nervous. But he had left his young son with her to keep her company. At that point, the stepmother jumped in to tell a story punctuating her predecessor's craziness. As the couple began to ridicule Chip's

mother, I thought Chip was going to come out of his chair
and throttle them both. A few sessions with Chip alone con-
firmed his anger at his father, and his protectiveness of his
mother. He was only seven when his father left, but since then
he has believed he was responsible for being the man in his
mother's life, her rescuer and defender. In the session yesterday,
I met with Chip and his father alone, and persuaded the father
to be more honest about the affairs he was having that led to
the breakup, about the various ways in which he had betrayed
his wife and his son, and about his defensiveness. He even
acknowledged the fear that his son would hate him for his
failures to be the man he should have been. The two guys
cried together and left with the father's arm on his giant son's
shoulder.

11:00 A.M. Doug is a man I have known for years. He
and his wife own the dry cleaners we use. We had watched
their children grow up behind the counter, and both of them
had done the family proud. Doug is a good man, honest,
cheerful, and helpful to a fault, always eager to replace broken
buttons or work a little harder on a stain. I never gave much
thought to it, but I certainly had no idea that Doug would
ever be unhappy. So it came as a surprise when he called for
an appointment. He came in and told me about the financial
disaster he was fearing. Now that the children were out of the
house, Doug's wife wanted a place in the country, but they
weren't making quite enough money. So Doug took out a big
loan and bought another location, which his older son could
run. The new store just didn't quite break even, and Doug
felt overextended emotionally and physically as well. He worried about his son, who was being frustrated by the business.
Doug's father's business had failed back when Doug was just
a child. His father had never recovered from the blow, had

sunk into a depression, and had committed suicide. Doug felt depressed now; he'd lost all interest in sex, avoided talking to his family, wasn't eating, and stumbled through his day with nothing to anticipate except sleep, if he could get any. He considered suicide, but knew he couldn't do anything that irresponsible. It bothered him horribly that he had not been able to set up his son in a successful business. But his greatest dread was telling the wife who had used up her life working beside him that he could not fulfill her dream of a place in the country.

1:00 P.M. Earl has sold his highly successful business and retired. His children have grown up and moved away. He and Elise, his wife of over forty years, are now alone. For all those forty years, Earl has been haunted by the fear that Elise did not love him. Shortly before they married, she broke their engagement and entered a strange and scandalous affair with an overtly unworthy man. Mercifully, the affair was brief, and soon thereafter she went back to Earl, married him, bore and raised his children, and remained faithful to him, as he has to her. But regularly for forty-five years, Earl has questioned her about various aspects of her affair with the man he refers to only as "the blackguard." And she has refused to answer his questions, since it seems to upset him so much. It has been a frustrating life for both of them. Earl's successes have meant little to him since he has not felt loved, and Elise has pondered leaving several times, but she really has no place else to go.

The couple, as they approach seventy, are still sexually active, but each time they have sex, Earl wonders whether Elise would prefer being with the blackguard. The couple has tried therapy before, off and on, and it has usually just stirred up more trouble. Elise insists she does not remember the details Earl is frantically seeking. Earl resents the fact that all the therapists they've been to quickly decide he is crazy, which I confessed was my reaction as well. How could a man waste a lifetime carrying on about something this insignificant?

Finally, I asked the question I assumed to be at the root of the problem: I asked Elise how big the blackguard's penis was. She could not remember after these forty-five years, and the sex had taken place in the dark, and she hadn't really looked too closely, etc. But the question opened up Earl's lifelong concern that his penis was so small that no woman could love him unless she had never experienced another man. Earl then told the horror story of his older brother's ridicule of him when he went through puberty late and not very impressively. Earl's emotions were fresh and intense, as if it were happening now, and Elise was gently reassuring. Her view of the situation is that she couldn't care less about comparative penises, but she has resented Earl's prissy self-righteousness and fussy control all these years, and she's glad she had at least a brief fling with "a man who didn't feel so goddam morally superior."

2:00 P.M. Fonville had been a wealthy bachelor in a small city near Atlanta, living well off the earnings of the truck dealership his father had left him. He mostly fished and played bridge with a group of men friends. He went out with women when the need arose, but he didn't really need a woman in his life until after his mother died. He was over forty when he married Fanny, a glamorous damsel in distress who had suffered at the hands of various mean or unpleasant husbands. Fanny was tall, dark, and exotically beautiful, especially when she got herself up in Chanel suits, at $3,000 each, or those even more expensive fantasy gowns she wore to the charity balls for the second wives of rich old men who wanted to break into Atlanta society.

Fonville just wanted to fish and play bridge as he always had, but Fanny wanted the social position her ne'er-do-well father had kept her from, and cost was no object. She designed and built the grandest of manor houses on an enormous country estate near the city, and Fonville threw money at her. But the mansion kept costing more than Fonville could afford, and every time he suggested cutting any of the frills, Fanny would pout and go to her room and lock the door. He was hurting Fanny's feelings, and his choices seemed to be to either give up the games he played with the other boys and actually spend time with Fanny as she said she wanted him to do, or keep shutting her up by stuffing money down her throat. Stuffing money was easier, at least until there was no more money he could take from his business or get from the bank. At that point he angrily refused to pay the builder any more money, and Fanny retaliated by getting into a flagrant affair with the young man. (In Atlanta society, women may have affairs with their builders or their tennis instructors without fear of criticism; they just may not wear the same dress twice.)

Fonville's feelings were hurt, though it wasn't clear whether he was more upset about losing Fanny or losing all the money he would have to pay to get out of his marriage. He was near bankruptcy and could see no end in sight. He kept thinking of his father's favorite song, "If you want to be happy for the rest of your life, never make a pretty woman your wife." As his father had told him so many times, "Son, ugly women do the same job for half the price." Fonville felt like a fool and didn't know what to do, other than just relax and accept whatever love he could get from this amazingly expensive woman, who was bleeding him dry but still turning him on. So each week, I see the couple again, and Fonville finds out what it would cost him to get laid this week. And I try another time to convince him that it might work better to throw himself at the woman he loved, rather than give away more of their financial security.

3:00 P.M. Garth is a successful plastic surgeon, and is his own best advertisement. He has had his nose and eyelids done, his love handles sucked, and little dots of hair stuck in rows all over his head. His mother wouldn't recognize him. And his wife, Grace, had been made equally bionically perfect, with sucked belly and thighs, and magnificent breasts pointing straight up to her perfectly molded new chin and cheeks. Their twin children, in braces and orthopedic shoes, were being made equally perfect. Garth makes lots of money, and the four of them used to go everywhere looking perfect.

But since Grace had the twins, she has gained weight in strange places, since the usual ones for normal fat to deposit had been sucked dry of fat storage cells. Consequently, she looked a little misshapen to Garth. It really didn't bother Grace much; she was so happy with her little family and the career for which she was going to graduate school. But Garth couldn't stand it. He kept picking on her, trying to tell her what to eat and how to exercise. She just seemed to get fatter. By the time the couple got to me, Grace was "fat" (perhaps twenty pounds over the ideal) and was miserable, not over the weight but because Garth was having temper tantrums and refusing to be seen in public with her.

Garth was beginning to be just like his father, although Garth insisted that his father had been out of shape and had never really made much of a living, and so the old man's efforts to control everyone around him were invalid. He, on the other hand, was physically perfect and financially successful, so he had the right to be bossy. Today I spent another hour with this couple trying to help Garth see that his father was mistaken about both the rights and the duties of men, and that while he had the right to make himself miserable in the pursuit of perfection, happiness comes not from getting everything right, but from accepting things as they are. He doesn't get it: his father's voice is still too strong.

4:00 P.M. Hank and Ian are a gay couple who have been together for almost ten years. Hank, a lawyer, is about forty and fell in love with Ian, a high school football coach, when the younger man was still in college. Both had given up heterosexual lives for their relationship; Hank had even given up a wife and two daughters. And the relationship between the two men has been good, though Ian from time to time would question whether this was the life he wanted, and would drift into affairs. Hank would always get him back, scurrying around frantically meeting all of Ian's needs while carrying on about all the sacrifices he has made for their marriage.

Ian, whose father had never been able to control his mother as much as he would have liked, could control Hank with ease. However, with the advent of AIDS, sleeping around with other men was out of the question. So as Ian approached thirty, he began to wonder whether he might like to marry a woman and have children. Hank offered his daughters for Ian to help raise, but they were practically grown and had little use for their self-absorbed stepfather. Ian pouted that he wanted a baby, his own child. His masculinity, which Hank worshipped, required it. Ian had found the one thing to want that even the resourceful but uterusless Hank could not provide. It looked as if Ian had won this round—he could be unhappy and Hank couldn't fix it, so like his hero Achilles he could repair to his tent to sulk, and with the mere sacrifice of his happiness could control the relationship.

*   *   *

5:00 P.M. Junior came in alone and miserable. He is a beautiful high school senior who had run away from home after a bad report card and another episode in the unending series of awful battles with Jeffrey, his father. Now he wanted to go back home but was afraid his father would ground him for a whole year. Jeffrey always threatened things like that.

Jeffrey, who worked hard and never made enough money, wasn't home much. When he was, he and his wife mostly just fought about Junior and debated whether they could afford to get a divorce. The mother wanted the father to be nice to the boy, but Jeffrey was outraged at such a suggestion. His father was a top sergeant and had never been nice to him, and he'd never messed up like Junior was doing, so why did Junior deserve love and approval? Jeffrey told his wife, "Why should I love Junior? Isn't he getting enough love from you already? I don't have any love to give. The only people who ever tried to love me either gave up or pissed me off somehow."

I'd been through all of this with this unhappy family before, but we always hit the same impasse: Junior wanted to be loved just for himself, whether he did things right or not, and Jeffrey saw that as encouraging weakness.

I called Jeffrey and told him I was sending Junior home to him, and Jeffrey agreed to negotiate some rules with the boy, but he insisted that he wasn't going to be nice to him until he straightened up, and Junior gave a look that insisted he wasn't going to straighten up until he felt loved. So I hugged the crying Junior and sent him home to face his punishment. And I'll meet with Jeffrey and try another time to convince him that men need love, too. Jeffrey knows he needs love, but he is so ashamed of it that it has never occurred to him that other men have the same needs as he.

*   *   *

At the end of the day, once a week, my longtime masseur, Rick, comes to my office. Rick grew up poor and black in Atlanta, and while his father was silent and grumpy, Rick was one of the few boys in the neighborhood with any father at all. He joined the Air Force and left home after high school, and married in England, swearing that he would do a better job as a father than his father had done. A series of medical disasters left his wife, with his two sons, back in England, where she can't leave the national health service and where he can't get a work permit. So he uses his enormous hands and gentle nature to relieve the stress of other men, while he can only send money to his children and hope to see them once a year. But he calls them once a week. I like to get my massage after he's just talked to his sons. Rick can pass on to me some male energy he feels from fathering, and I then can absorb more of the pain from all these shamed and lonely men who don't know how to feel man enough to do what they think it takes to be a man.

Men Need Love, Too

We have to help men find the missing parts of themselves, but first we have to soften the stranglehold of their masculinity training. It is possible to teach men a different model of masculinity, to free them from their shame and isolation, to share their vulnerability with other men, and even to go into a partnership with a woman. We can do it, but we have to keep several things in mind:

1. Masculopathic display indicates the man is frightened of his own inadequacy. The show of masculopathy is an

effort to scare off whoever is coming to measure his shortcomings.

2. Men who suffer from masculopathy cannot tolerate female anger. They will panic and run away or do something masculopathic, as if they think every angry woman is their mother come back to take their puberty away.

3. At the heart of the matter of masculine excess is a great longing for the love and approval of a father, a man who can tell another man that his masculinity is splendid enough and he can now relax.

Ultimately, we're not going to raise a better class of men until we have a better class of fathers, fathers who don't run out on the job. Our fathers didn't teach us how to live with our masculinity, and our mothers and our wives, no matter how hard they try, can't do it, either. So even if we remain terrified of women, we have to stop blaming them for what we've become, and stop expecting them to fix us.

We also need to consider what our passion for our masculinity is doing to ourselves, our buddies, and especially our sons. We can wait for our children to show us how to live with our masculinity, but we could also be bolstering one another's masculinity as father, as mentor, as brother, as Blood Brother, or just as teammate. And—let's be selfish—when we support and encourage other men, we are also bolstering ourselves. We are made whole by other men granting us our masculinity, dubbing us or anointing us or consecrating us "men." It is this act that we need to perform for one another; this is the heart of the men's movement.

And meanwhile, in families, in therapists' offices, in men's groups, and in the world, we must deal with the men whose masculopathy turns them from beautiful, vulnerable boys into PHILANDERERS, CONTENDERS, and CONTROLLERS.

TWO

Philanderers

"I've got those 'God-why-don't-you-love-me-oh-you-do-I'll-see-you-later' Blues"
—"Buddy's Blues" from *Follies* by Stephen Sondheim

What most wives don't realize is that their husbands' philandering has nothing whatever to do with them.
—Philip Barry, *The Philadelphia Story*

Perhaps half of the married men in our society have been unfaithful, or will be some day. Infidelity can take various forms—an accidental and uncharacteristic one-night stand; an overwhelming and disorienting passion that offers escape into fantasy from a reality that is coming on too strong; or a comfortably friendly adjunct to a marriage one can't get out of and can't get back into, either. Either men or women can have such affairs, but philandering is a special pattern—favored mostly by men—in which the compulsive, impersonal seduction of women reaffirms a man's flagging sense of his masculinity.

In the 1975 French film, *Cousin, Cousine,* Philanderer Guy Marchand complains about his wife. "She simply won't understand that a man has only one way to prove that he's a man, by sleeping with other women."

Philanderers require a steady change of sexual partners to protect themselves from making and keeping a commitment to just one person. They define masculinity in terms of sex (which doesn't make them oversexed but overgendered). They take gender and its stereotypes quite literally, and are uncomfortable in any situation in which they aren't displaying and even exercising the attributes of being a male. These gender attitudes and philandering pattern may come from the culture, or may come from the family, and are passed on from father to son, generation after generation.

Philanderers fear women. For a man who depends on women to define his masculinity, a woman is a dangerous and powerful foe. Philanderers handle their fear by believing that women are the "opposite" of men, are less important than men, and exist primarily to serve men in various ways, most crucially through sex.

For philanderers, masculinity is the determinant of status and security in life, the most important of virtues. Masculinity can be achieved in two ways—by competing with other men and by exerting sexual dominance over women. A man who is not defeating men and sleeping with women is not enhancing his masculinity and is losing status. The greatest loss of status would be to come under the control of a woman. Consequently, escape from female control is an affirmation of masculinity.

Philanderers may be hostile and cruel to women, using seduction to humiliate them, or they may be intimidated and frightened by women to such a degree that they use seductions to tame them. Even those who think they like women, and are friendly in their seductiveness, can depersonalize women by treating them as if they were replaceable and exchangeable. These men may have some awareness of the female person, but they are primarily aware of the female gender.

In popular culture, philanderers are seen as comic—bad little boys trapped in adolescence, trying to establish their manhood and defying their mama at the same time. In male liberation literature, philanderers are portrayed as tragic, as normal polygamists misplaced in a pervertedly monogamous culture. In feminist literature, philanderers are seen as villains, dangerous evolutionary throwbacks, creatures who have not quite differentiated from the chimpanzees. But whether we consider them to be in the wrong stage of development, the wrong culture, or the wrong species, we generally suspect there is something wrong with philanderers. They, on the other hand, regard their activity as quite normal. They believe they are envied and admired. They assume that every other man does as they do, or would like to do so if he could. They may assume women do the same, or would like to. They are often unaware of their anger toward women, protesting that they "love" women, and they consume them regularly.

Scoring

Kyle, a work-out buddy in his early forties, is an eager, proud, dedicated philanderer. In twenty years of marriage, he has had sex with approximately one thousand women—if we use his arithmetic, based upon the formula of one new woman a week. (He feels inferior to and rankled by basketball giant

Wilt Chamberlain, who claims 10,000 women, 1.2 new ones a day since age 15.) Kyle has made money in real estate, and despite his humble origins, he could do almost anything his heart desired, but he has found no activity that appeals to him quite so much as chasing women.

Kyle began this activity three days after his wedding, as he felt bored with his new bride and couldn't get his mind off one of the bridesmaids. He left the honeymoon early in order to pursue the bridesmaid, which he did successfully. Actually, the marriage brought no change in a pattern that had gone on since the age of fourteen, when he had his first girlfriend and then started sneaking around with her best friend. He goes now to singles bars, where he does not drink but buys drinks for women there. Within an hour he can find some woman who will meet him in the parking lot, or spend a few minutes with him in one of the houses he's showing, or accompany him on a trip somewhere.

Kyle makes it a rule never to see the same woman more than twice. He adopted this rule for himself after he had the bad experience of beginning to like one of them—a woman who worked for him, and who came by his office each afternoon for a quickie. He tells a joke: Q. "What is a romantic?" A. "A romantic is a man who suffers from the delusion that one woman is different from another."

In recent years, Kyle has noticed that sometimes he doesn't want to go through with the sex. Once the woman has agreed, the game is really over. He doesn't actually turn down the sex that is offered, though. He lives in fear that someone might think he was gay if it were known that he had turned down sex with a woman.

Kyle refers to his activity as *tagging* women. He has *scored* a victory by seducing them, or by making them care about him more than he does about them. But the concept of tagging also implies that the woman is now marked and filed for storage and will never be dealt with again.

Why, Kyle asks, would any man want things different? He is fairly relaxed, though unceasingly competitive with men. But he competes carefully according to the men's rules, so he is well liked by the men he knows. Around women who have not yet been tagged, he is tense and becomes stiff and formal, going through excessive rituals of good manners. He plays a little game that he hopes he never wins: he acts as if he is looking for a woman who is "better" than his wife, and he hopes he won't find one, because he wouldn't want to go through a divorce, with all the expense and bother. And anyway, he'd never find a woman as "dumb" as his wife, who hasn't suspected a thing in all these years (or so he thinks). He sees himself as a very lucky man. He has three children and has never had to change a diaper, go to a teacher conference or the pediatrician, or drive a car pool. He's had all the women he's wanted, never has to see any of them again, and is the envy of other men at the bars he frequents.

Kyle's father, unlike the usual father of a philanderer, was not a philanderer himself—Kyle says he was a wimp, never successful, never happy, and never able to please Kyle's mother. Kyle didn't want to be like him. He modeled himself after his mother's younger brother, a much married ne'er-do-well whom she adored and whom his pious father despised. Kyle assumes his father has been impotent for decades. He knew early on that he wanted to be a "real man," not a "limp-dicked, pussy-whipped wimp" like his dad.

Kyle derides Gary Hart and Bill Clinton for getting caught. He talks about President Kennedy and his affairs, and about the polygamous patriarchs in the Old Testament, and about the Mormons, though I would not think of Kyle as a

student of either history or religion. He has brought me cartoons from *Playboy* from time to time. He protects himself
successfully from the belief that there is something wrong with
what he is doing. At the center of his life—and the life of
other philanderers—is a determination to establish that he is
a normal man. The greater his difference from women, and
the greater his victories over them, the more clearly he is a
man.

Philanderers, Sex, and Women

I understand that in Jules Feiffer's original script for the
film *Carnal Knowledge*, the opening line had Jack Nicholson
saying to his prep school roommate Art Garfunkel, "Remember when we were younger and didn't like girls? We still don't.
We just like sex." Philanderers certainly don't like girls. But
they may not even like sex.

Philanderers like Kyle like to think of themselves as oversexed, as men who are so masculine that they just like sex too
much and too often. Most of them, of course, have a lot less
sex than do the people who have a very sexy marriage and
practice monogamy. There are a few, however, who are accustomed to two or more orgasms a day, with a variety of
partners in various combinations, exhausting themselves, rub-
bing themselves raw, in pursuit of some feeling they can't seem
to achieve.

Milan Kundera explored the question of what philanderers seek in his novel, *The Unbearable Lightness of Being*, about
a man who gives up everything for a woman he tortures through
repeated, compulsive, joyless betrayals. Kundera concludes
that there are two kinds of philanderers, the Epic and the
Lyric. The Epic Philanderer, like Kyle, seeks variety, a woman

of every sort, shape, color, and condition. He must have WOMAN in all her varieties. Each new woman excites him; he is unhappy if any one slips past him. If he has WOMAN, in her infinite variety, then he will finally feel like MAN. But the Lyric Philanderer seeks perfection and tries to fall in love with each woman, until he realizes she has some flaw. He is doomed to a life of disappointment. No woman is perfect enough to make him feel completely satisfied and totally man enough.

The prototypical Epic Philanderer is Don Juan, or in Mozart's opera, *Don Giovanni,* one of the great charmers of all time. In the opera, Giovanni has raped Donna Anna and killed her father. He is now hiding in the bushes with Zerlina, the peasant girl he has seduced from her own wedding. Donna Elvira, the fiancée he's abandoned, is chasing him, trying to get him back. His manservant, Leporello, entertains Don Giovanni's frustrated pursuers by cataloging his conquests. "In Italy six hundred and forty, in Germany two hundred and thirty-one, a hundred in France, in Turkey ninety-one, but in Spain there are already one thousand and three!" Leporello's admiration for his master is boundless. Leporello, an unsuccessful amateur seducer himself, particularly admires Giovanni's lack of discrimination. "He doesn't care a fig if she's rich, if she's ugly, or if she's pretty, so long as she wears a skirt." At the end, the stone statue of Donna Anna's father comes to drag Giovanni off to hell, telling him to repent, to change his mode of life. Giovanni refuses, saying that he will never be accused of cowardice. Giovanni would rather die than come under social control. His masculinity, as he defines it, is more important to him than his life.

A particularly charming, but rather rapid-cycling Lyric Philanderer explained to me, "All women are beautiful to me; each one I haven't had is a mystery and she obsesses me. I just can't stop looking at her and listening to her move and breathe, and I smell her and even taste her. All I want is to know her and give her pleasure. I will make her feel good— I'll tell her anything she wants to hear. It won't take long, and then I'll be out of her life forever."

There is an alarming innocence to philanderers' guiltless sense of entitlement and the childlike pleasure they take in doing whatever they like. Some are so seductive that few could resist them. Their confidence comes from being loved well and often. And these men may inflict some pleasure before they inflict the inevitable pain. Yet while a philanderer might initially satisfy a woman, he can never satisfy himself.

The Marriages of a Philanderer

Philanderers can't believe in monogamy and marital fidelity, or even negotiating a marital arrangement—any of those things imply gender equality. Such men recoil from the idea that a man would give a women enough control over him to determine such personal matters as who he has sex with. Such men may come from a religious or ethnic background that supports the belief that God Himself created man in His image and has commanded him to keep women and their dangerous sexuality under male control. Male domination and the double standard may be an article of faith for them.

However delightful they may be out in the world, philanderers can be domestic monsters. At home, they sense most intensely the danger of letting a female get control of them. The wife embodies all that is dangerous in women; she stands between him and the multiple seductions that he needs to reassure himself that he has power over women rather than women having power over him.

A philanderer sees his marriage as belonging to his wife, and she uses it against him to prevent his appropriate freedom. He may, of course, express his anger and defiance of her in other ways as well. He may reassure himself of his masculinity by controlling things, like money, or refusing to do things, like calling home or taking care of the kids. He divides the labor, and assigns status to his jobs. He may well be violent, if necessary, to maintain his expected level of control. He may go around "commanding" things or "forbidding" things so his wife can let him be the boss. He may complain a lot about liberated women, and he likes to tell stories about how stupid and inept women can be. The less successful he is in his own life, the more dependent he is upon women, the more likely he is to put women down.

A truly hostile philanderer may be multimarried, and adulterous in all his marriages. He may blame his wife for his sleeping around, and when he comes home from his philandering, he may berate her or even beat her up. The pattern may change for a while if he carelessly lets himself come under the control of a new woman who won't tolerate his nonsense, and who is willing to leave him if it continues. He may then give up the pursuit of new women and be more or less faithful to his new mistress for months or years, until she relaxes and begins to like him or trust him enough to tolerate him. Or until she marries him.

I saw a retired army officer, who had been in an affair for many years with the wife of his rich best friend. After the friend's death, he married the widow and let her support him, while he began other affairs. His latest conquest was the bride's niece. The wife learned of this while she was away from home and called her husband to confront him. She fussed. He explained that he would not permit a wife to fuss at him and would punish her by breaking her mother's china while she listened. He broke the china. She told him she would leave unless he saw me. When I heard the story, I clumsily referred to the china breaking as an overreaction. Whereupon the man stood up and informed me, "If you don't understand why I had to break that china, then you don't understand anything about how to handle women. The next thing you'll tell me is that she had the right to criticize me for who I slept with. I'm not going to put myself in the hands of a pervert like you." He walked out and, I am sorry to say, she followed.

A few years ago, when my book on infidelity, *Private Lies: Infidelity and the Betrayal of Intimacy*, came out, I went on Oprah Winfrey's television show, and was confronted by an audience of 150 men, who had volunteered to discuss their infidelities on national television. When Oprah asked me why men have affairs, I explained it was because they were afraid of women. The audience was displeased and began stomping and chanting and making animal noises. Immediately, a man leaped up and said, "I'm not afraid of any woman. You bring me any woman and throw her down and I'll jump right on top. I don't care who she is." Oprah assured the man that I wasn't accusing them of being afraid of sex, but afraid of coming under female control. Whereupon the man told the sad story of his brief marriage. He said, "Once I married this woman. I'd been living with her for three years, and she never got on me, but then we got married one morning, and as soon as we got back from the courthouse, I told her I was going up the street to play ball with the guys, like I always do, and she said, 'Aw, honey, can't you stay here with me.' As soon as I married that woman, she thought she owned me! So I went right out and found another woman. I'm not going to let any woman tell me what to do. What kind of man would I be then?" The other guys understood perfectly.

Ladies' Men

Philanderers see wives as the ultimate enemy, and they view women as objects more than as human beings, but they can get friendly with a "fucking buddy," a woman who has given up all romantic and idealistic expectations of men, and whose anger at marriage meshes with his own. One especially angry woman, who had such a relationship with several men, told me cynically, "All married men sleep around, at least everyone I ever went to bed with did." He cannot marry such a woman, of course, since the point of their relationship requires mutual independence and total lack of romance.

James Bond has been our most daring philanderer. He seems to risk his life regularly by bedding down the women who have been sent to kill him, and giving them such sexual pleasure they will betray their allegiances for him. His most famous conquest was Pussy Galore, a fascist lesbian assassin whom he converted on all counts. Bond will risk his life in any way, for any cause. What he won't do is go to bed with Miss Moneypenny, the safe, "wifely" sex object.

Competitive men who feel like failures often prefer the company of women they regard as inferior. In Woody Allen's *Interiors*, the failed husband of a successful poet seduces his sister-in-law, and tells her, "It's been such a long time since I made love to a woman I didn't feel inferior to."

In general, a philanderer is not likely to realize how much he hates and fears women, because he can always find one who shares his hatred and fear of all women, of herself, and of the basic gender equality that is marriage.

Homosexuality and Philandering

If the criteria for philandering involve (1) an obsession with masculinity, (2) determination not to come under the control of the "opposite" sex, and (3) sexual competitiveness with other men, the ultimate philanderer would be homosexual. The gay life used to center around phallic symbolism, polite avoidance of women, and frantic seductions of other men. It was remarkably promiscuous. AIDS has changed that. Now there are monogamous homosexuals who want to be married, but not to a woman. And there are many celibate homosexuals who use the gay world as sanctuary from the macho posturing and competition for women that obsesses the straight world.

Those who pay the enormous price for being gay in our society are making quite a sacrifice for the sake of their sexual freedom, so many have claimed their rights to the promiscuity they have bought. Gay philandering has been common.

A fair number of married men are actively bisexual, leading an underground gay sex life. Such a man may be so terrified of women that he must keep polite distance from his wife and can only relax sexually with the other boys. Or he may be quite comfortable sexually with women but wants variety, even more variety than a selection of other women would have to offer. He may just want to get close to a man, the way he could back in early puberty, and doesn't know how except through sex. But whether a man's sleeping around is with men or with women, it is still philandering, and it still, most likely, is an effort to feel like a man through sex while escaping a woman's awesome power to bestow masculinity and to take it away.

The Life of a Philanderer

> *The first betrayal is irreparable. It calls forth a chain reaction*
> *of further betrayals, each of which takes us farther and farther*
> *away from the point of our original betrayal.*
> —Milan Kundera, *The Unbearable Lightness of Being*

Once a man starts his career as a philanderer he has a lonely life ahead of him, and it isn't easy to turn back.

You've probably seen Lex on television and read about him on the sports page. Lex is a professional golfer. He doesn't often win tournaments anymore the way he did fifteen or twenty years ago, but he's steady and he makes a showing. He gets money and attention from the world. The press loves him. He has three fine sons, one an up-and-coming golfer himself, one an orthopedic surgery resident, and one a budding sports writer. He also has Louise, a beautiful, talented, loving wife, who gets a fair amount of press attention herself. They look like models, and they appear together in ads for sports clothes. Lex and Louise have everything, and they are both miserable. They have been for decades now. It's beginning to affect his golf game lately.

Lex grew up very poor in a town near Fort Worth. His parents had been just kids when his mom got pregnant and they got married. His father was a seventeen-year-old traveling man, darkly handsome, strangely dashing and breathtakingly confident, running away from God-knows-what as he landed in town. They said he was part Cherokee; he didn't seem to know. He'd left home after another of his drunk father's beatings, before anybody told him who or what he was. Lex's mother was a plain and shy but strappingly healthy twenty-year-old farmgirl, who had stayed at home after her father died and had taken care of her sickly mother and her sickly little brothers and sisters. She wanted somebody to take her away from it, and this young man seemed to know how to move. These two got together, she got pregnant and they got married.

Neither of them had more than an eighth-grade education, so they had trouble supporting themselves. Lex's mother started getting sickly as soon as Lex began to grow inside her. And Lex's father started looking for ways out. He would disappear for a few days, and Lex's mother wouldn't sleep or eat until he came back. But he always came back, sometimes with money, sometimes with venereal diseases, sometimes with nothing more than tall tales.

When Lex was nine, his father moved them to the city to a nice apartment overlooking a park. Lex got a fancy new bicycle, something far beyond his dreams, and his first golf clubs, and there were promises about how great it was going to be. But Lex's father didn't come home the next day, and his boss called and said that Lex's father had stolen some money and been fired. Lex's mother couldn't pay the rent and had never gone out and looked for a job, so she sold Lex's new bicycle and took to her bed. Lex kept the golf clubs. He managed to get a job shining shoes, and kept them going until his father came and took them away to a cheaper apartment. Lex remembers being angry with his father, but mostly he remembers being scared. He wanted to run away, too.

It was only a couple of years later that his father ran off with a woman from work and ended up in jail over a stolen car, so he wasn't gone long that time.

By the time Lex was fifteen, he had begun to feel some security that his father would stay. He'd almost forgotten about the times he had run away. His father worked as a salesman, traveled some, but was home enough to coach his little league baseball team. Always the charmer, he had arranged with a woman in the office of the country club for Lex to play golf and even to get golf lessons there. And then he was gone again. Lex supported himself and his mother as a caddy while he finished high school. He got golf scholarships to college, and his mother was all set to move back in with her invalid mother and grandfather. But suddenly his father arrived, too, after being gone three years. As always, Lex's father just flashed that killer smile, said, "A man's gotta do what a man's gotta do," and didn't explain.

Lex was so grateful to his father for taking his whiney, useless mother off his hands that he almost forgot to be angry about the long absence. He went off to SMU, became a hotshot golf star, and began getting things from people who wanted to sponsor him or hire him or just court him. But, more importantly, Lex could count on his proudly strutting father to be there to watch every match.

Lex had been dating Louise since junior high school. She lived with alcoholic parents who fought regularly, while she took care of things at home. During Lex's junior year at SMU, Louise's father turned mean and began to scare her. Louise's life finally became unbearable, just as Lex's career began to blossom. She talked him into marrying her. She was the only girl he'd ever slept with, and he wanted to take care of her. He loved the feeling: she, who had stabilized him through all those awful years with his father gone and his mother miserable and no money anywhere, was now a damsel in distress and he could be the conquering hero. He could be the man his father had never been.

After Lex married Louise, his father disappeared again. Lex left college, got backers to join the pro tour, and was soon making enough money to set up his mother in her own apartment. He's been supporting her ever since.

Lex and Louise were happy. They had their three sons in quick succession. Increasingly, Louise stayed home with the boys while Lex traveled alone. Louise took over the care of Lex's mother, who had nervous spells and had never been the same since Lex's father disappeared.

Lex always liked being with the other guys—it reminded him of those years when his father was coaching him and his buddies. The other guys on the golf tour drank a lot, and some of them used drugs. They entertained themselves chasing women, and there were always women chasing athletes—even golfers. The guys assured Lex it would be OK if he slept with these women, too, since Louise would never know, and, "What women don't know won't hurt them."

Lex would flirt a bit, but wouldn't let it go very far at all. To get the other guys off his back, he pretended that he was sleeping with various women. Finally, he found himself in a situation where he couldn't refuse without embarrassing himself, so he did it. The woman meant nothing and the sex meant nothing and went very fast, but he still felt a strange combination of shame and pride. He waited and watched for consequences, and nothing terrible happened. Finally he felt comfortable, so he did it again, and again. He tried to make it up to Louise by being nicer than usual for a while, and then he began to stay away more. He made up stories about what he was doing on the road, and soon he didn't have much to talk to Louise about.

Lex confided in a neighbor, and the neighbor told his wife Alice. And Lex's neighbor's wife, at a barbecue in the backyard, sidled up to him and told him she had heard he had hidden talents, and invited him over. Lex went. He kept seeing Alice off and on for a couple of years while they talked about themselves and their marriages. They knew they weren't in love, but they both knew they needed somebody with whom they could be honest. They were partners in sin. Alice told him she didn't love her husband, and he decided maybe he didn't love Louise. Lex prided himself on how he didn't run away like his father had. He remained a loyal, if not a faithful, husband, and a reliable father. His sons would never have to do as he had done.

In time, Alice and her husband moved away and Lex felt both relief and loss. He didn't have anyone to talk to about his underground life. He was interviewed on television by Babs, a glamorous lady who was one of the first big-time female sportscasters. Wherever there was golf, there was Babs. She seemed both desirable and unapproachable. He wanted to show off, so he made the pass, mustering up all the charm he'd learned from his father. It happened, and he felt like a conquering hero. He fell in love with Babs, but she was far more ambitious, and made clear that she was after a man with big money, not just one of the jocks on the tour. Anyway, she didn't want to be bothered with his children. Still, he would do for the time being. Babs broke Lex's heart when she did find the rich old man who had given up his own children and could devote himself totally to her.

Lex went through a few years of being mean and depressed. He spent more time with the boys, and less with Louise. Louise took care of everything for him, but he just didn't have anything to talk to her about. He didn't chase women for a while—he was really too busy with his kids. Sex was always fine with Louise, and he actually tried to make his marriage work by doing things for her and with her, but since they couldn't talk about any of the things he thought about, he always felt lonely. He wanted to run away. He had the feelings he'd had when his father had left his mother with him.

Lex got more irritable, got out of shape, and began to drink a bit too much and too often. He decided to get healthy and joined a spa. There he met Cynthia, the aerobics queen.

She wanted his fame and he wanted her body. Cynthia had just married again, and she didn't expect this marriage to last either, so she was shopping. They had great sex and great fantasies together, but she wanted him to leave Louise. He couldn't do that. She was supposed to be his "fucking buddy." How dare she ask him to betray his wife, to do what his father had done? He stayed angry with Cynthia the whole time they were together. She didn't understand at all what his life was about.

It was during the affair with Cynthia that he became obsessed with his father. He hired a private detective to find him, and did. His father, who had never been in the military, had gotten himself into a Veterans' hospital in Cincinnati, where he was suffering the consequences of a life of abuse and neglect. The old man was fifty-five, and he was burned out and ready for some peace in life. There were indications on his chart of another wife and family, but the old man assured Lex it was a mistake. There was no point in trying to get the truth from Lex's father, and Lex didn't really care. He brought his father home to his ecstatic mother and agreed to support them both for the rest of their lives—if they would only leave him alone.

Once he'd found his father, he was overcome with self-loathing at the resemblances he saw between himself and this awful old man he loved and hated so intensely. He told Louise of his affairs. She already knew. How could she not know: she loved him. Louise reminded him of what a perfect wife she had been, and what a shit he had been all these years, and then she forgave him. He broke with Cynthia and vowed he would be true to Louise forever.

But then, one by one, the boys grew up and left home. Louise remained chipper as always, cheerfully taking care of everything and seeming completely satisfied with what few bones Lex would throw her. She stayed busy with charity work, and liked to go to the theater. Lex was bored, but he wanted to be a good husband, so he would go with her. At a performance of Eugene O'Neill's *The Iceman Cometh*, Lex thought he was going to die of boredom and impatience as these men at a skid-row bar, men so like his father, talked bullshit to one another, pipe dreams of how their lives were going to be. They were all waiting for a salesman named Hickey, the successful member of their group. Finally, in the last act, Hickey arrives and tells them the story of his marriage to Evelyn, how Evelyn loved him and believed in him despite all the lies and the broken promises and the other women. She would always forgive him and take him back, reassuring him that she knew he would change. And each time, he'd let her down again. There seemed no escape. He thought of killing himself, but that would leave her in utter despair. He thought of just leaving, but that would just break poor Evelyn's heart. Finally he knew what he must do: he killed her, after she forgave him once too often. Lex's anger at Louise finally broke through. He could not live with a woman who would let him do to himself and to her what he had been doing.

He decided he would stay sexually faithful to Louise, but would find a platonic female soul mate. He found Denise. Denise's husband had just left her and the kids for cocaine and a stripper. Denise was depressed, Lex was depressed, and they had a lot to talk about. He told Denise everything, and her response was to get in his pants. Lex resented it, but once it happened he couldn't turn back.

He tried to resist this temptation to relive his father's history. Lex talked to all his friends, many of them athletes, the others mostly professional men in their forties. A few had been faithful all these years and seemed happy with their not very adventurous lives. Two had left their marriages for other women, or for alcohol and drugs, and that had not worked out well, and one of those had gone back home. The other stayed a mess. Most told stories much like Lex's, back in the '70s they bought the *Playboy* philosophy and tried screwing around. They liked it, but it made their marriages weird. Most had told their wives, some hadn't, most stopped doing it, some still did it from time to time, but they'd stayed married and they felt integrity and honor in their lives, even if passion wasn't always easy to work up. They were fairly happy. They all urged Lex to stay with Louise, to give up Denise, and just to mess around from time to time, if he could do it without caring about the woman. But they urged him not to do it if he had this tendency to fall in love and mess everything up. They saw Lex's romantic nature as a character flaw he should try to overcome.

Lex didn't know what he wanted, but his friends made him angry. They weren't lonely the way he was. They had sacrificed some freedom to end their loneliness and actually do the thing they used to ridicule in less masculine men — they settled in to a domestic life. Lex couldn't do that: he'd hurt Louise too badly to ever be a hero at home. He could not feel like a man with a woman he had to humble himself before: he felt trapped.

Lex talked to his sons. All three worshipped him, and his confessions came as no surprise. They disapproved, and they vowed they would never do what he had done. In the glib manner of their generation, they told him that if they found someone they wanted more than their wife, they would just get a divorce, or maybe they would wait until their kids were grown and then get a divorce, but then they weren't sure that was such a good idea, either. They were sure they would love him even if he left their mother, but they would not tolerate Denise, who had wrecked their family. This made Lex mad, too. They gave him permission to choose any other woman in the world, and it wasn't good enough: he still wasn't truly free.

Lex worked up a full-scale depression and talked about suicide, but neither Louise nor Denise would let go. He started being nasty to both of them, and still they wouldn't let go. He began to see his mother in Louise, and he realized he was even angrier at his mother for collapsing upon him than he was at his father for leaving him holding the bag. He felt this powerful urge to run away. He began to know what his father had felt. But he couldn't forgive his father, so he couldn't forgive himself.

He went into therapy and brought his father with him. His father tried to shed light on his pattern from long ago: he would just feel ashamed of himself about something, usually another woman, and would be afraid of upsetting his wife, so he'd run away until everybody forgot about it. He'd been doing it since Lex was nine. The old man felt good about what he was doing now, staying home and taking care of his sickly wife, and feeling pride in his son. He'd completely forgotten about any other wives and children he'd picked up along the way— he was going to do it right this time. He talked about how much more he had provided for Lex than his father had provided for him. He reminded Lex, one more time, of the golf clubs he'd given him almost forty years ago. He urged Lex to forgive himself for the things he'd done wrong and "straighten up and fly right." The old man had no guilt and no shame. Lex looked like he wanted to throttle him, until he began to realize that his father felt no guilt, because his father had stopped doing what he used to do that made him feel the guilt. He was now being honest, and it was working.

In therapy, Lex met his father face to face, came to understand his father, and therefore himself. In time he forgave

his father and risked getting close again, as his father set out
to face the ghost of his own father. Lex even made peace with
his mother, and his exaggerated sense of responsibility for her.
By leaving his father with his mother, Lex has become free
for the first time, but he is still surrounded by the mess he has
made of his own life.

Lex is living alone now. He tries to divorce Louise, and
give her everything, but he can't seem to divorce her as long
as he's involved with Denise, and he can't abandon the pathetically dependent Denise, despite his anger at her for caring
so little about the effect of this affair on him and his family.
He loathes Denise, but the more he hurts her by trying to
leave her, the more he feels guilt and responsibility for her,
just as he has felt for his mother and Louise. He wonders
whether he should look for a woman he hasn't hurt yet. He
says, "To go with Denise means giving up everything I have
and everything I am. To stay married to Louise means family
continuity, loyalty, and the approval of my family and friends.
It means stability and comfort and integrity. It means being
an adult. But I'm my father's son and I feel ashamed and I
want to run away, and I hate myself for finding him in me.
I'm trying to be the man he is now rather than the man he
was then, and those two men are at war inside me. I don't
know who I am anymore. I'm that nine-year-old boy whose
father ran away and whose bicycle had to be sold for rent and
who had to go to work to take care of his mother. Sometimes
I think I just want my turn. I don't really know how to be a
man. I can be a good little boy or a bad little boy—my father
taught me both of those—but I'm just now beginning to learn
how to be a man."

Chasing His Tail

I used to envy philanderers. I would hear stories about Epic Philanderers like Jack Kennedy having three women a day in the White House, or Lyric Philanderers like Warren Beatty having a short romance with every desirable woman in the movies. I had friends who were philanderers, and they seemed at first to have charmed lives. But whether through wisdom or cowardice, I did my philandering only in my imagination. It was a wise choice. The guys I envied then have not had an easy time of it. They have little comfort at home. They have not found love, and they have not found their masculinity. I don't think the preoccupation with sex has caused the unhappiness—sex beats hell out of most of the things men find to sacrifice their lives for. But philandering is a life that requires dishonesty, and philanderers spend their lives behind enemy lines, hiding and faking it, never really able to relax with someone who knows them.

Men who seek to find themselves as men through chasing women just lose more and more of the masculinity they are seeking. They sacrifice the wife who could know them and love them, and the children through whom they could know themselves, because they feel the power of WOMAN, and want to harness it to make themselves feel like MAN. But when each woman fails to bestow masculinity, the man feels betrayed and may despair over his failure or lash out in anger. He knows he doesn't have the power to turn himself into a man, and he can't believe women don't have that power either. The man going around in these desperate sexual circles is just chasing his tail.

THREE

Contenders

Winning isn't everything, it's the only thing.
—Vince Lombardi

Nice guys finish last.   —Leo Durocher

Contenders dedicate their lives to competition with the other boys. Full-blown contenders can compete about anything from their money to their golf score, from the amount of alcohol they can drink without throwing up to the amount of money they can spend without flinching. Everything from their wife's career to their kid's grades becomes part of the competition with the other boys. They may savor winning or they may merely fear losing, but they must compete to feel alive. And they must win or lose their sense of themselves.

These men are shadow-boxing through life, struggling all

alone in a competition against something in their imagination. Their audience, of course, is the father who didn't make them feel like a man, but who has forgotten all about it and has gone on to something else.

Contending with Life

I won't deny that I'm a contender; my competitiveness and my envy of other guys has cost me much happiness and comfort in life. I've never felt quite good enough about myself to shake it completely, but I've struggled to channel it into directions that are minimally destructive and minimally self-torturing.

By contrast, I grew up with a friend named Mark, who was as highly competitive as I was. But Mark wouldn't play right. Mark's father had been killed in the war when Mark was eight, and he'd been raised by his mother, his grandmother, and his aunts in a big old house with much antique splendor and minimal plumbing. Mark was the only child and was much loved by the women who raised him. He was careful about which competitions he would enter. His body, like mine, did not seem made for athletic glory. When we were younger, he was good at model building and board games, and later he liked to show daring in such things as tree climbing or shop-lifting. Mostly he had verbal skills: his specialties were dazzling wit and withering insults, and he could bait and deflate any of our athletic friends who were stronger, handsomer, and better loved by the world. Mark could write, and did, and was the first of my peers to be published.

Mark married Marcia, who had the biggest breasts in town and a wit almost as caustic and sarcastic as his. They went to London with some money she had inherited, and Mark wrote his first (and last) novel. It was autobiographical, and it told of our town, but Mark had made himself so heroic and glorious that the more competitive of his old friends laughed at him behind his back, even as we envied his opportunity to present himself to the world as he would have liked to have been seen. While in London, Mark and Marcia had learned even more tricks for making their friends feel inferior to them. They were frighteningly scintillating. They turned a cocktail party into a competitive sport.

Mark started a newspaper, which was literate and lively, but it never quite caught on. Mark's snide opinions were irritating. He put everybody else down. After that, he did restaurant reviews for a larger paper, and would brag about the great meals and service he got for free that way. I would see him from time to time, but he kept putting me down, and I didn't want to play that game anymore. I lost track of him.

Then Marcia called me. Mark hadn't worked in years. They had run through their inheritances, and now they were living on her earnings as a clerk in a toy store. As always, Mark had been drinking heavily; he had prided himself since high school on his ability to outdrink anyone in his weight class. But he was no longer holding it well. He refused AA or therapy, and Marcia finally got up the courage to kick him out, in hopes that would shock him into doing something about himself. Instead, he just moved in with his former secretary, who did drugs, and he started doing drugs, too. When the new woman went into a drug treatment program, he got very drunk and slashed his wrists and bled all over himself. Mark showed back up at Marcia's little apartment, covered with blood. She called me. I rushed over and found him in a dark, foul-smelling bedroom. When I walked in he rose up a little, and said, "Pitts, you old square. Still married to the same woman, huh? I bet I've fucked more women in the last year than you have in a lifetime." Then he vomited something green all over himself and passed out. Even at the moment of greatest degradation for him, Mark could not stop competing. Fatherless, he has wasted his life trying to win an adult victory to repair his sense of not being a boyhood success.

The Games of Childhood

Other animals, too, learn to compete with one another in play before they can face the real challenges of the grown-up world. Wolf pups begin play-fighting with littermates, male and female, when they are just three weeks old. They learn how to compete and they learn how to cooperate. Both males and females achieve status through size and aggressiveness. The alpha male and the alpha female learn to be dominant, and the others learn to join the team.

Boys do much the same as wolf cubs, competing over size and aggressiveness in games and sports. There is something almost passionately intimate and fraternal about these competitive relationships, and they are a necessary part of men's lives. It is probably unhealthy for boys to grow up without brothers, a deprivation that warps us. We only-sons undoubtedly miss those loving struggles for status that wolf cubs go through, struggles in which everyone survives and continues to love one another after the contest. We have to do it with kids in the neighborhood and classmates instead, always running the risk of rejection if we win too much or lose too much or play the wrong game. Through these boyhood games, we turn the other guys into our alternate brothers. It is an enormously important activity, and it has to be done right. It has to be done according to the rules.

Some boys, like my boyhood friend Mark, make the error

of not playing by the rules the other boys use. Mark wanted to make up his own game so he could win and make the other boys feel bad. That does not prepare boys or wolf cubs for life in the wild. We need to have alterbrothers that we know are on the same team with us, trying to make us look and feel good at the same time that they are competing with us to bring out the best in all of us. It may be that competing with the other boys on a structured playing field is all that keeps us from either killing them or falling in love with them when we get close to them later in life.

Boys Becoming Men

In time, after a dozen years of centering their lives around the games boys play with one another, the boys' bodies change and that changes everything else. But the memories are not erased of that safest time in the lives of men, when their prime concern was playing games with guys who just wanted to be their friendly competitors. Life never again gets so simple.

When puberty blossoms forth the boys begin to concern themselves with how well they can impress and ultimately satisfy a female. Boys desperately measure their peckers together, and compare their functioning, until they are sure enough of the splendor of their manhood to test it out on women. While the guy with the earliest puberty and the biggest penis wins the early rounds, the grand-slam winner is the first guy to get laid by a girl. We never get over those contests. The men who lost them and can't get quite enough reassurance of their masculinity may go on to set up contest after contest, sacrificing all else.

The ultimate contender is *The Great Santini,* from Pat Conroy's book about his own father. In the 1979 film, Robert

Duvall is Col. Bull Meechum. He commands his children to compete for the greater glory of their father. As the four young children sit on the front steps, Col. Meechum, in full uniform, addresses his four troops, calling them "hogs." The father tells his children: "You are Meechums . . . A Meechum is a thoroughbred, a winner all the way. A Meechum gets the best grades, wins the most awards, excels in sports, is the most popular, and is always found near the top no matter what endeavor he undertakes. A Meechum never gives up, never surrenders, never sticks his tail between his legs, never gets weepy, never gets his nose out of joint, and never, never, never, under any circumstances, loses sight of the fact that it is the Meechum family that he represents, whose honor he is upholding. I want you hogs to let this burg know you're here. I want these crackers to wake up and wonder what in the hell just blew into town."

In a later scene, Meechum and his oldest son Ben are playing one-on-one basketball while the rest of the family watches. When the son finally beats the father by one point, the father refuses to give the boy his victory, and demands that he must win by two points rather than one. The wife and the other kids scream at the father for being such a bad sport, and he runs them off. Then he turns on the boy who has defeated him, and calls him "sissy" and "girl" for refusing to continue the game. Meechum begins to bounce the basketball off the boy's head as he walks slowly and with great control up to his room. Meechum says, "I swear, Ben, you're my favorite daughter," to which Ben replies, "This girl just whipped your ass good, Colonel."

Needless to say by the end of the film, after being treated as a loser while required to be a winner, Ben has been kicked off the team for tackling an opposing player, which would be fine, but the game was basketball.

Fathers who compete hard with their kids are monstrous. The father, for a throw-away victory, is sacrificing the very heart of his child's sense of being good enough. He may believe he is making his son tough, as he was made tough by a similarly contending father, but he is only making his child desperate and mean like himself. Fathers must let their sons (and daughters) have their victories.

On the other hand, it seems inevitable, and perhaps ultimately empowering up to a point, that fathers will compete *through* their children. God knows my father competed through me and my sister, and I have competed successfully and enthusiastically through all of my kids, from the day they were conceived. Each of my kids, as I did, has gone through their competitions knowing they were carrying the family banner.

The military school I attended gave three medals at the end of the year: one for academics, one for public speaking, and one for military. My senior year my parents told me that if I won all three medals, something unheard of, they would get me a new yellow convertible. I was enthusiastic. I won the academic medal each year, maintaining my 99 average mostly as a game I played with myself, and a way of showing off without being an athlete. I entered the public speaking contest and won that too, reciting with great drama Victor Hugo's defense of Dreyfus, a case I did not understand in the least.

But then there was the compulsory competitive drill, which I'd never taken very seriously before. I, like my friend Mark, had made a show of not trying very hard at any competition we didn't think we could win. This time I worked myself up for it, and was unusually intense. I paid close attention and was sharp. It seemed to go on forever, but eventually the competition had been narrowed down to me and another guy in my class. We both just kept following orders without making a mistake, until the commanding officer gestured something to me. I assumed I'd made an error, so I dropped out of formation. I was mistaken. He had just wanted me to move closer to my competition. But I lost my rhythm and quickly made a real error, lost the medal, and did not get the yellow convertible. My mother got it for herself, and wouldn't let me drive it. She rubbed my nose in my failure. My father didn't, but he didn't protect me from my mother's need to compete through me. He did not look at my great success and tell me I was man enough and could stop competing now.

I had won scholarships to Harvard and to Yale, and I was so angry at my parents for pushing me to keep competing, to keep proving I *was* a man instead of just living as one, that I turned down both schools and went to Washington and Lee instead, where I hoped I wouldn't have to compete any more. As it turned out, the most pressing competition at W and L was social rather than academic, and I struggled to develop some social graces while I softened my competitive edge. It was a good choice. I'd never learned to lose gracefully, and I couldn't continue my life until I got over my need to be the very best, until I could just become one of the boys.

Contenders Manifested

There are many ways in which men can express their contending urges, and all forms of contending are not bad; some ways are even good for you as long as you don't overdo it. *Competitors,* who are always setting up contests and keeping score, lead stressful lives and may have trouble relaxing. And they might be obnoxious. *Enviers* are miserable, and they may be nasty as well. *Emulators* are always striving, so, if their champions are chosen carefully, they may develop a healthy masculine identity. *Adventurers* lead interesting lives, but may take on unnecessary risks. *Workers* are productive and useful, and they enjoy what they do, but they may work themselves to death, and even if they don't, they may not feel at home at home.

COMPETITORS

> *Nothing can seem foul to those that win.*
> —Shakespeare, *Henry V*

There are men who never get completely past the games of childhood. Even as adults, they may try to force competition on others, or even set up contests in their heads, keep score, and then gloat over their victories. Such vulgar competitors may announce their victories over you in contests you didn't even enter.

Nick and Nutley grew up deprived of fathers, money, culture, and social position, but they have been partners in a successful business, and think of themselves as one another's best friends. I've treated them both, though neither knows I've seen the other, and each is determined that the secret be kept. They have told me things they don't tell one another: their fears, their failures, their worries about their marriages and their children. When they get together with one another, they brag about how great their lives are. They always carry pictures of their exotic dogs, their winning horses, their vacation houses, their successful children, their skinny women. When Nick bought a new Bentley, Nutley rushed out to get a new Rolls-Royce. When Nutley bought a beach house in Florida, Nick had to have a chalet in Switzerland. When Nick went on a safari to Africa, Nutley had to dog sled to the North Pole. When Nutley got a thirty-year-old mistress, Nick got a twenty-year-old. When Nick's wife had a baby, Nutley was furious with his wife for not having twins. They keep striving for grander successes, exhausting themselves in the process, and making life quite difficult for their wives and children.

Nick and Nutley aren't close to anyone else. They have not lived up yet to the image they want to project of the man they think they should be, so they can't even relax with the man they consider to be their best friend. They carry so much shame from their past that they have not been able to stop competing for a lifetime, with any man, even the man who has been through the horrors of poverty and danger and now wealth with them, and who should be their Blood Brother.

They're willing to see me because they are both richer, smarter, and better looking than I am, as I constantly reassure them. I'm a little taller, so I scrunch down like a hunchback around them.

Some of us mild-to-moderate competitors, like me and most of my friends, are more subtle about it. We are not likely to bump into you and snort, "I can beat your ass," or lean over to you at the next urinal and chortle, "Mine's bigger than yours." We are rarely that blatant and basic. We do the same thing, but in a socially correct manner.

There are competitors who make a show of their impeccably attuned senses, doing such things as sending back the wine at fancy restaurants. They savor victories over us plebeians, who are made happy by whatever we get. There are competitors who build monuments to themselves, or put their names on things (like children, books, buildings, charities, or countries). They're striving for immortality, a hope of living on in memory after death—a posthumous competition with the men of the future.

While the boasting of competitors, especially at its most subtle, is irritating, it usually is not lethal. It is intended to deflate the competition rather than destroy it, and when men do it to us we know it is because they are still stinging from a contest they lost earlier in life, and they now fear we are winning an enviable victory over them.

It is painful to realize that men can't go back and win the contests they lost as boys. Those games are over, and they exist only in the minds of the losers. The winners of those contests may be thinking about later contests they themselves lost. It may be universal for men who have lost a significant contest to eternally ponder how the outcome might have been different, and how they could have achieved the higher status they desperately need right now.

A lovely little comedy, *The Best of Times* (1983), showed us the life of Robin Williams and Kurt Russell twenty years after Williams had fumbled the winning touchdown to lose their small town's championship game. The plot enabled them to replay the game, to try one more time to become winners rather than losers in life. It is a fantasy we all have, but one which takes over the lives of contenders, who believe their masculinity demands that the game be replayed, however many times it takes until they can be declared winners.

ENVIERS

> *Did ever anybody seriously confess to envy? Something there is in it universally felt to be more shameful than even felonious crime.*   —Herman Melville, *Billy Budd*

Men who have given up on winning envy the men who do, and get whatever status they can by trying to make those guys lose. Doubting their own masculinity, these guys want to whittle down the masculinity of the men they see as their antagonists.

All of us who were raised for competition are subject to

envy. Among the most uncomfortable of emotions, it is shameful and belittles the man who feels it. When we find ourselves drowning in our shame and treated as if invisible by those in favor with fate, it is unavoidable for us to distract ourselves from our own humiliation by falling back on anger at whoever seems to be winning contests lately. The object of the envy is merely confused by it, since he did not know there was a competition going on. Nevertheless, we may implore the heavens not to send us some manna but to rain on our victor's parade—or make him impotent.

Olaf was one of the most unpleasant young men that ever walked into my office. He assured me that I had so many important patients, I wouldn't have any interest in him, but that was OK since he had seen far more impressive therapists than I. He named a few, and I oohed and aahed on cue. But he told me that even they hadn't been good enough to help him, since they were all snobs. He told me I couldn't understand him because I'd probably had a father, and his had run out on him. He sneered that I must think I'm "hot shit," charging so much more than he made moving furniture. His boss had paid for him to see me because (he laughed) he had the habit of dropping and breaking the most expensive item in each move. He assured me that all the assholes in the world, the privileged little rich kids, the ones with daddies to take care of them and houses full of fancy stuff, kept getting in his way, firing him, talking about him behind his back, picking fights with him just because he wasn't going to play by their silver-spoon rules. He then put his feet up on my coffee table and scratched two deep furrows across the length of it, as he said, "All these assholes care more about things than they do about people."

I confessed that paranoid people, who go through life feeling like victims and envying the rest of the world so much that they see them as their persecutors, probably are so unpleasant they get picked on by everybody. I told him that I was already tempted to persecute him for being a rude, obnoxious jerk, who was so caught up in his own self-pity he didn't give a damn about anybody else. Olaf liked that, deciding that I was the first honest man he'd met. I even agreed to accept him as a patient. However, he smashed a priceless antique piano that afternoon and was fired. He still wanted to see me, but only if I saw him for free and paid his cab fare. When I couldn't accept his terms, he announced that I was an asshole like all the others. I fear I was no help to Olaf. Toxic enviers may be beyond help.

A man who loses every contest for a lifetime, who stays awake at night envying all the winners, can finally snap and shoot the driver who cuts him off in traffic, making him feel that he looks foolish. Rapacious tycoons or sadistic streetfighters play in different arenas, but they're playing the same game, less concerned with making themselves win than with making the other guy lose. In their envy they inflict pain on people they identify with the winners of the adolescent masculinity contests they themselves lost, still vainly hoping that hurting the winners will make them feel less like losers.

EMULATORS

> *Few men have the strength of character to rejoice in a friend's success without a touch of envy.*   —Aeschylus

It takes dignity to smile through your friends' victory celebrations. And yet we develop ourselves as men when we can vie with the competition and look to our rivals for models for ourselves. Emulation of men we admire can help make up for the fathers and brothers who failed to make us feel like men. Emulation is the cure for envy, and the mechanism by which boys absorb the character of their role models.

Emulation is generally a good thing, but it can go too far. Puckett was a young guy whose father had died at an early age. Puckett emulated an uncle who had made a fortune in the pretzel business and was rumored to have kept a mistress. Puckett made money in pretzels and chased women, but became disenchanted when he discovered the uncle was impotent. He promptly shifted his allegiance to a grandfather, who was revered for his self-restraint and religious dedication. Puckett gave up women and business, and took up church and proselytizing on street corners. He couldn't support himself, so he went back to school to become a lawyer, like his father's best friend. He gave up everything that wasn't like the lawyer, took up pipe smoking and even developed a limp similar to his. But he couldn't make the grades for law school, got depressed, and saw me. I tried to teach Puckett to mix and match who he wanted to be and what he wanted to do. Lately his clothes, like mine, look like they came from a fire sale in Brooks Brothers' attic, he's driving an ancient Jaguar like mine, he's getting a soft southern accent though he comes from the Bronx, and he's sitting behind me at the symphony. He still limps and goes to church, but he's doing well with the pretzels. Maybe he can get a little from each of us.

Models of masculinity can be found anywhere. Boys and men who have not been anointed by their fathers may be drawn to men who project a heroic image. Macho politicians—Harry Truman blasting his daughter's music critic or Ronald Reagan in a cowboy suit—are eminently emulatable. In New York City, Donald Trump served a term as the emulatable symbol of masculine success. And Ross Perot, with a mythic reputation of using his fortune to rescue workers being held hostage, seemed briefly to be the perfect combination for hero worship: a feisty western billionaire on horseback.

Sports remain the classic arena for masculine emulation. Sports fans, who emulate far more than they envy the accomplishments and glories of other men, can't be all bad. They respect the game that is played according to clear, fair rules. They emulate the character of players, who can operate within an honorable structure, who learn to accept victory and defeat without getting carried away by it, and who increasingly lead their lives amidst great fame and great wealth—enough to spoil those less disciplined. And sports fans are likely to emulate their heroes, warts and all. Emulators can deputize a surrogate to pinch-hit for them. They have turned their sense of themselves and their masculinity over to a champion who represents them.

At a different cultural level of masculine strivings, opera fans fight with one another over the relative merits of tenors Luciano Pavarotti and Placido Domingo, and I'd like to put in a word for Alfredo Kraus, who at sixty can match those young whippersnappers high C for high C. Such contests may lack the raw viscerality of athletic striving for mastery, for determining at the most basic physical level who is the better man, but they sound better.

Men who draw too much of their identity from their heroes, men who emulate too totally, may end up with a one-note male chorus and may not emulate with enough diversity to form a full-scale identity of their own. Sports fans fortunately are notoriously fickle and can switch heroes at the drop of a ball, but musical emulators tend to pick a model while they are young and never grow past it. It is painful to watch aging followers of The Grateful Dead, devoting their lives to following around their cultural and stylistic heroes. I read of conventions of people who spend their lives dressed as Elvis Presley. And I see pictures of Michael Jackson, who has had himself surgically reconstructed as Brooke Shields. All these guys, like Puckett, might do well to give up music and become sports fans.

ADVENTURERS

> That faculty of beholding at a hint the face of his desire and the shape of his dream, without which the earth would know no lover and no adventurer.
> —Joseph Conrad, *Lord Jim*

Adventurers' dreams and desires have a shape of their own; adventurers are turning themselves into men in their own image. The adventures may be frightening and dangerous for them, and are no less competitive than playing the game by the rules the other boys have laid down, but they make you your own person rather than leaving you at the mercy of the usual contests for masculine status. Sir Edmund Hillary did not climb Mt. Everest because "it was there," but because he was there, and in order for him to be the man he wanted to be, he had to do what no one else had done.

Quigley was an undertaker and an adventurer. He had had a brutal childhood, and a horrible first marriage to a woman who thought she might have been abused by somebody and spent the rest of her life abusing everyone who came close. He escaped the marriage, raised his children, and tried to find peace. He had spent a lifetime dealing with the frightening things about life, and now he felt most alive and least frightened when he was risking his life in the pursuit of adventures. Adventures exhilarated him, but they also gave him the feeling that he was in control of his life. He died unafraid on the summit of Mt. McKinley, as he would surely have wished. I thought of him as I was bungee jumping in New Zealand.

Some men eschew the competitions that are popular, often because they aren't really good at them and would not gain status from the competition, but sometimes because they see themselves as being above the competition with the other boys. What they do they may do alone, but they startle the other boys and men through their willingness to play far more demanding games than the usual assigned rituals for becoming a man.

I went through a period of taking crazy risks when I couldn't play the usual games that give a boy masculine status. My son Frank IV played all the usual sports and did fine at them, but didn't get real respect and accolades as a sports superstar until he found the overlooked sport of running, and made it his identity in high school. A decade and a half later, running is now a big deal, but in those years, it was so obscure at his school that he had to serve as his own cross-country coach. He and his team won the state championship anyway, and he became a bit of a local legend. He was brutally competitive, but only in competitions of his own choosing.

My nephew Harrison grew up on a golf course, and soon was the state junior golf champion. He didn't go on adventures with the rest of the family, didn't go climbing mountains or shooting rapids or digging down into caves with the rest of us. He just played golf and never wanted to be away from that fountain of his masculine identity. But after giving up on a career as a professional golfer, he worked for a few years selling leather furniture, and made enough money to celebrate his thirtieth birthday by taking off a year for the adventures he'd missed during a boyhood of competing at more structured games. He called from Bali after rafting uncharted rivers in

Borneo to tell us he'd decided he wanted to go into teaching like his mother and stepfather, preferrably coaching golf for inner city kids.

I have savored Harrison's competitive successes, but winning contests, for either money or glory, gets boring and pointless in time. I'm eager to live vicariously through Harrison's adventures into the world and into the spirit. As he seeks a worthwhile outlet for his fierce drive and his poetic nature, he'll share it with me.

Adventurers eschew competing with the other boys and are contending against the forces of nature or society or reality. But adventuring can become such a solitary, antisocial pursuit that men who dedicate themselves to it can miss the brotherhood-making teamwork the other guys savor. Life becomes both dangerous and time consuming for men who don't feel man enough as they're growing up and have to go to so much trouble to get it later. As Bilbo Baggins complained in *The Hobbit*, "Adventures can make you late for dinner."

WORKERS

> *The man who dies with the most toys wins.*
> —Bumper sticker

The primary contest for grown men is not sports or penis size anymore but is economic. Grown men are measured by the size of their net worth. And contending men, not content with merely making a living and having a life, want to improve their position in the pecking order by flashing a bigger checkbook. They can always try to steal money, or inherit it, or marry it, or win it, but most often they will try to make it through work. As long as they are working, they can feel themselves contending to finally, however belatedly, become a more alpha male in the pack.

Contenders like to believe their success is part of a contest against the other guys. Actually, of course, most work is an exercise in cooperation and teamwork, in which their competitiveness may serve them badly. I routinely see men who have failed at noncompetitive nuturing jobs, as teachers, coaches, or managers, because they found a competitive aspect they could run with and they let that overwhelm the job itself.

Contenders may just compete to see who can work longest or hardest, who can sacrifice the most. These guys stay up all night to best the competition, maybe to win the prize, maybe just to keep the competition from winning it. Those who really like to win can struggle with enthusiasm and optimism, and the game can be fun for them. But those who are desperate not to lose go through it with tortured anxiety, and with envy of whoever was relaxed and enthusiastic enough to win.

Workaholic Contenders may well love their work, but they may not love the rest of their lives. They may not feel at home at home. They may find their wives and children to be distractions. Men sometimes try to convince themselves that they work *so* hard and make *so* much money for the sake of their wives and children. They can't admit to themselves that their work is just part of that old schoolyard competition with the other boys.

Rooker had dropped out of school and started a clever, creative business that he sold for a million dollars when he was only twenty-five. He felt on top of the world, having done better financially than the workaholic father he barely knew. He planned to use his money to make even more money. He was ecstatic. But his wife, at that point, started an affair with a mechanic and left him. She wasn't going to spend her life "lorded over by a millionaire." I tried to work with them, but I never actually saw Rooker. We scheduled several appointments, but each time he had to cancel because some business deal just came in. He suggested that we could get together on a Sunday before his golf game with customers, or at dawn before his breakfast meeting with his lawyers. I tried to explain that his marriage didn't seem to have a very high priority, and he said, "But this is business, for God's sake! You can't expect a man to let a woman's feelings interfere with business! The sort of man who would leave work to go talk about marriage is a loser. He's never going to have any success." She got the divorce.

The Contender's Tragedy

We all have some of the contender in us. No boy who grows into a man can escape the sense that his status and his dignity and maybe even the love and money of his life depend upon his success at competing with the other boys. We all know this about ourselves and about one another, and we try to tolerantly respect it, and we can do so as long as everyone plays by the usual rules. But men who don't feel man enough can get desperate and can contend recklessly, illegitimately, obnoxiously, destructively.

There is a tragedy here not just for all the rest of us but for the contenders themselves: the more successes they have, the less other people will feel the impulse to give them the reassurance they are really seeking. By growing up they have lost any parental audience for their masculine strivings, and they're not likely to find anyone again who cares very much about how they're doing as men.

One intermittently successful man I know, Spike, tells

me that he got his restless drive from his father, a miserably depressed alcoholic who saw happiness as a sign of weakness. He feared his three sons would relax and be satisfied before he had become the best he could be. So he did all he could to make them insecure and ashamed of themselves. He threw them into such competition with one another that they've never been close. Spike was the youngest, his father's last hope to produce a champion. The old man would humiliate Spike in any company, beat him routinely, convince him he was stupid and worthless, and present him with tasks he couldn't possibly perform. He would excoriate him for any sign of human sensitivity or compassion, for intellectual or aesthetic interests, or for being friendly. He brutalized young Spike in an effort to turn him into a contending brute: he emotionally attack-trained his son.

Spike grew up with such extreme self-doubts that he had to prove himself in every arena. He was a champion athlete, then a war hero, then an entrepreneur, then a famous writer, finally a powerful politician—he lived the life of Walter Mitty, but for real. However, he couldn't get close to anyone. He certainly couldn't get close to another man, since every one of them was either part of the competition or an impediment to the game. He couldn't be faithful to his wife, since seduction of women was part of the competition. He couldn't be around his children, since that was time wasted from the crucial competitions. Any time he spent with his children was disastrous, anyway, since he didn't know how to be a father except by doing what his father had done. He had no friends, of course. He never had.

Spike didn't seem to know that he hurt people with his efforts at shaming them. He didn't know he had been hurt. He assumed the only comfort and pride a man could achieve would come from making every other man feel more ashamed than he was. One might think Spike's unusual talents and profound successes could help him overcome his shame. They didn't. The taunting and ridiculing voice of his father overwhelmed the rest of his male chorus.

For relief of his shame, Spike had to identify his father as a monster, who had himself been shamed and brutalized into his brutality. He had to recognize how he looked at other men, including his brothers, how they reacted to his successes, and how they reacted to his insensitive, brutal nastiness to them. He, even at his age and level of success, had to seek out mentors from among the men in the world he admired. He had to relearn who he was and what a man was.

Men who were ridiculed and shamed instead of loved and approved by their fathers have to either compete for favor, or give up and live in defeat. Both the chronic struggle for glory and the lifelong defeated withdrawal are fueled by shame.

For contenders, there is no end to the contest. Their status as a man, however many medals they win or women they seduce or toys they accumulate, remains pretty much where their fathers left it. To move it past that point becomes a lifetime struggle.

But contenders, no less than philanderers, are looking for their masculinity in the wrong place. Women don't have it, and the other boys don't have it, either. They can only make a man feel like one of them, can only let him join the team where he can find reassurance that he is no better and no worse than the others, and that should be enough. If just being one of the boys doesn't make him feel man enough, he is in for a lonely struggle.

FOUR

Controllers

And God said, Let us make man in our image, after our likeness: and let them have dominion over the fish of the sea, and over the fowl of the air, and over the cattle, and over all the earth, and over every creeping thing that creepeth upon the earth. —Genesis 1:26

The great act of faith is when man decides that he is not God. —Oliver Wendell Holmes in a letter to William James

Heads of the Household and the Divine Right of Control

Men have felt called upon by good authority to control things. In our blessed little heads, we have felt a divine responsibility to conquer and control nature, to conquer and control men who are in some way different from ourselves, and, of course, to conquer women, who otherwise would surely go out of control and create disturbances and disorder.

Dominion over people and things had passed on from

God to Adam to Dad to us. The chain was broken in recent decades as women and children rebelled against men's divine authority, as fathers became increasingly peripheral, as men rejected fathering and ran away from home, leaving their sons to grow up in the image of whatever rock star or sports hero was popular that day.

Even in the early '40s, patriarchy seemed dated and the object of ridicule. The classic play *Life With Father*, by Lindsay and Crouse, was based on Clarence Day's story about growing up at the turn of the century with a father who thought he should control things, and couldn't quite get control of his wife, who wanted him baptized. Mr. Day resisted this female challenge to his masculine authority.

In the 1947 version of the movie, William Powell is the father and Jimmy Lydon is the young Clarence. My favorite scene takes place in the father's study, after Clarence has just had a confusing encounter with his first girlfriend, who has run through the room in tears. Father attempts to pass on to his adolescent son the wisdom he has gained about the nature of women. He sits Clarence down in the oak and leather library of the Edwardian house and sagely informs the boy: "Clarence, women aren't the angels that you think they are! Well, now— first, let me explain this to you. You see, Clarence, we men have to run this world and it's not an easy job. It takes work and it takes thinking. A man has to be sure of his facts and figures. He has to reason things out. Now, you take a woman— a woman thinks—no, I'm wrong right there. A woman doesn't think at all! She gets stirred up! And she gets stirred up over the damndest things!"

Father reassures himself that he will not be baptized, that he will not undergo submission of his authority to any power greater than himself. He declares, "Clarence, if a man thinks a certain thing is wrong, then he shouldn't do it. If he thinks it's right, he should do it. Now that has nothing to do with whether he loves his wife or not. . . . Women! They get stirred up and then they try to get you stirred up, too. If you can keep reason and logic in the argument, well a man can hold his own, of course. But if they can *switch* you—pretty soon the argument's about whether you love them or not. I swear I don't now how they do it! Don't you let 'em, Clarence. Don't you let 'em!"

Clarence solemnly accepts his father's wisdom but wonders what a man is supposed to do when a woman cries. Even Father acknowledges befuddlement, but reaffirms his recommendation: "You just have to let them know that what you're doing is for their own good. . . . The thing to remember is— be firm!"

Clarence nods and marches out, having learned all he needs to know about women, and about men's need to control the world around them.

Everything about the patriarchal position looks pretty silly in retrospect, and men who claim that St. Paul has appointed them Head of the Household will get only laughter in most circles nowadays. But being a patriarch at least gave fathers a role at home where they could be known by their children. There is no more important job for a man than raising his children, and you don't have to be godlike to do it, but many men don't discover how little it takes from them, or how much it gives back, until they have already thrown it away.

For instance, Sturdivant considered himself a modern man, unlike his rigidly patriarchal, thoroughly domesticated father. Sturdivant was not going to lead a boring life at home. He didn't try to run his household—instead he dropped by to make sure things were going just as he had ordered. He wanted everything to be set up just to his specifications, and everything run according to his schedule, even though he was rarely there except to inspect and make sure all was to his liking. He made all the decisions about how and where the family would live, what sort of clothes they would wear, what sort of food they would eat, and what sort of games they would play. And he kept the emotional atmosphere nice and calm and respectful—he would hear no complaints, especially about him and his control and his absence. After all, he paid for everything and the only reason he was away was to work or to make business contacts or to get some well-earned relaxation after working.

For years, no one dared complain. Now Sturdivant's marriage is busted, after years of his heavy drinking and intermittent philandering. He lost his money when the market collapsed, his wife has filed for divorce and found another man. Sturdivant has been sober for over a year, struggling to make a living, and faithful to his new girlfriend. He is baffled about how the wife he loved and controlled and ignored for so many years could turn away from him now that he has changed. But Sturdivant is a charmer and was always optimistic that his charm would prevail. He felt sure that at least he'd be spending "quality time" with his children.

Then an event happened that made him see what he had really lost. His three-year-old son spent the weekend with him. As he and the boy were taking a leak together, the little tyke looked up at his daddy and said, "Roger says to always shake your pee wee." Sturdivant burst into tears for the first time through this whole awful process, shaken by the horrifying realization that another man would be teaching his son how to be a man. He had spent his time with his children possessing and controlling and even dictating, just like his patriarchal father whom he despised, but he hadn't done what his father had done: he hadn't been there, living out his life with his family, sharing the experiences. He'd missed the important part. He'd done the destructive things Patriarchal Controllers do, without any of the benefits of being a "hands-on" husband and father.

Control of Women and Their Dangerous Sexuality

No matter how old-fashioned the underlying concepts, I still see men and boys who get their sense of their masculinity from their control over women. Teenaged boys, sometimes pumped up on steroids but certainly pumped up on testosterone and insecurity, strut through shopping centers wearing muscle shirts and holding the hands of tiny, heavily made up cheer-leader types. The boys try to look fierce. They get into ex-travagantly recounted fights with other boys who go sniffing around their girl. And if the girl should encourage, however subtly, attention from another guy, she's dog meat.

Boys have committed homicide or suicide when they have failed in their responsibility to control a girl sexually. Othello was a fierce general, and governor of Cyprus, but he was still shattered over his failure to control a woman. He strangled his beloved wife, Desdemona, when his envious lieutenant, Iago, convinced him she was being unfaithful enough to give a handkerchief to another man. I have seen a man kill a woman over a Kleenex. (In all fairness, I've seen women kill men for even less.)

Back when I was working in the emergency room of At-lanta's public hospital, we could count, on busy Friday nights, sewing up men and women who had been cut or shot by jealous lovers after real or imagined betrayals. Jealousy can get espe-cially intense in young men, or poor men, or men who feel like failures in life. If a man is to feel like a man, he's got to have control over something, and for men who don't have anything else they can control, a woman seems a natural.

In the movie *Rambling Rose,* based on Calder Willingham's southern gothic novel, everyone in the depression era southern town is agog over Rose's unbridled sexuality. Rose (Laura Dern) is a victim of incest and assorted mistreatments by men, but her sexual promiscuity is seen by the adolescent boy and his mother as a liberating force. The father and the family doctor, both of whom have fallen victim to Rose's sexual freedom, feel threatened by it and conspire to neuter Rose in hopes of drying up her sexual juices. Similarly, in other times and places, clitoridectomy or a cult of virginity would serve the desired purpose of keeping female sexuality safely under male control. The current effort to remove women's rights to chose abortion is another attempt to put female sexuality safely back under the control of men.

Incidentally, when Rose finally finds Mr. Right, a policeman whose thumb she has bitten to the bone when he tried to break up a fight between two of Rose's other suitors, he, too, wants to control her. We know the marriage is doomed at the wedding reception when she giddily delights in what she calls a "picnic," and her new bridegroom insensitively deflates her by explaining that this is a "barbecue," since a picnic does not offer roast meats, and roast meats are being served here.

Thor, an enormously brutish and painfully ugly patient of mine, went through life feeling especially insecure. The other boys had made fun of his fat face and bug eyes until he got too big for anyone to mess with, and then they just stayed away from him. He was poor, fatherless, and lonely, and he dreamed of the love of a woman. But he had always feared he would never be able to find a woman to love him. This insecurity about his sexual attractiveness wasn't relieved when he made money in the plumbing business, but more women did make themselves available to him. He never trusted their love, though.

When I saw Thor, he was supporting a wife, a mistress, and two ex-wives, and had to keep them all under his control. He would pay unexpected daily calls on each to inspect and make sure no other man had been there. One of the ex-wives in his stable acted up by letting the teenaged boy next door come over to watch television with her. When Thor found out about it, he took a shotgun and blew away both the television and the sofa. His rationale was that he had, through alimony, paid for both, and he wasn't about to let another man have that victory over him.

Thor sobbed that he just wanted to be loved, and he couldn't understand why women like his ex-wife didn't love him the way he wanted, even after he had been so generous with her. Thor was perhaps certifiably insane, though he had been extremely successful in the world. Inside he was little different from other men who get their sense of themselves from their control over women.

The newspapers tell us daily of men like Thor, who blow away the ex-wife or the teenaged boy rather than the sofa or the TV set. The man who threw the fire bomb in the Happy Land Social Club, and burned alive eighty-seven people to become the most successful mass murderer in history, was just trying to get back at his girlfriend for not paying enough attention to him and paying too much to other men.

I've seen men in my practice who were devastated by their wife's affair, but the grown-up ones have rarely left the marriage or killed themselves or anybody else because of it. Instead they obsess over why she chose someone else over him. Even when the wife is apologetic and returns enthusiastically to the marriage, the husband can lose all sense of power when "his" woman proves to be "her" own person. This obsessive or violent jealousy is fueled in part by competition with the other man (every man who has been sexually betrayed by a woman wants to know the penis size of the man who has cuckolded him, but some are afraid to ask). And his jealousy is fueled also by his firm belief that his masculinity requires that he be in control of women.

Fathers, who generally delight in their son's sexuality, may feel called upon to control the sexuality of their daughters. Perhaps it is competition with the boys over control of the girl, and more than one man has told me something as alarming as, "I'm not going to let any other man sleep with my daughter as long as I'm supporting her. They're not going to pick the apples off my tree." But the other element is the man's sense of stewardship, as if God has appointed him to keep Eve from eating apples, and to keep daughters from losing their virginity until they marry.

Underbush, otherwise a sane, solid, slightly boring man who worked too hard and drank too much from time to time, had felt his mission in life was to keep his daughter Virginia chaste, just as he and his wife had been when they married. Underbush considers this mission crucial to his sense of himself as a man.

While Underbush's mean-spirited and embittered father had passed on few social graces to his sons, he had passed on a fear of social disgrace. Underbush had heard him ridicule an otherwise more fortunate neighbor whose daughter had an illegitimate child, thereby dropping the neighbor a few pegs in the unspoken competition with Underbush's father. Accordingly, Underbush had carefully censored the TV shows Virginia could watch, had made sure she went to Christian schools, and only had friends from the most proper families.

When Virginia was fifteen, she went on a trip to visit

her father's brother and his daughter. Underbush's niece turned out to be a bit wilder than Underbush thought proper, and he did not like some of the entries in Virginia's diary. He raised hell with his brother and broke off all contact. He began to follow Virginia around, spying on her in movies. He tapped her telephone and obsessed for hours daily on the meaning of each fragment of conversation. He mostly kept her on restriction and under close surveillance. He even had her taken to a doctor to confirm her virginity. Finally, his wife got so alarmed she sent the girl off to a strict boarding school with specific instructions to keep the girl from losing her virginity.

Once Virginia was off at school, Underbush lost all interest in whether she remained a virgin or not, since it was no longer his job to protect it. It was no longer a determinant of his masculinity. He didn't make up with his brother, though. He savored that victory—his daughter was under better sexual control than his brother's daughter.

Control of Whatever Women Do

Women don't even have to drop their pants or bat their eyes to alarm some men, who seem to have built-in "female motion detectors," as if anything a woman does is likely to be out of control. These men seem to stay on duty all the time, alert to their responsibility of keeping women from doing things, spending things, or even eating things of their own choosing.

One of the most frustrating husbands I've met was Victor, a hard-working chiropractor whose father had died when he was young. On his death bed the old man had bidden Victor to keep his mother from blowing the family fortune. Actually, the mother had run the family hotel and the family farm and handled the money quite nicely all these years, but Victor decided, like Adam, that his father had bidden him to control all women, money, and things. He made himself and his mother miserable for years, until he married and set out to keep his wife from spending anything. She really was a frugal bargain shopper, and squeezing nickels became a full-time job for her.

Victor was a rich man, with expensive investments, but he prided himself on how well he kept his wife under control: at home, there was no air-conditioning, the holes in the wall went unrepaired, the stuffing was coming out of the sofas, and the chairs with broken legs were propped up on books. The television was black and white, the can opener was manual, and there was only one set of sheets. He slept in a moldy basement on a rump-sprung couch. He explained proudly that if other men ever come by the house, they would be impressed with how well he controlled his wife, and would have thought he was quite a man. Victor's father would be pleased with him.

Men frequently try to control what a woman eats and how much she weighs. To some men, how a woman looks is a reflection of their masculinity, and therefore something they should control. They might prefer their wives to maintain the level of stylish skinniness Tom Wolfe in *Bonfire of the Vanities* ascribes to the "social X rays," women starved to the bone. Men obsessed with a wife's weight may get quite pudgy themselves. Men who carry on wildly when their wife gains a few pounds may have affairs with women who are quite zaftig. It doesn't seem to be a sexual thing at all; it is a matter of the man's control over the woman.

I saw one woman who had never been able to get her picky husband off her back about her big bottom. She finally went on a fast, got addicted to starvation, and became severely anorexic. She was skin and bones, and her husband was embarrassed that she looked so awful, but as she started back eating he asked her if she could get a diet from her dietician that would keep her from putting the weight back in her hips, and take off a little more in the ankles. At that point she realized he was endangering her life.

Controlling the World

Obviously, if men can stake their sense of themselves on their ability to control a woman's sexuality or weight, they are willing to try to control anything. And sometimes they do. They may try to battle nature and rid a lawn of any living thing they themselves didn't put there. They may try to make their surly kids become champions at whatever interests the father. They may even battle against traffic and try to make sure all the other frustrated drivers behave with impeccable manners. Some battle over time, getting huffy if someone is running late to see them, as if the punctuality of others were a measure of their worth as men.

It is enlightening to watch men watch sports. Some of them think they can influence the game through the television set. And I've even known men who tried to control the weather. My own particular need to control centers on audiences in movies and concerts. I'm determined to make the rest of the audience behave, and I get into verbal fights with people who whisper—it's never quite gotten physical, but it's come close.

The need to control may appear selfish and intrusive to the objects of it, but the men who are doing the controlling see themselves as fixing things, correcting them, or getting them back on track. A man would feel irresponsible and ashamed of himself if he let things go out of control when he had the chance to make them "right." And while most of us want to be loved, controllers are willing to forgo love if that's what it takes to be the boss. In *The Prince*, Machiavelli wrote that "the question arises whether it is better to be loved rather than feared, or feared rather than loved. It might perhaps be answered that we should wish to be both: but since love and fear can hardly exist together, if we must choose between them, it is far safer to be feared than loved."

The Heroic Posture

Wise men, especially as they set forth to control others, feel they should first of all control themselves. But not quite wise men may overdo the self-control, and turn themselves into machines. They may even rid themselves of emotion. That was the Heroic Ideal when I was coming along.

The heroes on the screen were strong, silent types in the John Wayne/Gary Cooper tradition, men who never shed a tear or muttered a complaint as they were screwed over or blown up. Back then, boys were expected to play football and be put through pain, deprivation, and humiliation until we overcame human emotions. At the first sign of loss of control, those boys whose families could afford it sent them to military school. Those whose families couldn't, sent them to the military. Those without families went to reform school that were run on a military model.

I spent four years at military school. My father was just back from World War II, and I had been raised by women; now I needed to be toughened up. I didn't want to be beaten into the manly model of the day, probably because I couldn't imagine that I would fit. I wasn't the real thing, but I learned to fake it. I was neither strong nor silent. I felt things that real men were not supposed to feel, and I ridiculed the things we were supposed to worship.

Girls wanted me to be different, too. They urged me to talk less and smile less in hopes people would see me as dumb and brutal, or at least dumb and moody, so other girls would envy them when they were seen with me. But, no matter how I tried, I was not the anesthetized, strong, silent type and not likely to be.

We were trying so hard to be heroic, we didn't notice that the hero we emulated was so devoid of emotion that he could not savor his victories. Years later, when I've seen the more heroic adolescents I envied growing up, I've come to realize that they weren't aware of what was happening—they were only doing their duty, following the rules, and trying to live up to other people's expectations of them. Boys can only be heroes unawares. Awareness is unheroic.

Homoclites and the Control of Emotions

Most people are satisfied with controlling the *behavior* of themselves and others. The even more dangerous ones, the ones I call "homoclites," want to control *emotions* as well. For them, it is not good enough that people *do* the "right" thing, they have to go so far as to *feel* the "right" things, too. The ideal is merely to do what is "right" and be so far beyond emotion that they don't feel anything at all.

Back in the early '60s, when the world hadn't gone through puberty yet, psychiatrist Roy Grinker set out to prove that there were at least a few normal people in the world, people who were not experiencing any emotional distress. He applied the currently popular psychological tests to various groups and found that the ones who showed up "normal" were a group of young men at a church-related men's college for the earnest and the not very intellectual. These guys represented the societal ideal of the post-WW II Eisenhower era: they were dutiful, unimaginative, unemotional rule followers. They came from stable homes and they sought stability in their own lives. They never doubted, never questioned, never rebelled, and just did what they were told. They were happy with the world they had been given. Grinker called these young men "homoclites" to distinguish them from "heteroclites," a scientific term meaning "exceptions to the usual rules." These guys were not exceptions to any rules. Grinker followed these young men for many years, and sure enough they married women much like themselves and raised children in the same image. They have lived uneventful, unimaginative lives with which they were uncomplainingly content.

I know these men. Many of the boys with whom I grew up have been expert homoclites. They can't think and feel at the same time. They try not to think about how they feel and they try to stop those around them from stimulating any emotion. They are disoriented by issues that can't be settled by choosing True or False; they really hate essay questions because they don't tolerate doubt. They want life to be like baseball, played dispassionately with incontestible rules, lots of statistics, referees in every corner to make sure everyone does the right thing, and the game played out until there is a clear winner.

Stomping Out Emotion

Among my earliest memories are the visits from my great-uncle Walter and my great-aunt Ramona. These visits were marked by a recurring pattern of interaction that haunts me still. Uncle Walter was a calmly cheerful man who liked to fix things. He would always bring me tools—hammers, axes, and saws. I had a formidable hardware collection before I was old enough to walk. Aunt Ramona brought stories and drama. She wore flamboyant clothes, with lots of shawls, fans, and feathers. She had no children of her own, and unleashed a lifetime of maternal affection upon me and my sister. She entertained us with a vengeance, telling fantastic stories and laughing too loudly.

After a while Aunt Ramona would wind down and begin to sob about how much she loved being with us. We felt loved, and happy to make her happy enough to cry over us. But Uncle Walter would seem uncomfortable and would whisper, ever so gently, "Now, now, dear. Don't get upset." Aunt Ramona would say fiercely, "Don't tell me how to feel!" Uncle Walter would calmly and rationally explain that it was "wrong" of her to "excite" the children, and he would ask her to "calm down and just be cheerful." That was when the feathers hit the fan. Aunt Ramona would cut loose, and once she shouted out defiantly, "I may want to feel happy or I may want to feel sad, but I'll never want to feel just calmly cheerful."

Homoclites are totally comfortable and find it unfortunate that everyone close to them sinks into a state of dithering despair. One homoclite's wife said she was worried about something with one of the kids. She couldn't get her husband to discuss it and said, "I don't know how you feel about it." He justified his bland emotional palette by saying, "I don't. If both of us fall apart in this marriage, then we don't have a prayer." To him, any emotion was loss of control, and he was clearly too worried about the situation to indulge himself in emotions and loss of control. When men don't have any feelings about something, it may not be because the issue is too insignificant, but because it is too unsettling.

Cartoonist James Thurber understood all of this and wrote about it in *Men, Women, and Dogs* and *The War Between Women and Men*. One of his classic cartoons shows a woman kicking over the furniture, while her husband calmly reads the newspaper, with a smirk of superiority. She is screaming, "Why did I ever marry below my emotional level?"

A homoclite can drive someone who takes him seriously quite mad. However, since he seems so secure, correct, and normal, he attracts people who doubt themselves and feel security in his supposed strength. They attach themselves to him and grow increasingly insecure as they find themselves reacting "incorrectly" to life's events.

A homoclitic man is likely to point out to a woman that she is feeling more (i.e., colder, sadder, more worried, angrier, or just more annoyed by the loud music) than he is, and therefore there must be something wrong with her. In Harold Pinter's play *The Homecoming*, a man brings his wife home to meet his family for the first time. He is so anxious about the visit that he fails to notice that she is perfectly comfortable. He busies himself trying to calm her down. Finally, she announces she's stepping outside for a breath of fresh air. He panics: "But what am I going to do? The last thing I want is a breath of air. Why do you want a breath of air?"

A patient of mine could never acknowledge feeling anything: he identified himself in terms of what he didn't feel. Wilkes had grown up as the pampered, adored prince of the town his family had owned for generations. Wilkes's mother was a flighty lady, whom her father adored but disdained, and his father was a man of great dignity and presence.

Wilkes's father never relaxed, never unbuttoned his starched collar, never revealed anything about what it felt like to be the boss of everyone in town. He had inherited the family cotton mill when his father died at an early age, and he had struggled to hold on to it through the Great Depression so he could support his family and his town. Wilkes was his only son and was expected to take over the mills in due time.

Wilkes had always been perfect, the president of the Student Body, the valedictorian, the captain of the football team, the pitcher on the baseball team. He was not the captain of the basketball team, since he was only 5'8" tall and constitutionally unable to shine in that one activity. He played hard at it, though, and always felt he'd betrayed his heritage by not growing taller and playing basketball better. He went off to the state university, where he did well, and made his father proud, and then he went into the army. Wilkes's father died when Wilkes was in Vietnam; the mills were in great debt, and had to be sold. Wilkes's life since then has not been the life that had been planned for him, but he has no feelings about that.

Wilkes says he wasn't frightened in Vietnam—"It's in God's hands"—but he began having anxiety attacks there. When he came home, he says he wasn't ashamed of having been in Vietnam—"I did my duty, and part of my duty was not to ask why we were there"—and he wasn't angry at the protestors: "Free speech was one of the things I was fighting for." He went on to law school in the city, and joined the firm of his father's old college roommate. He did well and moved up in his prestigious firm, until he discovered that his mentor and senior partner was involved in some shady dealings. He assures me he wasn't angry: "Only God can judge the actions of others. He was an old man, and I'm sure he was just confused." Instead he set up his own little law firm, which has done OK. "I grew up with money. I've had that, I don't need it now, and I'm sure the kids are better off without it.

It was wonderful for me having such generous parents. But the times are different." He doesn't feel under pressure: "I was raised to work hard. I like a challenge, and I'm used to working eighteen hours a day."

Wilkes has started having all manner of stress symptoms. He's baffled by that since he doesn't feel any stress at all. The symptoms have gotten so bad that he hasn't been able to function at work for a while, but he goes in every day, and smiles, and pretends that he is functioning. He doesn't want to look like a loser for fear other people will think he's in bad shape, and that might make him feel bad about himself and his condition.

Wilkes explains that his football coach in high school taught him that "losing comes from having a losing attitude. If you never give a thought to the possibility of losing, then you're sure to win. It's dangerous to be afraid. If you're afraid, all sort of bad things can happen."

I know this man. My father was much like him. One day at work at the cotton mill, my father was showing his bosses a new cotton combing machine that separates the fibers and lines them up straight before they are twisted into yarn. Dad reached out with an unusually expansive gesture and got his hand caught in the machine, ripping off one finger and shredding two others. He wrapped a handkerchief so deftly around what was left of his hand that no one noticed the blood, until it began dripping out of his pocket onto the floor. He hadn't wanted his bosses to notice how careless he'd been to lose his finger, and he certainly didn't want anyone to think he was sissy enough to cry over something that was past, like a lost finger or two. Men don't cry, or complain, or ask for sympathy.

Showing No Doubt

Homoclitic men also don't show any doubt, which would deliver them into the control of others. There are men who require that they be kept informed about every detail of living, but they themselves will not call home if they are running late. It makes them feel controlled. And they are afraid they will be fussed at for not being punctual.

Men are also notoriously unwilling to stop and ask for directions. My father would rather circumnavigate the globe underwater than admit he was lost, turn around, or stop and ask. I realized this as we were all dressed up going to a wedding in the strange town of Cordele—a south Georgia town otherwise famous only for the prodigious number of frogs that hop into people's houses after a rain. The bride's parents had told my parents how to get to the restaurant for the rehearsal dinner. Dad was driving and was sure Ruth and Russ had told him to turn left at the Baptist church, Mother was just as sure they had said to turn right.

At the intersection, Dad signaled left and Mother signaled right. Joanna and I could see the restaurant off to the right, but Dad had already turned left. We couldn't convince him, so Mother insisted Dad stop at the filling station and ask for directions. Dad huffed out an explanation that he had never had to do something that degrading and he wasn't about to start now. Mother demanded that Dad go back, but Dad only did what Mother demanded when she was drunk, and unfortunately she was sober this time. We all sat calmly and waited for Dad to decide he was on the wrong road. His usual way of dealing with such situations was to find a road that circled around and then announce he'd taken the scenic route. Unfortunately, the road he'd taken went straight into the swamp, with not a side road for ten or twelve miles until it suddenly dead-ended in the yard of a farmhouse.

Fortunately, there was a little stand with a kid selling boiled peanuts, so Dad, in his tuxedo, tried to save face by buying some boiled peanuts. He told the kid, "It's been a long drive, but we couldn't go to the wedding without getting some of your boiled peanuts." The kid said, "Yeah, lot of guys get on the wrong road. Keeps me in business." Joanna and I sat real quiet and ate boiled peanuts all the way back to the restaurant, and went to the rehearsal dinner with peanut juice all over our fancy clothes.

I grew up thinking this peculiar resistance to acknowledging error applied only to my father. Eventually, though, I began to notice that I had friends who couldn't ask for directions, and I chuckled to myself about their absurdity.

As soon as I began to drive, I began to get lost, and I began to experience this same phenomenon. Even when I knew it was absurd, as soon as I sat behind the wheel, I felt I must know everything, must show no weakness, must not look lost or in doubt. I hated to slow down for the car in front of me, as if that car had won a victory over me, or was holding me hostage—I would rather risk my life by passing. I hated to slow down sharply for a traffic light, as if I hadn't planned properly and was taken unawares—I would rather gracefully run the red light. I would get angry if anyone noticed that I wasn't parallel parking smoothly enough. If I was distracted and drove past my driveway, I would pretend I did so purposely, and would think of an errand to run before returning home. When I was in the driver's seat, I was a different creature altogether.

I've gotten over this symptom with driving, but it's popped up in my writing. I like to be edited, and I've loved all my editors through the years. Betsy, of course, is the first to see everything I write, but I am paralyzed with writer's block if she reads it over my shoulder as I write it. I fear I'll make an error and look like a klutz to my own wife, for God's sake, who knows after thirty-two years just what a klutz I am and loves me anyway.

Men are raised to feel a heavy and lonely responsibility to do everything right, to leave their mothers and go forth into the world to do it alone. If we ask for help, it is a sign of weakness, dependency on another man or woman: we've failed. It's dumb, but people have been hit, yelled at, and even killed because they committed the unforgivable and saw a man's masculine shame over needing directions.

Malignant Homoclites

Youngblood is among the most uncomfortably homoclitic men I've ever known. When he was a child, his mother had been sent to an asylum. They knew she had gone crazy because she stopped taking care of the house, and there were dirty dishes in the sink and piles of dirty clothes in the bedroom, and Youngblood's father seemed to be so domestically incompetent that he sent his wife away rather than clean up the mess himself.

Youngblood was the oldest child and took it upon himself to keep everything in order so no one would know the family had a crazy mother. He very much faulted his father for the embarrassing situation and determined that he would never let his life go out of control again. He grew up to be a neat, punctual little man, who kept everything in order. He tried marriage a couple of times but could not tolerate anyone else's noise or clutter, and it drove him nuts to have children around the house. He made his second wife send her children off to boarding school, but then he couldn't tolerate having them around for holidays, and he couldn't get them to make the grades he thought they should make. He finally got so uncomfortable he divorced her.

Youngblood wanted to try marriage again, but realized he was just too uncomfortable with the disorder. In therapy, I tried to get him to loosen up. He was finally able to keep a dirty coffee cup in his sink, but when I had him leave his bed unmade, he went into a panic and had to leave work to go home and make it. His fear was that a repairman would come to the house, see the unmade bed, and think he was as sloppily incompetent as his father had been.

A recently popular domestic horror movie was *Sleeping With the Enemy,* in which Julia Roberts is terrorized by a picky husband, who would hit her, unemotionally of course, to help her see the importance of keeping the canned goods lined up in alphabetical order. She fakes her own death, runs away, and begins a new life, but the blood-chilling moment occurs when she finds the hand towels in her bathroom lined up just right and knows that her insanely neat husband has found her.

Many women have tried to live with such men, who "inspect" the housekeeping, perhaps by putting on white gloves and running their fingers over the tops of the doors and windows looking for dust the incompetent woman has permitted to accumulate. One such man wanted the faucets polished daily to be free of fingerprints. (It really seemed important to him, so I encouraged the couple to see that as his hobby rather than her responsibility.)

HOMOCLITIC VIOLENCE

> *The tendency to identify manhood with a capacity for physical violence has a long history in America.*
> —Marshall Fishwick

Men who have been raised violently have every reason to believe it is appropriate for them to control others through violence; they may feel no compunction over being violent to women, children, and one another.

When I ask men why they did violent things, they tell me that the object of their violence made them do it. They don't experience their violent acts as having been chosen—the violence was not motivated by thought, or even by emotion, but was an automatic, knee-jerk response to someone else doing something wrong. A woman had gotten upset and wouldn't back off, a man had crossed a boundary—the violent man sensed something going out of control. His masculinity snapped to attention and his body, not his mind, jumped to the defense. When a man gets violent with a woman, he may not feel he has lost control of himself—he may feel instead that he has lost control of someone it is his duty to control.

Hypermasculine Despair

Like the philanderers who run from wives and compulsively seduce strange women, and the contenders who won't join the boys' team because they have to win their victories alone and by their own rules, controlling men who must change the world to suit them and rid it of unsettling emotions are doomed to go through life lonely and ashamed, driving away those who would be close, and protecting themselves from being known and understood. It hasn't worked, it doesn't work, and it's not going to work. These men, beneath their hypermasculine shells, are the same beautiful, vulnerable boys they were, and if you look deep inside you can still find them, in great pain, hiding alone, guarding their precious masculinity.

What went so horribly wrong? To understand that, we have to look at the history of masculinity, the myths of men's heroes, and the way in which boys are raised into men—what happens between a boy and his father, a man and his mother, and the world a guy shares with the other guys.

II

BECOMING A MAN

FIVE

Growing Up Male

Snips and snails and puppy-dogs' tails;
That's what little boys are made of.

—Anonymous

All men were once boys, and boys are always looking for
ways to become men.   —James Dickey, *Deliverance*

A Boy and His Penis

We know from the beginning that we're supposed to be
boys, but the Y chromosome doesn't show. The only visible
sign of our maleness is a useless little peanut we're told to keep
hidden. So we have to wear boy clothes and play with boy toys
and try to act like boys act. When the other boys are with us
we practice being cowboys or soldiers or football players or
space jockeys. We practice pissing off the porch, rolling in the
mud, whatever we can think of that boys do and girls don't.

We have to show that we don't fit in at home. We're too loud or messy or crude or clumsy. We clearly belong out there in the jungle with the wild animals who don't scare us because we are one of them, and we have the protection of the magic peanut and an invisible chorus of males to give us the courage to battle fiercely.

We aren't big yet, or strong, and we can't make the muscles grow very much, so we substitute courage. Long before our peanut becomes a pecker, we are trying to reassure ourselves that we have balls.

We go around pretending to ourselves that we're big, powerful men, but our mothers keep reminding us that we are still little boys. When we are prepared to test our bravery against the forces of darkness in the night, mother tells us to brush our teeth and go to bed. Mother treats us as if she, not we, owned our bodies and our lives. Mother isn't even fazed by our magic peanut. We're still her baby, and as much as we love that when we're hurting or when we need her service, she can bring us back from the soaring fantasy world of masculinity to the inglorious little life of a child.

We long for our father. We wear his clothes, and actually try to fill his shoes. Anything of his is charmed and can endow us with his masculinity. We hang on to him, begging him to teach us how to do whatever is masculine, to throw balls or be in the woods or go see where he works. We spend so much more time with our mother we begin to fear that she will tame us from being the wild animals we now we must be. We want our fathers to protect us from coming too completely under the control of our mothers. We fear that femaleness might be contagious and we don't want it to rub off on us. We want to be seen with Dad, hanging out with men and doing men things.

We practice our masculinity, trying to develop enough of

it. We feel a bit foolish with it, like imposters, so we practice it in front of mirrors and around strangers, trying to learn how to swagger, trying to mimic the men we admire. We always overdo it. If we have a father (or uncle or grandfather) we know and admire, and we can find him in ourselves, we can imitate him. If our older brother will give us the time of day we can use him as a model, though he probably hasn't gotten his act polished yet, either. We may have to imitate stars or sports heroes and we may have to look to the other boys our own age—also posturing—to tell us when we're overdoing it.

As boys without bonds to their fathers grow older and more desperate about their masculinity, they are in danger of forming gangs in which they strut their masculinity for one another, often overdo it, and sometimes turn to displays of fierce, macho bravado and even violence.

The Disorientation of Puberty

> *I wonder why men get serious at all. They have this delicate thing hanging outside their bodies, which goes up and down by its own will. If I were a man I would always be laughing at myself.*
> —Yoko Ono

A boy's puberty is a strangely unsettling transition, perhaps not quite so dramatic and definitive as menarche (though a boy's first ejaculation can be every bit as frightening as a girl's first menstruation), but a great deal more disorienting because it involves such total change in the boy's body. Prior to puberty the bodies of boys and girls are similar enough to be easily interchangeable except for the insignificant little genitals. Much is made of those little genitals from birth (or nowadays even before birth), and they become the determinant of everything in life, but for the first twelve or fourteen years they have little significance except as predictors of future events.

Early on, girls begin to menstruate, which is dramatic but not obvious to their playmates. They grow taller and rounder, but underneath their makeup they are still recognizably themselves. For boys it is far more disorienting. Puberty comes later, sometimes much later, and its delay is humiliating. While the tall, round girls are getting themselves up like grown women, the prepubertal boys, with their featureless, hairless bodies, are just dirty little kids who could pass for the children of the hypermature girls.

The genitals are the first part to change. First there is a little pubic hair and then, with alarming suddenness, the penis blossoms into its full glory, utterly inappropriate to the little boy body from which it projects. A boy's penis seems enormous and hard to hide, far too big yet still too small, always too small. It has a life of its own, responding to all the wrong things at all the wrong times, intrusive and embarrassing, yet utterly honest in its responses. It requires much time and attention, much measuring, exploration, and comparison with the other guys, and much concern about how it is going to behave in the presence of girls. The boy has little control over it, and for a few years it is not clear who is in charge of whom. He must masturbate constantly to keep it down. But beat it down, however many times a day, and it will spring back up just when it is least welcome. Yet when it is needed, it is nowhere to be found; with any anxiety it will run away and hide. The boy has become one of Siamese twins, with this other, independent person attached to his body, a constant, unreliable companion.

While the boy is preoccupied, learning to ride this willful creature, thick hair has started at his ankles and is moving relentlessly up his body. All this is happening inside his trousers and does not show to the outside world, until his voice changes, and his pants one morning are a foot too short. The hair reaches his pimply face, and his body gives off goatlike odors, and his muscles bulge—again never enough—and the boy bears no resemblance to who he was a year ago or even yesterday.

Parts of his body look like a man, and the impatient girls who got into puberty before him expect him to act like a man so they will feel like a woman, but he doesn't feel like a man and his parents don't treat him like one. His parents may not even be aware of what is happening inside his pants or inside his head. And he certainly dosn't know how to talk to them about it. At the beginning, he clings to the other boys who are going through the same exciting, terrifying changes, and they form a separate society, really a very intimate one, alternately avoiding and examining the sexuality that obsesses them and passing on fantasy, fears, and lies about sex.

A man's relationship with his penis is rooted in that pubertal experience when his masculine identity is between his legs. His penis is the first and, for a time, the only part of him that seems truly masculine, and since he has grown up in awe of the masculinity he is suposed to develop, he worships this first confirming symbol of it.

Boys with models of masculinity can learn to keep their penises under control. But a boy without models may consistently defer to his penis, which seems so much more masculine than the rest of him, and then spend the rest of a lifetime being a slave to an insensitive, noncommunicative, unreliable, utterly self-centered, spineless piece of flesh.

In time, as his measurements and comparisons establish some confidence in his physical normality (though he's still sure that it's not big enough), a boy dares to put himself in the hands of equally excited and terrified girls. Some of the boys, less sure of their capacity for masculinity, more daunted by what they believe to be the requirements or the expectations or the dangers, may postpone this test of it, perhaps skip the process entirely and spend years or lifetimes keeping their penises safely out of the hands of women. Once we entrust our sexuality to women, we leave the safe company of the boys.

Losing Our Cherry

> The introduction to sex is . . . complicated and difficult . . . 'The first time' remains an emotional, guilt-ridden, bewildering and not wildly erotic moment.
> —Karl and Anne Taylor Fleming, The First Time

The classic coming-of-age joke tells of a tenderfoot trying to gain acceptance in a rough-and-tumble Alaskan mining village. He is told he'll be accepted by the other men if he 1) chugalugs a gallon of 180 proof local rotgut, 2) screws an Eskimo girl, and 3) wrestles a bear. He drinks the whiskey and stumbles out of the bar to accomplish his next ordeal. When he returns, bloody and battered, he announces, "I did the bear. Now where's the Eskimo girl I'm supposed to wrestle?"

The scariest step in a boy's quest for manhood is sexual. The twins must make it with girls. They may not want to get close to girls yet, but the point of screwing girls is not to get close to them but to prove heterosexuality so the boys won't have to feel unmasculine in their closeness to one another. So our boy, trying to hold his grip on his throbbingly impatient little twin, shouted onward by his male chorus, marches forth in search of a female who has the power to save his magic wand and turn him into a man. To whom will he entrust his nascent masculinity: a prostitute; a curious friend who wants to examine it and find out how it works; an insecure girl who wants to curry favor; a compassionate older woman who feels gratified when she kisses tadpoles and turns them into princes?

At first, we need girls who don't scare us, who don't threaten our budding masculinity. We feel safest with girls who are younger, smaller, weaker, perhaps damsels in distress who collapse upon us and make us feel strong and important. Yet our male chorus may propel us toward the girls who are "popular" and beautiful, trophies that announce our masculinity to our fellows. A virginal fifteen-year-old-boy's dream woman might be a beautiful, popular, undersized, slightly mentally retarded, depressed fourteen-year-old anorexic (with big breasts), who is running away from an abusive family.

These experiences are at least as traumatic and crucial for the girls as for us, yet we are barely aware of one another as we go through this—physically together and emotionally worlds apart. In times past, a "nice girl" tried to hold on to us by holding us off. She somehow knew that the audience for these sexual experiments was still the other boys and the invisible male chorus, and her primary power lay in frustrating us. How tortured we all were, and how grotesquely we overvalued sex as a result! We might even think we were in love with whatever girl would frustrate us most maddeningly.

What enormous power children grant one another! The two combatants are sure to have very different agendas, the sex is bound to be a disappointment if anything beyond survival were expected, and there is no way a horny little boy will respect anyone but himself in the morning.

Mating

> Woman is the sun, an extraordinary creature, one that makes
> the imagination gallop. Woman is also the element of conflict.
> With whom do you argue? With a woman, of course. Not
> with a friend, because he accepted all your defects the moment
> he found you. Besides, woman is mother—have we forgotten?
> —Marcello Mastroianni

Once we've passed the hurdle of our own virginity, we don't really *need* women for sex: we might prefer them, but we can do that for ourselves, and we do. Mostly we need women to affirm our masculinity. They can do so by responding to us sexually, by reassuring us that we are strong and powerful, by loving us and offering us nurturance as our reward for being masculine enough—or our solace for not being.

When we must choose a mate, a partner for a lifetime, should we choose the woman who makes us feel good, or the one who makes us look good to our relentless male chorus? Our male chorus demands that we honor our masculinity before we can consider our comfort, our humanity, our soul. So we must consider what woman will make us seem more masculine—perhaps someone younger, weaker, poorer—or we can try for status. Our male chorus may drive us to compete for the trophy. Or we may display our masculinity by clutching our balls and escaping each eligible candidate just before the wedding bells—perhaps a real partner will make us look "pussy-whipped."

Our ability to fall in love requires enough comfort with our masculinity to join it with someone's femininity and feel enhanced. In order to do it, we must find a woman who doesn't scare us. If our mother scared us by depending on us too much or because we depended on her too much, if we felt her to be a threat to our freedom to be men, we have to find someone very different from her. But if our mother made us feel secure and proud in our masculinity, then we want to find that again in our wife. If we are really comfortable with our mother, we can even marry a woman who is a friend rather than an adversary, and form a true partnership. In the best of all possible worlds, mating is a coupling of equals, where we look after one another.

What we need most in a mate is someone who can enable us to see and understand all those things to which our masculinity blinds us. Dare we find in a woman the lost part of ourselves, and by marrying become whole, or are we still just measuring peckers with the other boys? Even the most important decision in our life is a compromise between our instinct for survival, our search for meaning, our pursuit of pleasure, and our masculine mystique.

Do we want a girl just like the girl who married dear old Dad, or more like the girl he eventually ran off with? Even in the most important choices of our lives, it is our father's voice that leads us.

Father Knows Best

> *Like father, like son.*   —Latin Proverb
>
> *It is a wise father that knows his own child.*
>   —Shakespeare, *Merchant of Venice*

Of course, it is a wise, lucky child that knows his own father. Whether we know him or not, we can't escape him. We know, before we can walk and talk, that we're destined to grow up to be like him, and if he's there and we're not paying close attention, we'll end up just about like him. If nothing interferes, we'll just grow into him without really trying. He doesn't have to do a thing but be there, perhaps giving a little approval from time to time, and whether he is paying attention or not, we are spending our childhood studying him and creating ourselves in his image.

But if we find something in him that doesn't appeal to us, with a little conscious effort, we may be able to correct that in ourselves. We don't have to repeat our father's errors—if we know they are errors.

Our father has an even more important function than modeling manhood for us. He also has the authority to let us relax the requirements of the masculine model: if our father accepts us, then that declares us masculine enough to join the company of men. We, in effect, have our diploma in masculinity and can go on to develop other skills.

If he's not at home, we can only model ourselves after the life we imagine our father is leading out there. We may become what we imagine him to be and do what we imagine him to do.

If he is dead, we can invent whatever mythology suits us and imagine his acceptance, but if he is alive but gone for whatever reason, then we only feel his lack of acceptance. We may spend our lives seeking that acceptance, and with it a reprieve from the masculine striving. We become dependent upon the company of men to overwhelm our father's rejecting voice.

Without a father, we are forced to find mentors and heroes to model masculinity for us. Every man who gets close enough can do a little of it for us, can replace some of the mythological heroes of our desperate puberties and the raucously pubertal voices of our male chorus. But the professional models of masculinity that appeal to deserted adolescent boys tend to overdo it. Without a "father in residence," we may go through life striving toward an ideal of exaggerated, even toxic, masculinity.

The fathers who are most likely to produce masculopathic sons out to rape, pillage, and plunder for the greater glory of the masculine mystique may not be the hypermasculine fathers who mistreat the family—those monsters intimidate and repulse their sons—but may be the ones who aren't there because they are somewhere else. Some of them were merely passing sperm donors; others ran away with another woman or another man; others still technically live with the family but are too busy with work or play, enhancing their own masculinity, to be much concerned with the masculinity of their sons.

Every boy was supposed to come into the world equipped with a father whose prime function was to be our father and show us how to be men. He can escape us, but we can never escape him. Present or absent, dead or alive, real or imagined, our father is the main man in our masculinity.

Making Room for Daddy

> You don't have to deserve your mother's love. You have to deserve your father's.   —Robert Frost

I now know that my struggle with masculinity is little different from that of other men, and it is not the most dramatic, certainly not the most painful nor the most successful such struggle I've seen today, but it is the one I know best. Like every man's struggle to be a man, the central figure is my father.

I had a wonderful father, a good, hard-working, loving man, who was totally devoted to his family. He performed his fatherly duties exactly as he thought he should.

My earliest memory is of my dad taking me to the hospital to see my newly born sister when I was two and a half years old. I have many memories of Dad when I was little. He was usually at work, running the cotton mills in the little towns we lived in. I remember the excitement when he would come home. I was just a child when he went off to the war. Mother and Joanna and I had to get along without him. We moved back to Griffin, Georgia, where we lived with Mother's mother. I didn't have a room of my own at Grandmother's house, so I spent a lot of time with Dad's parents, who lived a few blocks away at their funeral home, and they had a room for me next to the caskets.

My dad was gone, but he had brought me to his father so my grandfather could take his place. Pops was hot-tempered and impatient, and he thought I talked too much and asked too many questions and made things too complicated, but he did his duty. He would take me out of school to go hunting with him, and we'd sit around a fire all night listening to the dogs bark. We'd have to be very quiet so he could tell which dog was barking and whether it had treed a raccoon or a possum. But Pops wasn't accustomed to dealing with live people who wanted conversation. He never talked to me. Pops died when I was ten, and Dad was still somewhere in the Pacific.

Dad came back after the war was over, but I never quite found a use for him, and he didn't seem to find a use for me. I needed something from him that I wasn't getting. I didn't know how to ask for it and he didn't know how to give it to me. I kept trying to get him to tell me the secrets of being a man, and he kept avoiding talking to me.

Mother told me what a good father I had, and he was a good man—far, far better than my friends' fathers. Several were alcoholics who stayed home drinking and trying to act like the Head of the Household. One friend's father was an alcoholic who had disappeared long ago, and his pictures had been taken down, and each time he'd see a drunk passed out on the sidewalk he'd wonder if that were he. He envied the guys whose fathers passed out at home. Another father was a paranoid schizophrenic who had been married eleven times, and was now into religion. From time to time he thought he was God, Abraham, or Jesus, so he would drop by and try to sacrifice his son. The strangest father was a professional wrestler and legendary underworld figure who appeared on his son's sixteenth birthday to give him a flashy new car, a pistol, a blackjack, a set of brass knuckles, and a case of rubbers: "all the things you'll need to be a man." My friends thought I had the best father in that section of Alabama. I have no doubt that I did, but I still felt I was missing something.

Dad was always reliable, and he took care of everything that went wrong, like when I was smoking in the bathroom and set the shower curtain on fire, or when I ran my car into the slot machine salesman. He even got me a car when I was thirteen and didn't like riding a horse to school.

Dad was perhaps the most respected man in Prattville, Alabama, where we lived. People always told me of his athletic accomplishments at Georgia Tech. Those were his days of glory. He would come to life talking about sports and war. I couldn't be athletic. I had been born with a heart murmur, and Mother was afraid it would kill me to play sports. I knew Dad was crushed. It's strange, but the heart murmur began to go away when I was grown, when it was too late for me to play ball with my dad.

Dad had gotten used to noise, working at the cotton mills, and he didn't like silence. He could relax best if there were three radios going, all at the same time, with different ball games on each of them and my mother screaming over the top of the athletic ensemble, trying as always to get his attention and ending up having another drink instead. My younger sister, Joanna, did better with him, I think. She just sat in his lap and pretended to be interested in whatever he was interested in—usually just listening to ball games. Mother and I kept trying to get him to pay attention to us, and we'd stay angry with him because he wouldn't. I couldn't share sports with him, so I'd show him the things I'd written, and he'd read a few paragraphs and say I was too smart for him and go back to his baseball games on the radio. Finally, I defied Mother and tried sports, and Dad just looked disgusted at my clumsiness. I *knew* he wanted me to be like him, and I wasn't, and I *knew* he was disappointed in me. My mother and both my grandmothers and both my aunts seemed delighted with me, but Dad didn't pay much attention.

Dad was not much of a talker at the mills, either. I worked there in the summers, toting bales of cotton, loading and finally driving trucks, sorting yarn, inspecting, testing—but he wouldn't let me work on the machines. (He'd lost a couple of fingers on one, and I was the only member of our church who could play the organ on Sunday.) I watched how he ran things. At the beginning of each shift, he'd look at the production figures from the day before, and walk through the mills. He'd smile at some people, and frown at others. The mills would hum along smoothly. I would try to talk to him about how he knew who to smile at and who to frown at, but he pretended not to know what I was talking about. He would then frown at me. He had apprentices who were learning to assist him, and one of them would walk through the mills frowning at some people and smiling at others—apprentices usually frowned more—and the machines would start clanking and the yarn would get tangled and people would get their fingers caught in the cotton combing machines.

I was much more taken with Mother. Much of the time she was drunk and took to her bed. She was outrageous and often frightening, but she was damned good company, and she talked to me. I had fun with her and felt the security of always knowing exactly what was on her mind. I wanted Dad to keep her sober and sane, and he expected me to, and neither of us could. I knew I felt helpless with it, and maybe he did, too, but he wouldn't talk about it.

I looked to my uncles. Mother's sister, Aunt Emily, was a writer (the first female sports editor for a daily newspaper in this country!). She was married to a surgeon, Uncle Harry, who was a great golfer and bridge player and war hero. They didn't have children, and joined in parenting us. I knew Uncle Harry loved me—he delivered me, and circumcised me, and gave me a choo-choo train when I was a baby—but he never talked to me, either. Aunt Emily said he was most comfortable with people who were under anaesthesia.

Things would get rather wild at home, and we would be sent off to stay with Dad's sister and brother-in-law in Mississippi, Aunt Josy and Uncle Mac, who already had six kids and a houseful of animals and wouldn't notice two extras. I always loved that. Uncle Mac was a great story-teller. He was a dentist, so he wasn't used to having people talk back to him. And then, on top of that, he became deaf. He became an accomplished monologist. And that was a lot more interesting than listening to Dad's baseball games.

The best of times for me were when I could get my teeth worked on. I could get up in the big dental chair, and Uncle Mac would put metal things in my mouth and talk just to me. In retrospect, I think it would have been better if I could have talked back some of the time, and he might then have listened. But since I'd never had a conversation with a man, I didn't really know what I was missing.

When I was sixteen and went off to college, I finally began to get some words from my father. Mother would write long, drunken epistles detailing her miseries and my short-comings. She would scream through the pages of a letter, usually about my failure to pay her enough attention. Those letters would come at irregular intervals, and some of them were written over a period of weeks. Mother's letters told me how I should feel and think and act, and what were the deficiencies in my character, and which ancestor was the source of each deficiency.

And every single day for four years, I got a letter from my father. The letters were usually very short. They'd say:

Dear Son,
We're fine.
Love, Dad

Sometimes his letters would be newsy:

Dear Son,
Jack and Leonard brought us some birds they shot. We had them for dinner. We're fine.
Love, Dad

Once or twice, his letters would be philosophical:

Dear Son,
Lots of high school kids getting married. Must be an epidemic of morality. Too many preachers in town. We're fine.
Love, Dad

After fifty years together, Mother died, and Dad married her best friend of fifty years, and was happy for those last few years. He then began to die himself, and finally was willing to talk with me about his life, though by then he barely had the breath to talk. Dad and I even had a conversation before he died. I have it on tape, but I haven't listened to it during these ten years since he died. What he said wasn't important: the important thing was that he talked to me. He said he'd known all along that I wanted him to talk to me, but he didn't know what to say. He saw I was different from him, but fine, and he thought Mother had done a good job of raising me, and he was proud of me, but he didn't know what I could want him to do for me. He just couldn't understand what I might need from him.

I think I finally realized what an uncomplicated man he was, and that he loved me simply. I realized that I had known everything there was to know about him all along. He'd been very close to his father and had spent his childhood sitting in the dark with him, listening to dogs bark, and that was all he needed. He could never understand why I made things so complicated. He just did his duty and hoped for the best. He was glad to be alive, and when he was dying he couldn't think of anything to regret. I'm sorry we didn't get together while there was still time. I think our relationship, like Mother, was a casualty of World War II.

What I did not realize until I became a father myself was that there really was very little to talk about. There was no secret to fathering, no magical answers about masculinity that are passed on from generation to generation. Boys just learn to be men by being with their fathers, experiencing the world and living life. But if they haven't had that experience, they may never feel comfortable with an awareness of what it means to be a man, what they are supposed to do with their masculinity, and how they can become fathers themselves.

SIX

Father Hunger

How sad that men should base an entire civilization on the principle of paternity, upon the legal ownership and presumed responsibility for children, and then never really get to know their sons and daughters very well.
—Phyllis Chesler, *About Men*

The family history of fatherhood has followed an inexorable pattern as the world has changed over these last few generations.

We are in the declining years of patriarchy, a system of male dominance and privilege in which the world and domain over it was passed from God to Adam to father to son. As patriarchy wanes, so of course does the patrimony. For a couple of hundred years now, each generation of fathers has passed on less to his sons; not just less power but less wisdom, and less love. We have finally reached a point where most fathers are largely irrelevant in the lives of their sons. The baby has been thrown out with the bathwater, and the pater has been dismissed with the patriarchy. Everyone seems to be floundering around not knowing what to do with men or with their problematic and disoriented masculinity.

Zach Yardley V is a young man I've been treating off and on for years. His family is much like my own: his ancestors and mine had adjoining farms in Telfair County, Georgia. The history of his family parallels the tragedy of the American father. Zachariah X. Yardley, Sr., was a farmboy from south Georgia who had fought in the Civil War, and had lost a leg when he was still in his teens. He came back home to the poverty-stricken family farm, where he hobbled around feeling sorry for himself and drinking too much until his father died. He was almost forty by then and hadn't done a lick of work for a lifetime. He had an elderly mother and two unmarried sisters, and it took all of them to take care of him, to bring him his bucket of beer before he would get up in the morning, and to pick him up when he fell down. But now they required that he be the man of the house, so he found Jesus and gave up the bottle. Pretty soon Old Zach married a very young girl from the adjoining farm. They had a flock of kids, and he built a church on the road between his family's farm and hers. He never left his property. He'd seen war, and it was hell, and he'd just as soon stay home for the rest of his life. He prayed a lot with his children, and he could barely part with them. The family story is that he would lock himself up in his bedroom so no one could see him cry as he sent each of the boys off to college. He kept the girls at home, of course, and didn't let them out of his sight until they were married and some other man was watching over them.

Zach Jr. went off to Mercer College in Macon, stayed for a year, and came home to get married. He stayed at home for a while, and then got it into his head to open a general store over in the town of Helena. He and his wife and their three kids lived upstairs over the store. Zach III was waiting on customers before he was as tall as the counter. Zach Jr. had too many children to go to World War I, but his younger brother went. After the war, Zach Jr. took on his returning veteran brother as a partner in the store. The family built a house a few blocks away, but went home only to sleep. Zach Jr. was one of the few men in the county with a college education, so he was elected to the state legislature. He would have to travel to Atlanta from time to time, and would write a long letter of good advice to his children each night. But he died quite young.

Zach III was a great football star at the University of Georgia. He was also quite a hellraiser in his youth. When he was twenty-one, four things happened: he made All-American, he flunked out of college, his father suddenly died, and the Great Depression hit. He was horribly ashamed at letting his father down, and privately thought that his school failure had brought on his father's early death. He was broke, and too proud to ask for money from his uncle, who took over the store and the care of his mother. But he was quite a salesman and managed to support himself, and in time a wife and a child. He didn't want more children—he was too busy working to spend much time with a kid, and he wanted to make sure he was supporting his family in style.

Zach III was thirty-two when he went off to World War II—he didn't have to, but he thought it was his duty as a man. After the war, he never really made a success of anything. He had to travel a lot, so he wasn't usually there for his only son's games. Although the world saw him as a sports legend, Zach III never felt he'd made a success of his life because he hadn't gotten rich. In one of the few conversations he had with his son, he urged Zach IV not to waste his energies by marrying and having children. Instead, he should give his first priority to making money.

Zach IV didn't like his father. He was embarrassed by his father's failures and cringed when the old man would bore people with football stories. When he got out of Georgia Tech in 1956, the year Eisenhower was re-elected, he decided that what he wanted to do in life was to be rich. He married a woman with the right social contacts, went to work with her father, and joined a country club where he could play golf. He had a nose for wealth, and while everyone else was trying to change the world and fight for good causes, he made a fortune from other people's money. It has never been enough, so he continues traveling the world making deals.

Zach IV wasn't home much and was careful to leave the childraising to his wife. He got fat and out of shape. The only exercise he got was riding around in a golf cart smoking cigars. His wife wanted to see a marriage counselor, but he could never work the appointments into his schedule, and she gave up.

A few years ago, Zach IV left his family for a young woman at the office. The great romance cooled, but by then he was divorced. Zach IV and his wife have an arrangement about the kids. He'll get involved if there is a problem she can't handle herself, but he'll make her pay for it. As much money as he gives her, and as well as she lives, he thinks she should be able to manage without him having to do "woman's work" as well.

Zach V and his sister were good kids. They had a devoted mother to take care of them, a widowed, retired grandfather to entertain them, and a father who provided spectacularly for the family. Strange how Zach III discovered fathering once he had retired. Zach V's best memories are of sitting in a bass boat with his grandfather on a muddy lake hearing tales of football glory. By the time he was grown, he knew the scores of every game his grandfather had played. Zach V did well at sports. God knows he tried, but he never could get his father's attention. He did feel close to the man across the street, the father of his best friend, who would take the two boys on trips, and he felt close to his coaches, but closest of all to his grandfather. The old man died when Zach V was a freshman at college. His father decreed that he should not come home for the funeral, since the important thing was for him to keep his grades up. By the end of the quarter, Zach V had flunked out of college.

I've watched as Zach V has created whatever crisis he needs to get his father involved in his life, and yet he mostly gets his father's impatient disapproval. His sister is doing OK in school and wants to be an investment banker like her father. She blames everything on her mother for spoiling Zach V and swears she'll never marry and have children. Zach IV has sent everyone in the family to therapy, but he can't seem to fit it into his schedule. He doesn't understand what his son wants from him, what this boy must have from his father before he can go ahead and be a man. All the men in his family have been successful at something, but the most recent bearer of the family name seems determined only to fail.

As the Yardley family moved away from their rural roots, the men spent less and less time with their children. Zach III felt he'd failed his father by flunking out of college and not getting rich. Despite his athletic successes, he felt he was a failure as a man, and he was too busy, trying to make enough money to feel like a man, to be much of a father. He wised up in time to be a wonderful grandfather, but the damage to his son (and thus to his grandson) had already been done.

Zach IV, no matter how much money he makes, can never have the glory his father had, so he can never be man enough. In his desperation for a sense of being man enough, he's become a woman-chasing, money-making machine who has left his own son floundering in a series of attention-getting crises.

The greatest tragedy about the Yardley family is that it is not deviant—this has become the norm, and the dilemmas of Zach IV and Zach V are almost universal once the father-son bond is broken.

The Rise and Fall of Patriarchy

> And Adam said, This is now bone of my bones, and flesh
> of my flesh: she shall be called Woman, because she was
> taken out of Man.   —Genesis 2:23

If we didn't look back a long way into our roots, we would think patriarchy was natural for the human animal. Actually, according to Gerda Lerner in *The Creation of Patriarchy* and Riane Eisler in *The Chalice and the Blade*, the human animal seems to have developed as a peaceful hunter-gatherer with equal but slightly different genders. Men would hunt; women would gather. But once women invented farming, and began to keep and breed animals, they discovered the crucial function of the rooster in the henhouse. Fathers suddenly gained a function, and could do what only women had been able to do for all those millions of years—point at a child and say, "That is *my* son" "That is *my* daughter." Patriarchy quickly followed, beginning about five thousand years ago: a very short time in the development of our species, but covering all of recorded history.

The history of the creation of patriarchy is well known—

it is described in the Old Testament. The first step was to invent a male God who created the world without female help, a God who created Man first and just threw in Woman as an afterthought. Then the patriarchs made Woman/Mother Eve the villain when she did anything either sexual or independent of Man. This new God of war believed in son-killing, and in hellfire and damnation, but was terrified of female sexuality.

This patriarchal power is accepted, and not even seriously questioned, in the Old Testament, and in Homer and Greek myth. Under patriarchy, men were expected to be Gods, and to pass divinity from father to son. To prove their worthiness for such divine power, fathers had to show willingness to sacrifice their sons, and sons had to show their willingness to be sacrificed. Under patriarchy, men's dominance is a gift from God to reward their willingness to die for this masculine authority. In this worldview, it seems natural that Abraham would sacrifice his son Isaac to God, and that the boy's mother, Sarah, would not have a voice in the matter. The creation of monotheism seems to have occurred when Abraham proves to this son-killing god that he's willing to kill the boy.

Under full-blown patriarchy in ancient Rome, the father had power of life and death over the members of his household, including his children. At birth every child would be placed on the floor before his or her father, and the child would not be considered to have been born alive until the father picked it up. Babies without fathers would be placed outside the city gates, where they could be picked up and adopted by any free man. Every Roman child must have a father. And the father could, at any time, for any reason, privately condemn his son to death.

Family life in Western society since the time of the Old Testament has been a struggle to maintain patriarchy, male domination, and double standards in the face of a natural drift toward monogamous bonding. Young men have been called upon to prove their masculinity by their willingess to die in warfare, and young women have been called upon to prove their femininity by their willingness to die for their man. Women have been asked to appear small, dumb, and helpless so men would feel big and strong, brave, and clever. It's been a trick.

Fathers Matter

> Death ends a life, but it does not end a relationship, which struggles on in the survivor's mind toward some resolution which it may never find. Alice said I would not accept the sadness of this world. What did it matter if I never loved him or he never loved me? Perhaps she was right. But still, when I hear the word "father," it matters.
> — Robert Anderson, I Never Sang for My Father

John Demos, in Past, Present, and Personal; The Family and the Life Course in American History, traces patriarchy into eighteenth-century America. In colonial America, the father was the primary parent. "Books of child-rearing advice had been addressed to him; the law had preferred him (to mother) in the matter of child custody; and all parties affirmed his superior 'wisdom' in understanding and nurturing the young. (Women were considered too irrational and unsteady to take the lead here.)"

During those millennia between the creation of patriarchy and the destruction of the patriarchal family by the Industrial Revolution, men were busy being fathers. Patresfamilias wore many hats. Demos looks over public and private writing from that period, and lists a few of the things that were expected of fathers:

- Father the *Pedagogue*, imparting the rudiments of his own literacy;
- Father the *Benefactor*, allotting portions of family property to help his children get started in their own families;
- Father the *Controller*, keeping children on a short leash until they showed sufficient maturity;
- Father the *Moral Overseer*, restraining the powerful, natural passions of the young;
- Father the *Psychologist*, perceiving the wisdom of his children;
- Father the *Example*, modeling good character and right behavior;
- Father the *Progenitor*, strongly personally identified with the prospects of their sons;
- Father the *Companion*, hanging out with the kids, working and playing as part of the family;
- and, of course, Father very much the active *Caregiver*.

FATHER THE PROVIDER

Over the past two hundred years, each generation of fathers has had less authority than the last. The concept of fatherhood changed drastically, rapidly, and radically after the Industrial Revolution in the nineteenth century. Economics dictated that somebody had to go out from the home to work. Men were usually chosen, since they couldn't produce milk (once more, biology is destiny and makes men the expendable creature). Maybe the men would come home at night or just on weekends. Masculinity ceased to be defined in terms of domestic involvement, skills at fathering and husbanding, but began to be defined in terms of making money. Men had to leave home to work. They stopped doing all the things they used to do. Instead they became primarily, in Demos's phrase,

Father the *Provider*, bringing things home to the family rather than living and working at home within the family.

Gradually fathers found other roles to fulfill when they visited home after working somewhere else. Visiting fathers found different functions: Father the *Disciplinarian*: "Wait till your father comes home!"; Father the *Audience*: "Tell Daddy what you did today."

And, of course, mothers and children discovered that they could manage without a grown man around the house. Fathers ceased to be idealized and showed up in tragedies as Father the *Intruder*, disrupting the female realm of the family life, or as Father the *Abdicator*, the man who got away and gave no child support whether he was at home or gone. Fathers were the stuff of comedy as well, as Father the *Anachronism*, embarrassingly representing old-fashioned codes of behavior; and on innumerable TV sitcoms and TV commercials as Father the *Incompetent*, out of place in the business of the home, serving no useful domestic function, just getting in the way and looking foolish.

FATHER THE FAILURE

Father the Provider is a sad figure, leading a life without dignity or rest, and certainly without the glory and reverence his paterfamilias grandfather had known. If all a father's functions were economic, if all his status was measured by how well he provided, the rich and economically powerful father became a potential tyrant, but the father who wasn't rich and famous was an inescapable failure, a disappointment, a buffoon. As Demos puts it: "The husband-father, for example, was not just the breadwinner for the entire family; he was also its sole representative in the world at large. His 'success' or 'failure'—terms which had now obtained a mostly economic significance—would reflect directly on the other members of the household. And this was a grievously heavy burden to carry. For anyone who found it too heavy, for anyone who stumbled and fell while striving to scale the heights of success, there was a bitter legacy of self-reproach—not to mention the implicit or explicit reproaches of other family members whose fate was tied to his own." The father's position in the family was no longer determined by how well he functioned as a father, but was scored by his status in the eyes of the world, in a set of economic contests in which there were few men winning by being the richest of them all, and most men losing.

Any respect a father got was mixed with pity, and even a bit of defensiveness. The frustration and resentment mothers and children had harbored through millennia of patriarchy, when their own lives were sacrificed to the glory of masculine privilege, were dumped on men who suddenly had no power and were straining to get through a day of seeking success and meeting only failure, in hopes of finally collapsing at home with loved ones who appreciated a man's struggle.

What a drastic reversal of gender relations in family life! Fathers were demoted from the central patriarch of family life to the bum who drops by to leave money and to be abused by his family for not making a big enough success in the competition out there and, at the same time, for not being at home to hear everyone's complaints about how hard life is for a family with such a failure for a father.

Some men—particularly when they feel like failures—have understandably tried to hold on to their patriarchal positions and act like the Head of the Household, even after patriarchy proved too inefficient and expensive to maintain, after their wives demonstrated that they could handle things at home quite nicely without the men being around, and after the whole family decided they would be willing to do without all the other functions fathers perform if the fathers would just go out into the world and make money. These men can seem monstrous to their children.

There are men raised on modern military bases, or a few generations ago out in the country somewhere, untouched by twentieth or even the nineteenth-century attitudes of freedom, and bolstered by fundamentalist religion and perhaps a few generations of in-breeding. They may defend what they were taught about masculinity. When they feel like failures in their own lives, they may fall back on the patriarchal tradition of their childhood and try to act like the Head of the Household. They really believe they are doing their duty as fathers, operating from the model they learned, and they have been such cultural outsiders that they have never questioned it. They won't understand when the world sees them as monsters.

Abner was such a man. I saw Abner after he was violent to his son for failing to feed the chickens. Abner's wife had left him, and he had lost contact with the son. He recalled his own childhood out in the swamps. When he was eight, his father had left him for a while by the side of the road with a truckload of watermelons to sell. When a customer came by and offered a lower price for the whole truckload, the boy had never seen so much money all at the same time, and took it. He thought his father would be pleased, but he had not done just as his father had ordered him to do. His father beat him, and then he tied a rope around his ankles and left Abner hanging from a tree over the swamp all night long, and warned him that if he cried, bears would come and eat him. His mother concurred in the punishment, as did the preacher, who saw that the devil was in the boy and would have to be beaten out. Abner ran away from home, supported himself by stealing for a while, and finally found an old woman who took him in and sent him back to school. He had heard of peaceful men who raised their children gently, but had never known one.

FATHER THE SUCCESS

Once a father had moved out of family life and become part of a work crew, family values ceased to be his primary definers of himself, and he adopted instead the values and job descriptions of the other workers. His work ceased to be something he did for the sake of his family and became work for the sake of work.

He soon stopped striving to support his loved ones. He didn't slow down when he'd achieved a level of sufficient comfort; instead he strove even harder to get the approval of his fellow workers, and to earn glory in their eyes. He worked because he worked; that was what he did because that was what he was. He was no longer *paterfamilias,* he was *homo-laboriosus.* In the endeavors and identity dearest to his heart and heaviest on his schedule, he was a working man, and his family should understand that their claims on his time came second at best. In his mind, he had moved out. He had gone to conquer the world.

Some men, of course, did become successes. When a father's position came from God or heredity or family tradition, it could be passed on to and incorporated by the son. But when the father's victory was caused by the man's special personal ability, then his victory over other men was also a victory over his sons. For this reason, the sons of some successful men have a hard time seeing anything they do as good enough by comparison, and they are at risk for giving up and becoming consumers rather than producers.

Once society decided that raising children was woman's

work, and making money was the single-minded point of men's lives, fathers were too busy for their children, and boys began to grow up without fathers. That would not have been critical if there were uncles and cousins and grandfathers and older brothers around to model masculinity for boys. But our ideas of mental health and the goals of the housing industry required that families trim themselves down to the size of a married couple and their children. Reducing the family to such a tiny, isolated nuclear unit made it mobile enough for the purposes of industrial society. Workers were no longer rooted in the land or the community. Nothing now came between a man and his job. Companies could extract the utmost loyalty from employees by making them a part of the family of work and cut them further away from the family of home. Men on the Daddy Track were severely penalized, much as women on a Mommy Track are now.

The classic movie on this subject is *Kramer vs. Kramer* (1979). Meryl Streep gets depressed from staying at home trying to raise their son alone while her husband, Dustin Hoffman, dedicates himself to his job. She leaves, but leaves the child to his father. Hoffman, domestically incompetent, doesn't really know his son—he has to ask what grade the boy is in. Hoffman's boss encourages him to send the six-year-old off to a military school so he won't interfere with his father's job. The movie chronicles Hoffman's efforts to handle both his job at work and his job at home. The obvious point is that this impossible juggling act is required routinely of working mothers, and makes it harder for them to get ahead on the job. Our economy is set up with the assumption that men aren't going to give much of their energies to their children.

In *My Life as a Dog*, a gentle 1985 Danish comedy easily indicative of American life, twelve-year-old Ingmar lives with his dying mother, and takes it upon himself to keep her cheered up. As she is about to go to the hospital, and he is about to be sent off to an orphanage, his little girlfriend expresses her regret that he will move away, and asks where his father is. Ingmar tells her that his father is off on the equator somewhere loading bananas. She looks rather disgusted and offers the opinion that he should be here with him and his mother. But Ingmar cheerfully tells her, "Somebody has got to load the bananas. It's an important job and it has to be done just right." The children of this generation may well have seen so many fathers run away that they may grow up with the idea that a father's life is his work, and his family should not expect anything more from him.

I recall one man I saw about the problems of his son. He said, "I don't know what Betty could have done wrong in raising that boy. I know it wasn't anything I did, since I was busy working and left it all up to her. I barely saw the kid so I couldn't have done anything wrong."

FATHER HUNGER

After men were forced out of their homes and into the work force to provide, there were still wars to fight to give them a sense of worth. WWII gave men courage that masculinity would be respected again. But so many men went off to war, the women learned they could do all the things men had been doing out there in the masculine world of work. Women got educated, too, and saw that their lives were being wasted. When the men came home they went back to work, declaring the home as Woman's realm, and the rest of the world as Man's realm. Women revolted.

Men, movies, and fashion tried to push women back into the kitchen with hooped skirts and virginity, but the women who went back were depressed at their pointless lives, and had fantasies of "having it all": both the domestic lives their mothers had known and the worldly lives their fathers had known.

By the '60s, the fathers hadn't really been part of life at home since the Great Depression. They went to work and sent money, and spent the rest of their time celebrating V.E. Day and having dreams of gloriously dropping more atom bombs on whoever challenged them. These same fathers then dreamed up a war in Vietnam, in which they would sacrifice their sons in time-honored patriarchal tradition. But the kids rebelled and ran away from home and from the trappings, symbols, and responsibilities of traditional masculinity. They still wanted the privileges of patriarchy, though.

Forgetting about all those millions of years of evolution, they decided they were by nature chimpanzees and that promiscuity was the natural order of things. Hooking up with women who were terrified of a life like their mothers', they had a sexual revolution that effectively ended the human family by sacrificing marriage to the glory of frantic, suicidal narcissism. Therapists came along to assure the world that the problem was the family, and that the family must be sacrificed for the sake of everyone's mental health, narcissism, and sexual freedom.

Men, who had rejected the duties and responsibilities of acting like fathers and husbands, or doing anything beyond "money and death," still expected women to serve them. So we had a gender revolution, too, and the women began to leave home as well. In time, nobody is going to be at home. Noel Coward sang plaintively, "What's going to happen to the children when there are no more grown-ups?" We're finding out.

Life for most boys and for many grown men is a frustrating search for the lost father who has not yet offered protection, provision, nurturing, modeling, or, especially, anointment.

All those tough guys who want to scare the world into seeing them as men, and who fill up the jails; all those men who aren't at home at home, who don't know how to be a man with a woman, only a brute or a boy, and who fill up the divorce courts; all those corporate raiders and rain-forest burners and war starters who want more in hopes that more will make them feel better; and all those masculopathic philanderers, contenders, and controllers who fill up my office—all of them are suffering from Father Hunger.

They go through their puberty rituals day after day for a lifetime, waiting for a father to anoint them and say "Attaboy," to treat them as good enough to be considered a man.

They call attention to their pain, getting into trouble, getting hurt, doing things that are bad for them, as if they are calling for a father to come take them in hand and straighten them out, or at least tell them how a grown man would handle the pain.

They collapse on women, and then are furious with the women for making them feel weak and dependent. They force women to take care of them in whatever way they think will make them feel like a man.

They compete with the other boys, but they don't get close enough to let the other boys see their shame over not feeling like men, over not having been anointed, and so they don't know that the other boys feel the same.

They seek out mentors, and try to please, or try to get taken care of, and they are outraged when the mentor or the boss doesn't give them enough notice or enough honor. And, since they are still just lost little boys, they pout.

In a scant two hundred years, in some families in a scant two generations, we've gone from a toxic overdose of fathering to a fatal deficiency.

Men naturally blame women. Sigmund Freud queried:

"The great question which I have not been able to answer, despite my thirty years of research into the feminine soul, is 'What does a woman want?' " D. H. Lawrence deplored "that's the thing about women—always seeking self-importance through love." Sam Keen confides: "The secret men seldom tell, and often do not know, is the extent to which our lives circle around our relationships to WOMAN." Most of the guys I talk to at the health club would blame women for the plight of men. But even the most cursory reading of Freud's life, of Lawrence's thinly veiled autobiographies, and of Sam Keen's book reveals the Father Hunger. It's not that we have too much mother, but too little father. We can't forgive our mothers for taking the place of our fathers until we are ready to see that the point of a man's life is to be a father and a mentor, and we can't do that because we don't know how we would be a father or a mentor when we never had one. So we just blame women and run away from the challenge of our life as a man in the chain of men passing manhood from generation to generation.

Poet Robert Bly has become the patron mentor of the men's movement. In Bly's autobiographical poem, *Fifty Males Sitting Together*, he describes the son who turns away from his father's alcoholism and mother's unhappiness, "loses courage, goes outdoors to feed with wild things."

Bly looks at the "soft" men he sees, the "Sensitive New Age Guys," and he believes they aren't life-giving—they lack what he calls "fierceness." Their fathers were remote from them and they didn't get initiated into manhood by the older men, so they remain dependent on women to define them.

Bly says, "When we stand physically close to our father, something is exchanged that can't be described in material terms, something that gives the son a certain confidence, an awareness, a knowledge of what it is to be male." Without this he learns a woman's way of feeling, and a woman's view of men. He learns to be ashamed of himself, and he learns to distrust men who would be fathers.

Bly describes the earning of manhood as a four-stage initiation process that boys go through over and over again as they move deeper into awareness of themselves as men. Bly's four stages are 1) bonding with and breaking away from the mother; 2) bonding with and breaking away from the father; 3) finding a mentor, a "male mother" who will "care for the boy's soul"; and 4) passing "beyond the realm of the personal mother and father" to achieve "spiritual mating with the universe."

Bly, struggling to escape an alcoholic father who was too present in his life, may be closer to patriarchal times than many of us. Most men of recent generations are trying to get closer to the remote father, rather than trying to break away from the oppressive one. I have a couple of friends and a few patients who don't cry when they see movies like *Field of Dreams*, about finding the lost father. Like Bly, their fathers were psychotics or alcoholics who presented an ominous presence they couldn't escape.

According to Bly's formula, the boy who would be a man must feel his mother's love and her blessing and then he must leave her. He must feel his father's love and his blessing, and then he must leave him and go alone into the forest, or the unconscious, or the unmapped world, and find his manhood.

The impasse in Bly's formula comes when there is no longer a father to bond with the boy and anoint him and let him go. The boy can't escape his father if there is no father to escape, and he has trouble escaping his mother if she must be left alone. Fatherless boys are then at the mercy of their mentors. But a boy who couldn't get anything going with his father may be reluctant to entrust himself to a mentor. He's more likely to get stuck in his competitions with the other boys or his seductions of women. In a world without fathers, mentors are crucial, but a society that discourages fatherly attitudes does not produce very nurturing mentors, either. Where's a man to find a good mentor any more? Bly cries out for fatherless men to mentor one another, and this has spawned the Men's Movement.

It's not easy for any man to achieve Bly's final step in becoming a man, which Bly calls something like "achieving spiritual union with the universe." One way of achieving that spiritual union, of making yourself part of the succession of generations, part of the past and the future, is by raising children. But it is hard for a man to be a father, not just a sperm donor or provider or protector, but a father in a spiritual sense, until he has come to peace with his own father.

Robert Bly is an heroic figure, symbolizing the father so few of us had, but he can't be the father of us all, or even our personal mentor. I'm with Bly in believing that, in the absence of fathers, what the world needs is not more distant mothers or more subservient wives but a better class of male mentors, something each of us can do for one another. While Bly calls it the "male mother," what he is striving for is a more nurturing model of masculinity.

Post-Patriarchal Myths of Masculinity

As patriarchy fades away, so do the myths based on patriarchal relationships with the dangerously powerful fathers boys need to escape or overturn. Stories in which the father is a king no longer quite create the appropriate mythic tone. How can you escape a father who has already run away, who might not know you, might not remember you, or perhaps is just too busy for you?

To be mythic, a story must connect with something primordial, deep within human consciousness; it must offer some profound, shared insight into the human condition. It is a story which is so true it transcends the mere words. Myths not only enlighten us, they connect us. And as the world changes, we change, and our myths must change, so we get a new crop all the time, and some of them work, so we keep them. Our modern mythmakers are busy tackling the relationships between fathers and sons, to find connections between pre-patriarchal and post-patriarchal consciousness, between the old fear of the too powerful father and the new longing for a father to love and teach and anoint us.

The pain and grief and shame from the failed father-son relationship seem universal. The blockbuster movies of the past couple of decades—*The Godfather* trilogy, the *Star Wars* trilogy, and the *Indiana Jones* trilogy—had father and son themes that overshadowed anything going on between the men and women.

In *The Godfather* (1972), Vito Corleone (Robert De Niro, then Marlon Brando) sees his father killed in Sicily by gangsters, so he comes to America and becomes a highly successful gangster himself. He wants only that his youngest and best son, Michael (Al Pacino), be clean and straight and able to restore respectability to the Family. But a crisis occurs in which Michael must kill a cop in order to save his father's life. One brother is killed and the other is incompetent, so Michael is drawn into the Family business, and becomes the new Godfather, both to the Family and to his sister's baby. He kills off his brother-in-law during the baby's baptism.

In Part Two, Michael gradually loses his soul and his wife, and turns into a dangerous and lonely patriarch like his father.

When he tells his widowed sister, "If you marry this man, it will disappoint me," our blood is chilled by the homicidal threat. He is finally forced to kill his own brother in order to protect the Family.

If Part One was Francis Ford Coppola's *Hamlet* and Part Two was his *Macbeth*, Part Three is his *King Lear*. Michael tries to give up his kingdom, lets his only son go his own way, tries to protect his daughter, and becomes mentor to his warrior nephew. Wracked with guilt over the murder of his brother, he turns to a fatherly priest for absolution, and the priest is made pope and then killed. At the end, Michael's beloved daughter is also killed. There is no escape. He withers away and eventually drops dead, too.

The Godfather trilogy, which started only twenty years ago, takes place in an anachronistically patriarchal family. Its mythology is warning us about the sins of the father being visited upon the children for generations, but also about the dangers of stepping into your father's shoes. The Family centers around the omnipotent father, who has the power of life and death. He grants many goodies and great emotional security, unless you try to leave the Family. In exchange you owe it your life. This was the perfect myth for a society in the early '70s, which distrusted authority, and was running away from family life and patriarchy with all deliberate speed, fearful of the power of the family, yet nostalgic for the sanctuary. This was the post-Vietnam message about masculinity: "If you kill to save your father, you will become a killer like him, and you and all your love will die, so run away from the anointing and refuse to become a man."

George Lucas's *Star Wars* trilogy began five years later, in 1977. It had the emotional tone of a comic strip, the look of a futuristic hardware store, and the pace and spirit of eternal boyishness. While *The Godfather* told a patriarchal nightmare about the terrible things that would happen if you became a man like your father, *Star Wars* told a prepubertal fairy tale about how hard it is to become a man if you don't have a father. Luke Skywalker is the idealistic young space jockey who is mourning his lost father, a hero who has been killed by the evil Empire of Darth Vader.

In order to become a Jedi knight, Luke must become disciplined and selfless enough to attain The Force, the spiritual power that will make him feel like the warrior he needs to be. The Force, which only the men seem capable of attaining, is the energy field that binds the universe together and can even control technology for good or evil. The Force, clearly, is masculinity.

The movies are technically dazzling episodes from Luke's intergalactic puberty rituals. There is much comic relief from tomboy heroine—Princess Leia—with whom Luke boyishly bickers, and practical mercenary—Han Solo—who savors his pleasures, isn't really into sacrifice and idealism, but becomes a rescuing hero at the end. But the central story involves Luke's training with the mentorly counsel and comfort of the venerable Obi Wan-Kenobi. As Luke goes to war against the evil forces of Darth Vader, he depends on his mentor's counsel and comfort.

By the end of the third film, after Luke has repeatedly proved himself a hero and gained The Force, the voice of Obi Wan-Kenobi tells him to "turn off your computer, turn off your machine and do it yourself, follow your feelings, trust your feelings." Luke feels The Force coming from inside himself. He defeats and unmasks the evil Darth Vader and discovers it is his long-lost father who, like the universe, combines both good and evil. Now he can even be nice to Princess Leia, who turns out to be his sister. Once he knows he's a man he doesn't have to be afraid of women, but he looks tired and worried and lonely, with all those responsibilities of being a man.

The *Star Wars* trilogy is a coming-of-age myth, like *Hamlet* or *Godfather* Part One or *Iron John*, and as always in such stories the boy has to defeat, replace, or avenge the father in order to prove himself a man so he can take the father's place. But by the late '70s and the early '80s, the hardest part of the job was to find the father, who had run away from home and is still hiding from his family.

Indiana Jones is the hero of three Steven Spielberg films in the '80s. Our hero (Harrison Ford) is a droll, swashbuckling anthropologist who travels around the world dodging danger while constantly risking his life in cliffhanging, breathtaking stunts for which he shows his continuing distaste. The plots don't need to make much sense—they are merely an excuse for the derring-do. The experience is more like a roller coaster than a movie, but the character is fascinating—a man who isn't impressed with himself as a man, even as he goes through these amazing muscular rites of passage.

The secret of the character is finally revealed in the third film, when his father appears, played by an actor who exudes even more masculine bravado than Indiana Jones himself, Sean Connery—the original and real James Bond. The senior Jones is a pedantic biblical scholar who has devoted his life to seeking the Holy Grail. He is the only man alive who is not impressed with the youngster. He calls him Junior, even as he waits impatiently to be rescued by him. The father takes his son's talents for granted, feels license to slap the boy for blasphemy, and shows no awareness of the son's need for the father's approval. It's the son, not the father, who is threatened by the revelation that they have each slept with the heroine. The father is likewise impervious to the son's efforts to make him feel guilt over his detached fathering. Junior says, "We never talked." Senior says, "You left just when you were getting interesting."

The mythic message seems to be that no man is ever enough of a man to get his father's approval, so men are doomed to go through life constantly risking their lives in their effort to prove their masculinity.

These father-son myths attracted huge audiences in the '70s and '80s. Men feared being like their fathers, but they wanted desperately to bond with them even if they could never really please them enough to feel anointed.

FIELDS OF FATHERS

The film that set the tone for the Men's Movement was *Field of Dreams* in 1989. Many women thought it was just a dumb fantasy about baseball. But baseball, with its clear and polite rules, and all its statistics, and its players who are normal men and boys rather than oversized freaks, is a man's metaphor for life. In this magical fantasy, Iowa farmer Kevin Costner tells us his life story: how his mother died when he was two, so his father gave up his efforts to play pro baseball in order to raise his son. The boy grew older and didn't have time to play catch with the old man, who died after the boy left home at seventeen to protest war and all the things his father stood for. Now the son is grown, with a wife, a daughter, and a farm in Iowa. But he feels something is missing in his life.

Costner hears a voice from his cornfield telling him, "If you build it he will come." He understands that to mean that if he moves his cornfield and builds a lit baseball diamond, his father's hero, the long-dead and even longer disgraced Shoeless Joe Jackson, will appear and play baseball with him. He does. The voice then tells him to "go the distance." Costner drives to New York and finds his own hero, J.D. Salinger (refashioned as James Earl Jones). The voice comes again and urges him to "ease the pain," whereupon Costner and Salinger find old country doctor Burt Lancaster, regress him to adolescence, take him to Iowa, and watch him play baseball with Shoeless Joe. Shoeless Joe and J.D. Salinger, the heroes of the father and son, become buddies and disappear into the cornfield. Something is healed.

Then Costner's dad appears in his baseball uniform, and father and son solemnly play that belated game of catch. Father and son don't talk much, except to wonder whether Iowa might be heaven, "where dreams come true." They just play catch with total solemnity. And it is quite enough. That is one of the prescribed anointing rituals. If fathers who fear fathering and run away from it could only see how little fathering is enough. Mostly, the father just needs to be there.

Field of Dreams did amazing things to grown men, who soaked themselves in sobs. Some couldn't walk out of the theater when the movie was over. The theme in this or in any other movie that draws the most tears from grown men is unquestionably the lifetime mourning for the father they couldn't get close to.

One of our central myths is that of the son who could not get his father's approval, so he turned violent and killed his brother, who had been more favored by the father—familiar as the story of Cain and Abel. John Steinbeck, in *East of Eden*, gives it a happier ending. In the 1955 film, Adam (Raymond Massey) was the patriarch who had banished his bad wife and was raising a good son and a bad son. Cal, the bad son (James Dean) can never get his father's approval. He brings him money that will save the family farm, but his righteous father scorns it. Cal smites his goody-goody brother Aaron, gets him drunk, and sends him off to war. Adam has a stroke and is dying, and

Cal tries to apologize but gets no response from his stuporous father.

Abra, the boy's girlfriend (Julie Harris), intervenes. She goes to the bedside of the paralyzed old man and gently tells him, "It's awful not to be loved. It's the worst thing in the world. Don't ask me how I know that, I just know. It makes you mean and violent and cruel, and that's the way Cal has always felt all his life. I know you didn't mean it to be that way, but it's true. You never gave him your love, you never asked him for his. You never asked him for one thing . . . You have to give him some sign that you love him or else he'll never be a man. He'll just keep on feeling guilty and alone unless you release him. Please help him. I love Cal, Mr. Trask, and I want him to be whole and strong, and you are the only one who can do it. Try, please try. If you would ask for something, or let him help you so that he knows you love him, or let him do for you . . ."

The father whispers into Cal's ear that he wants the boy to fire the nurse and stay with him and take care of him. Cal straightens up, feeling like a man who has been anointed by his father, kisses Abra, who has brought about this crucial ritual, and takes his chair beside his father's bed for the film's fadeout.

What It Takes to Be a Man

What goes on between the father and son, and what does not go on between them, is surely the most important determinant of whether the boy will become a man capable of giving life to others, or whether he will go through life ashamed and pulling back from exposure to intimacy with men, women, and children.

But it is not enough for the boy to win his father's love and anointment and be declared man enough by his father. He must also satisfy his mother, pay her back for her sacrifice for him, and break free with honor and comfort from the maternal symbiosis.

Even that is not enough. He must become a man among men. He must establish sufficient brotherhood with his buddies to join the men's team in life.

And finally he must find mentors and myths of heroes to inspire him and show him the way to go beyond the model of his father and his peers, and what he has learned from them. And he may be inspired to develop his own masculine heroism.

It takes the fulfillment of all those relationships for a boy to become a man who is able to live in peace and cooperation with his community and to give something back to his family. But if there is a failure in the father-son bonding, the rest of the boy's tasks will be distorted. If his father has abandoned his mother, he may find her impossible to satisfy and leave. The unanointed boy is likely to feel shame or distrust with the other boys and shrink away from their brotherhood or compete with them too fiercely. If his Father Hunger is too intense, he may choose unattainable heroes and take them far too literally.

Without a father, he may never become a man.

SEVEN

Mother Love

Male rule of the world has its emotional roots in female rule of early childhood.
—Dorothy Dinnerstein, *The Mermaid and the Minotaur*

The world, like the family and like our collective unconscious, had long been ruled by the Mother Goddess, who creates life and sustains it with her body, while men go out and make themselves men by taking lives and offering their own. Gerda Lerner, in *The Creation of Patriarchy*, says: "Metaphysical female power, especially the power to give life, is worshipped by men and women in the form of powerful goddesses long after women are subordinated to men in most aspects of their lives on earth."

With the invention of warfare, by which men could conquer what they could not produce, matriarchy and the Goddess gave way to patriarchy and the Judeo-Christian-Moslem god of war. But, as men gained power in the world, women gained power at home. Margaret Mead, in *Male and Female*, explained that Woman left the main responsibility for history to Man, as compensation for her more important contribution to the species, that of the Childbearer. That was certainly important enough. But somewhere along the way, Woman became also the Childraiser.

In the life of the child, the father, however revered, is likely to be a shadowy figure, while the mother is the source of all that is good and pleasurable, of life and comfort and security.

Rudyard Kipling bowed to this healing of power of mothers:

> "If I were damned of body and soul,
>   I know whose prayers would make me whole,
>   Mother o'mine, O mother o'mine."

I think of Eleanor Roosevelt, the Great Mother of the Depression and WW II years, who went wherever she had to go to give comfort to the downtrodden, even to the bottom of a coal mine in West Virginia. The Great Mother has the power to kiss it and make it well.

George, a friend of mine who used to play fullback for the Cleveland Browns, weighed 230. His mother, a Czech immigrant, weighed only 110, but she still believed she should be taking care of her little boy. Once in a game when he was returning a kick-off, he was hit head-on and knocked out. He came to looking into the face of his little mother in a babushka leaning over him on the fifty-yard line. She said pleadingly, in Czech, "Buddy, is my baby all right?" George snapped to, and with great embarrassment, said, "Mom, you *can't* be out here on the football field." To which his mother slyly replied, "But I *am* here." Mothers will be wherever their children are in need.

The Great Mother is the life-giving, life-sustaining, all-nurturing heroine of stories about families facing troubled times. She seems always to rise to the most dreadful occasion, healing and comforting her beleaguered family.

In Steinbeck's *The Grapes of Wrath*, a family of Oklahoma dirt famers leaves their Depression-era dust bowl to seek their fortune in California, where they find rejection and disaster. While the other family members shrink and fall away, the matriarch, Ma Joad, thrives under adversity. In the 1940 film, she explains to her husband what it is like to be the Great Mother, as they drive off in their dilapidated truck in search of work.

> PA JOAD: You're the one that keeps us going, Ma. I ain't no good no more. Seems like I spend all my time these days thinking about how it used to be, thinking of home. I ain't never gonna see it no more.
>
> MA JOAD: Well, Pa, a woman can change better than a man. A man lives sort of—well—in jerks. A baby's born and that's a jerk, he gets a farm or loses it and that's a jerk. But for a woman it's all in one flow like a stream— eddies and waterfalls, but the river goes right on. A woman looks at it that way.
>
> PA JOAD: Maybe, but we sure taken a beating.
>
> MA JOAD: (Laughing) That's what makes us tough.

This Great Mother is exultant over the opportunity to test her mettle by wrestling with reality and surviving. And all her strength and power flows into her child.

But as Dorothy Dinnerstein describes in *The Mermaid and the Minotaur,* the Great Mother is also "the overwhelming external will in the face of which the child first learns the necessity for submission, the first being to whose wishes the child may be forced by punishment to subordinate its own, the first powerful and loved creature whom the child tries voluntarily to please."

The Goddess

> On the spiritual level, women can kill with rejection . . . Women's most feared power over men, then, is the power to say no. To refuse to take care of men. To refuse to service them sexually . . . To refuse to worship their God. To refuse to love them. —Barbara Walker, *The Crone*

However patriarchal the world, at home the child knows that his mother is the source of all power. The hand that rocks his cradle rules his world. And if she smiles upon him, he feels blessed and secure. His life is in the hands of Woman, and he must fear and pacify her, seduce her into taking care of him, entice her to let him live. The son never forgets that he owes his life to his mother, not just the creation of it but the maintenance of it, and that he owes her a debt he can not conceivably repay, but which she may call in at any time.

The Goddess or Great Mother exists in at least three mythic forms, the Creator of life or Virgin, the Preserver of life or Mother, and the Destroyer of life, the Crone or Witch. All these manifestations of Woman have power over us. The nubile Virgin awakens our sexuality, points it out toward herself, and turns us from boys into men. She can create life from her body. The Mother, whether she is our wife, our mother, our secretary, our doctor, our nurse, or our therapist, takes care of us, keeps us fed and watered, and makes sure we do the right thing. The all-sacrificing Mother doesn't just nurture us and adore us, she tends our moral development, extracting from us guilt in exchange for her sacrifices on our behalf. The Crone or Witch, who may be the Mother after we try to get away from home, or may be the Virgin after we've been married to her for a few decades, is also the Wise Woman. She knows us and the world well enough to give us the wisdom we need. But her understanding of us can enslave us, as we look to her to tell us how to run our lives, and as we offer our life in payment.

Christianity mixed and matched the Virgin and the Mother into Eve, mother of mankind but still less than Man, and Mary, Mother of God but still less than God. The patriarchal effort to keep the Great Mother subordinate hasn't worked. People still pray to Mary. And when a shadowy image of the Virgin Mary is seen on an oatmeal box or a billboard, people will come from miles around to kneel and be healed.

Mother Eve enters our mythology as the seductress and the betrayer, the cause of pain and death and mortality, living out her life in shame, while Mother Mary has become enshrined in our mythology as the giver of life, the symbol of moral purity, the source of healing, and the pathway to some sort of victory over death. The Crone lives on as the witch, knowing too many secrets, wielding too much power over men, pulling us back toward the earth and nature.

The classic mother-villain, Medea, exists in all three forms as Virgin/Mother/Crone. Medea was the sorceress who used her magic to enable Jason to win the Golden Fleece. She had to betray her father and kill her brother to effect Jason's escape, but he had promised to marry her. His promise was binding only if she were a virgin, but he slept with her before the wedding and reneged on his promise. Medea and Jason had two children nonetheless, and when Jason left her to marry another woman, Medea sent the new bride a poisoned dress that burned her alive. When Jason still wouldn't come home, Medea killed their children and sent them to him. Medea is the Greek myth for our time, as children are routinely sacrificed when their fathers run away from the power of their mothers, and try to connect with women to whom they owe less.

The more power Woman has over us, the more intimidating these archetypes. Dinnerstein says, "The crucial psychological fact is that all of us, female as well as male, fear the will of women. Man's dominion over what we think of as the world rests on a terror that we all feel: the terror of shrinking back *wholly* into the helplessness of infancy. Sinking back *partly,* on the other hand, is delicious; it is the basic form of play that makes the adult human condition tolerable."

Overthrowing Matriarchy

> Every person's passage from nursery to society is an overthrow of matriarchy.
> —Camille Paglia, *Sexual Personae*

Mother has the power of both life and death over us, and either her absence or her presence can be a threat. The two most terrifying scenes I recall from the movies of my childhood were both in cartoons. In *Bambi* (1942—I was seven) the young deer's mother was shot by hunters, and Bambi was left alone in the forest without a mother to take care of him. In *Snow White and the Seven Dwarfs* (1937—I must have seen it in re-release, but I was still young enough to hide under my seat), the Wicked Stepmother/Evil Queen, the Great Mother as

Crone, had turned the natural world into something malignant, and was chasing Snow White through the forest to kill her. Mother was necessary for life, but she had the power to kill us if we tried to get away from her.

MATERNAL GUILT

> Guilt: *the gift that keeps on giving.*
>
> —Erma Bombeck

The aspect of the Great Mother that is most powerful in the lives of boys and men is her position as our conscience, the careful cultivator of our character, and thus our guilt. Jules Feiffer, the cartoonist who chronicled the gender wars of the '60s, much as James Thurber had chronicled those of the previous generations, had a comic strip hero he called Hostile Man. He used his magical powers to counter the force of his archenemy, Marsha the Enormous Mother, whose guilt could paralyze and even kill.

Morally superior women used to teach an "epic style of domesticity" that aimed at imposing female virtues on wild men. Critics of this moral "Momism" argued that women "dominated husbands, emasculated sons, effeminized schoolboys, and made them unfit" for the predatory world of men. Mark Kann, in *On the Man Question*, says: "The ideal mother taught her sons to discipline unruly passions and resist profligacy, to assume the traditional obligations of manhood, and to 'prefer home and the companionship of pious women to the temptations of bachelor life.' " In other words, when the masculine mystique is pulling boys and men out into the world to growl manly noises at one another, the only power with a stronger pull on the male psyche is maternally induced guilt.

The guilt is quite necessary for our moral development, but it is often uncomfortable.

My mother worshipped me and I adored her. She was witty, scintillating, and beautiful. She was fun; she was inspiring; she made me feel loved. But she did not want me to grow up and leave her. And I felt a special responsibility for her, not just because she had to stay in bed for nine months to have me but because she held me somewhat responsible for her "accident."

When I was seventeen and home from my freshman year in college, I enlisted my sister and we finally felt secure enough to talk Dad into standing up to Mother. For the first time in their twenty-five years together, he actually said no to her. He refused to give her a drink one morning. She was so outraged she flung herself off the balcony and was crippled for the rest of her life. She always blamed her invalid state on her ungrateful children. We were expected to achieve glittering success in her honor, but at the same time she expected us to push her wheelchair forever. She wanted to teach me that a man must never fail to meet a woman's needs. It made me feel both powerful and helpless, as I sincerely tried to live up to everyone's expectations. It wasn't until I was a father of adolescents that I learned to respect the limitations of my power and responsibility.

I was nearly forty before I could protect myself from her. I had tolerated her drunken telephone calls for all these years, but I finally installed a "breatholyzer" on my telephone. As I explained to Mother, "The phone just automatically hangs up when it discerns that someone has been drinking. I have no control over it. So if it hangs up, don't bother to call back until the next morning." She hung up and didn't call for a while. How pitiful I was! I could run the mental health services for the city or design the mental health services for the nation, but I could not deal directly with my mother. I don't know whether it was because I loved her too much, or because she loved me too much.

MOTHERS IN DISTRESS

Sons are the anchors of a mother's life.
—Sophocles, *Phaedra*

One of the legacies of patriarchy is the guilt of sons over their father's degradation of their mothers. Mary Catherine Bateson, anthropologist daughter of Margaret Mead and Gregory Bateson, came to a Networker Symposium a few years ago and described Arab cultures, in which women are not considered fully human, and have no equality and little power in their marriages. Lucky women have sons, and these sons feel such guilt over their mother's degraded state that, as soon as they can overthrow or outlast their fathers, they elevate their mothers to positions of great power in the household, reigning regally over their daughters-in-law, providing the conscience for the sons, and making sure the sons don't get too close to their wives. The women without sons are considered accursed, since they have no access to power. But Bateson insists that women with sons would never give up their power for mere gender equality.

We think of Hamlet as a wimp. He dithers around, indecisive, not able to decide such a simple question as whether to be or not to be. He couldn't go about his job of being a man, i.e., killing his Uncle Claudius and making himself king, because he was still controlled by his mother's feelings. To Shakespeare, in *Macbeth, Othello, Anthony and Cleopatra,* etc., the man who is swayed by female emotionality is not yet a fully heroic man. Hamlet is wimpiest of all; he can handle Ophelia, but he is still tied to his mother. However, with his father dead, Hamlet had to protect his mother. Poor, foolish Queen Gertrude could not protect herself. What is a poor boy to do?

As with foolish Queen Gertrude, it is not strong mothers who hold their sons hostage, but weak ones. If the mother is sickly, or depressed, or abused, or abandoned, then the son has no way to achieve his masculinity: he can't leave her without feeling both the failure and the guilt, and he can't stay with her without sacrificing his hopes of going on a hero's journey.

Mothers who are strong people, who can pursue a life of their own when it is time to let their children go, empower their children of either gender to feel free and whole. But weak women, women who feel and act like victims of something or other, may make their children feel responsible for taking care of them, and they can carry their children down with them. Battered and abused mothers may insist they are staying in monstrous relationships "for the children's sake." These women are, in effect, asking their children to rescue them. It is not uncommon for an adolescent boy, wanting to be his mother's champion, to pull the shotgun off the mantel and blow away his abusive father or stepfather, sacrificing his own future in his frustrated quandary about how to rescue a mother who won't rescue herself.

Depressed mothers are hardest for a son (or a daughter) to leave. Duke had such a mother, and he was one of the most outrageously hypermasculine men I've known. He was a professional wrestler who wrote books on how women could protect themselves from rapists. He posed for the pictures of the rapist, lurking around corners, brutally attacking, fiercely leering. His mother was a homeless person in Newark—what we called in those days a "bag lady." Duke had tried for a lifetime to rescue her, and she had spent a lifetime making sure she wouldn't be rescued. She was miserably unhappy, and complaining constantly, but she could find something wrong with any arrangements he made for her; she seemed happy only when he was by her side. Anything he did, short of joining her on the streets, was a betrayal of her. Since Duke could never satisfy her enough to get her blessing for his own independence, he went through life as a male impersonator.

A man who is to escape a mother in distress may panic and throw his money, his children, or even his wife at the mother who is holding him hostage with her insatiable need for a son to love her enough to give her life meaning.

CUTTING THE CORD

> The mother must not only tolerate, she must wish and support the child's separation.
> —Erich Fromm, *The Art of Loving*

> You love me so much, you want to put me in your pocket. And I should die there smothered.
> —D. H. Lawrence, *Sons and Lovers*

When a boy goes through puberty, the tension between him and his mother mounts, as he wants to leave her and stay with her in widely divergent ways from the ways in which she wants him to both stay and go. He may want to be taken care of like a child by his mama while he acts like Head of the Household, and is granted the privileges of being a man whose life away developing his sense of masculinity takes priority over anything going on at home. She, on the other hand, may want him to remain a boy under her supervision while he uses all that new masculine energy to make her life more comfortable and to keep her company. If there is no father or stepfather strong enough to come between the boy and his mother, the boy may achieve peace by giving up part of what he must do to become a man. Or he may join the other boys at this stage of development and leave home before either he or his mother is ready.

What we see in fatherless ghettos and increasingly in the rest of the society is young men who run away from the Great Mother, overdo their masculine display, get into trouble, and bounce back to Mama. Mama can give him security that he will be taken care of, but she can't make him feel like a man. So he soon has to leave again, fail again, and come back. It becomes a lifelong cycle for "homeboys" who, lacking domestic models of masculinity, don't know how to be man enough to make it in the world. Only if the boy can leave the mother, and become a man among men, can he return as a man for a different level of relationship with her.

Freud pointed out that "a man who has been the indisputable favorite of his mother keeps for life the feeling of a conqueror, that confidence of success that often induces real success." But the painful reality is that he can't make use of that confidence unless he cuts the cord to the mother who has instilled it in him. Breaking free from the delicious security of mother love can be a painful rupture for either mother or son. Some boys can't do it. Some mothers can't let it happen because they know the boy is not ready to leave her; others are simply not ready to give up their sons.

I've even encountered one case of a mother willing to love her son to death. Bair was schizophrenic. He was pitifully dependent, but he couldn't tolerate closeness. With his fuzziness about boundaries, his mother made him uncomfortable. I urged her to respect his privacy. When Bair became psychotic again, I asked her how well she'd done in maintaining the boundaries. She admitted that she crawled into bed with him each morning to watch television, and told him how much more beautiful his body was than his father's. I told her she was killing him. She apologized, telling me that she couldn't help herself since "I love him to death."

Another mother in my practice was in a battle with her rather weird son, Custis, because he insisted upon wearing underwear that was too big for him. It had some symbolic meaning for him. But as she had fussed at him about it, Custis just bought larger and larger underwear. When I first saw him he was wearing enormous boxer shorts bunched around his waist above the belt, like a big white cummerbund. I convinced his mother to let him dress however he liked, since her efforts to control him produced just the opposite results from the ones she desired. She agreed not to mention the underwear anymore, but after they left the session, they called back with an emergency. On the way to the parking lot, the mother decided Custis was breathing irregularly, so she insisted that he breathe in rhythm with her own breathing. When she started fussing at him for breathing out of synchronization with her, Custis hit her. Such examples of engulfing mother love are rare except in the psychiatric literature, and in the collective unconscious of men. The myth of Oedipus is alive and well.

Despite the rareness of such examples, the fear of inescapable mother love is alive and well. Perhaps somewhere in the collective unconscious there still lurks the incestuous myth that spawned the story of Oedipus. Perhaps at puberty there lurks in the hearts of men a craving to overthrow their fathers and mate with their mothers. At puberty a powerful struggle ensues between the boy and his father, in which the father must win, and the boy must either leave or buckle under. But, in reality, lately the father leaves home instead. Nothing is quite so horrifying and paralyzing as to win the Oedipal struggle and to be awarded your mother as the prize.

In the 1970 absurdist Carl Reiner film, *Where's Poppa?*, George Segal wants to marry, but he can't until he gets rid of his demanding, senile mother (Ruth Gordon). In the film's original ending, Segal finally gives up, breaks off with his fiancée, and falls into bed with his mother. Preview audiences rejected that ending in favor of a fantasy in which Momma goes to a lovely nursing home where she finds a man she thinks is Poppa. Either way, the point is clear: a boy is not free to find a partner of his own as long as he must be the partner to his mother.

The single mother and her fatherless son may fear that her love will hurt her son. She may pull back from him, and thus withdraw the only parenting the boy ever got. In protecting him from what she believes to be her dangerous love, she may inadvertently turn him into an orphan. She may believe his masculinity would be damaged by her discipline, so she may let him run wild or even bully her. She may believe that only a man should control her son, so she may belittle female authority, and bring in a stepfather to beat the boy into shape. Single motherhood is problematic for both mother and child, but the mother must parent her son, discipline him, and love him. If her son does not have a father, he needs a stronger mother, not a weaker one.

Whether she is weak or strong, in order to become a man, he must break free of her. If she gives him a Blessing of Independence, he does not have to desert her, or even leave her forever in order to be a man. At the right time, one of them merely has to cut the cord, and then they both can experience their independence of one another.

THE GREAT DEED

To become a separate person the boy must perform a great deed. He must pass a test; he must break the chain to his mother.   —Gilmore, *The Making of Manhood*

But how in the world can we leave our mother?

A boy does not become a man just by running away. He would be hounded by guilt and shame and self-doubt forever. First, the boy must pay his mother back for giving and sustaining his life. That is a hell of a debt to pay off. The classic solution to the mother-son dilemma is for the boy to go off to war to protect the mother he leaves behind. He is thus leaving her, joining the other boys, taking on an adult role, and fulfilling his responsibilities to his mother by offering up his life for her in payment for the life she gave him.

An alternative is offered in the tale of Jack and the Beanstalk, wherein the foolish boy sells his widowed mother's cow for a handful of beans, which dashes the poor woman's hopes for the future. She has lost her only marketable asset and she has been forced to realize that the son she relies on is an idiot. But Jack plants the beans, and a beanstalk grows up to the heavens. He climbs up there, finds a giant to kill and a goose that lays golden eggs, or a golden harp that sings or whatever, kills the giant, steals the gold, and returns in triumph to his mother with the money to make her secure. More importantly, she has a son who is now a man and a success and a source of pride. We assume the mother and son live happily ever after, since he has earned his manhood and has purchased his life back from her.

Of course, there are simpler great deeds. The boy may achieve a great success in the world that makes his mother proud. The young millionaire professional athletes I see may have to buy their mothers a mansion and a Rolls-Royce before they can leave home and get married. Tom Hanks in *Nothing in Common* is a successful advertising genius with parents who collapse on him. He tells his girlfriend, "I used to wish I could be a great success and have a big mansion, and my parents would come and say, 'What a pretty mansion! We're proud of you, David.' And then they'd go off and die. Does that make me an asshole?"

The boy who wants to ransom his life from his mother may have to settle for a different kind of great deed. He may simply bring home a wonderful daughter-in-law, who makes both him and his mother happy. He may even send his new bride over to do the things a dutiful child would do.

Of course, best of all, he may bring home grandchildren who will give the mother some connection to the future. Becoming a man and a husband and a father, while still being a son, is all his mother could have hoped for anyway. But does he know that that is quite enough?

A real man doesn't have to run from his mother, and may even have to face the reality that no great deed is going to be great enough for him to ransom himself completely, and he may always be in his mother's debt. If he understands that, he won't have to run away, he won't have to feel guilty, and he won't have to please her completely. He can go ahead and be nice to her and let her be part of his life.

The War Against Mothers

> The book of Genesis is a male declaration of independence from the ancient mother cults.
> —Camille Paglia, *Sexual Personae*

For millennia men have been trying to overcome their fear of female power by controlling the lives of women. Men have tried worshipping Woman as Goddess, and men have tried burning Woman as Witch. Gender history is not just the story of how men have consolidated their control over women; it is an account of how men have banded together to keep the power of women from paralyzing them.

MOTHER BASHING

> *A boy's best friend is his mother.*
> —Anthony Perkins as Norman Bates
> in Alfred Hitchcock's *Psycho*

The fear that the mother, who has given so much, will want repayment seems primordial in myth, but that fear becomes imminent in a world in which childbearing is considered "women's work," in which marriages no longer hold, and in which single motherhood, however abnormal, is becoming the norm. When men pull back from family life, it causes a critical overload on the relationship between mother and child. Without father, mother is never enough but always too much. This fear of mother love, this mother bashing, is the aftermath of men who don't feel man enough yet to become husbands and fathers.

We perversely see mother love as the problem—when it is all we have to sustain us—rather than blaming the fathers who have run out on our mothers and on us. We seem willing to forgive fathers for loving too little even as we still shrink in terror from mothers who love too much.

My God, what we expect of mothers!

Mother is so powerful in a boy's life, she is held responsible for everything: his successes, his failures, even his mental illness long after the child has become a man and his mother has met her maker. We feel in our guts that our mother is responsible for us and all the good and all the bad we do; we read from our experts that our mother is controlling our minds all our lives. It's all her fault.

Freudian psychology got twisted into a frightening message that imperfect mothering was dangerous: mothers were expected to provide unfaltering, adoring care for a certain number of years, followed by unfaltering, adoring distance for the rest of the child's life. We began to blame all our troubles on mothers who were either too present or too absent. Mental health professionals became the exorcists in a holy crusade to free tortured psyches from the mothers who held them hostage, enslaved by guilt. Mother bashing was de rigeuer in mental health circles for decades.

Psychoanalysis even brought bad mothers into the movies. There were distant, unloving mothers in the misunderstood teenager movies like *East of Eden* and *Rebel Without a Cause* in 1955. In those days we thought that bad mothers were the ones who were insufficiently dedicated to mothering, and who didn't hover lovingly enough. "Working Mothers" were the villains.

By the '60s our culture and our movies reversed our position on what constituted bad mothering. We decided it wasn't cold, distant mothers who were to blame: it was mothers who loved us too much. We began to see mother love as toxic and crippling. In these nightmares of inescapable mothers, the frightening moms used guilt to keep their sons from growing up.

Of course every man incorporates the mother who has suckled him and taught him guilt. She is always inside him ready to keep him from doing anything she wouldn't want him to do. The most dramatic cinematic example was *Psycho,* in which Norman Bates dresses up as his mother (whom he keeps dead and mummified in his bed) and slashes to death any woman who sexually tempts him and threatens to take him away from Mom.

Between *Psycho* (1960) and *Mommie Dearest* (1981), mothers replaced vampires as the stuff of nightmares. The heroes of the sexual revolution were the guys who fought back against the power of mothers. In Mike Nichols's 1967 film *The Graduate*, Dustin Hoffman was Benjamin, who graduates from college and comes home, where he is promptly and efficiently seduced by his parents' best friend, Mrs. Robinson (Anne Bancroft). Benjamin loses his innocence in their emotionless couplings, and then Mrs. Robinson refuses to let him date her daughter Elaine (Katherine Ross). Benjamin finally invades the church where Elaine has just been married to a blond medical student, stands silhouetted as if being crucified in the church window, and calls, "Elaine!" All eyes turn to him as Mrs. Robinson gloats, "It's too late," and commands Elaine not to respond. Elaine, angered by her mother's tyranny, says defiantly, "Not for me!" and runs out of the church while Benjamin swings a giant cross at the congregation, barricading the church while he and Elaine make their getaway together on the back of a bus. This bravery in the face of "mother power" as embodied in Christianity, marriage, and maternal control of male and female sexuality, was one of the symbolic heroic acts of the sexual revolution of the '60s.

But by the '80s, in films like *Terms of Endearment* and *Steel Magnolias*, mothers came back into favor. As women gained more power in the world, children felt less guilt about leaving them, and the culture no longer had to imagine mothers as dangerous. Mothers who run for governor, take up painting, or find a new husband seem safely powerful; the mothers who languish at home alone and helpless seem threateningly powerless, and therefore in need of their children's lives to make their lives complete.

But we seem most afraid of mothers if they have no life except us. We are able to forgive our mothers anything except loving us more than they love themselves. We are willing to enshrine our mothers in positions of honor only if they are too busy with their own careers and their own affairs to come to the ceremony.

Living with a Woman

> *A man—should he not know everything, excel in manifold activities, initiate you into the energies of passion, the refinements of life, all mysteries? But this one taught nothing, knew nothing, wished nothing. He thought her happy, and she resented this easy calm, this serene happiness, the very happiness she gave him.*
>
> Gustave Flaubert, *Madame Bovary*

To escape Mama, we have to leave her: leaving her is one of the steps toward manhood. But we can't leave her until we have made her satisfied with what we have done with ourselves and for her: that is another of our steps toward becoming a man. Then we must find a woman of our own who will honor us with her sexuality and thus help us pass another test of masculinity. Our sexual knighthood, in which we are dubbed Man by a woman, need only be performed once, though some men aren't sure it will hold, so they go through the ceremony repeatedly.

To be a real man, we must do more than bed a woman, however expertly: we must *mate* a woman. We must actually *partner* a woman. This can be confusing to men: on the one hand we gain our manhood by escaping a woman, and on the other hand, we gain our manhood by putting ourselves in full and equal partnership with another woman. How can that be? Aren't all women the same, just incarnations of the same Virgin/Mother/Crone that has been seducing, terrifying, nurturing, dominating us all along?

A steady refrain from the men's chorus keeps singing music from *Samson and Dalila*, warning us of how a woman can shear us of our masculine glory and thus rob us of our strength. We approach each woman as if she were our mother, come to punish us for independence by taking our puberty away. It takes balls to get all the way into the partnership of marriage. It isn't easy to explain this to a woman, because it sounds too dumb, but women don't hear the same incessant voices men hear.

The garden variety of men who can't commit are suffering from hypermasculine panic, in which they are still waiting for their penis to get bigger before they dare put their balls in the hands of a woman. To feel fully masculine, a man must not only win a woman, he must satisfy her. A woman can utterly deflate a man by refusing to be aroused, or if things get to that point, by refusing to be satisfied. ("I am the Earthmother and you are all flops." "I know the game. If you're not a stud, you're a houseboy." "Which are you, baby? Houseboy or stud?" So goes Martha's test in *Who's Afraid of Virginia Woolf?*) Many men live even more dangerously, by requiring that a woman respond orgasmically to his penis, of all things! He's orgastic over his penis so he assumes she should be, too.

In marriage, we are playing a new role, discovering the female perspective and the limitations of being male. Are we able to be partners with someone whose perspective is different from our own, and then go through a lifetime with binocular vision? Or must we protect ourselves by choosing hierarchically and protecting our maleness from her femaleness, playing our male role to her female role, going through life marching to the tune of our militant chorus? We know how powerful our mother was when we were little, but is our wife that powerful to us now? Must we relive our great deed of escape from Mama with every other woman in our life?

Each man may have to remind hmself, as many times a day as necessary, that he is now and forever a man, that this woman beside him is not his mother, that she is not the source of his masculinity, that she can not take it away, and that he will not enhance it by escaping her. Maybe if he sticks around for a while and opens up to her a bit and gets to know her, he may even discover that she's not feeling especially powerful, either.

EIGHT

The Brotherhood of Boys

And the men that were boys when I was a boy
Shall sit and drink with me.
　　　　　—Hilaire Belloc, "The South Country"

"Now I feel," he said cautiously and intensely, "that if you
and me was mates, we could put any damn mortal thing
through, if we had to knock the bottom out of the blanky
show to do it."
　　　　　—D. H. Lawrence, *Kangaroo*

Boys who would be men must leave the company of women. If they're lucky, they'll have fathers and mentors to model masculinity for them, to nurture them through the tests of manhood, and to anoint them when they are man enough; they'll have heroes to inspire them and point the way; and they'll have companions on the path to manhood. One's buddies may be the most encouraging voices in any man's male chorus, or they may be the most rigid and demanding. But without those voices, masculinity is lonely indeed.

Man has been bred as a group hunter; man, for his seed

to survive over those millions of years of evolution, had to be monogamous enough to remain bonded to his woman while he was on the hunt and committed enough to come home bringing the bacon; but he also had to work and live cooperatively and intimately with the other men on the hunt, and to desire that adventure enough to face the dangers of the mission.

"Men court men," as Lionel Tiger explains in *Men in Groups*. Tiger describes male-male courtship patterns as men seek status among other men and form groups with them. Using as an example the street gangs in *West Side Story*, and the song "When You're a Jet, You're a Jet," Tiger notes that "at times the commitment is almost like a marriage." Certainly the lives of boys are tied to their playmates and their teammates. And the models of male bonding for grown men, in work groups and play groups, are rooted in the brotherly bonds of boys. Teenage gangs are closely akin to bowling leagues, poker clubs, and law firms.

Grown men will eventually need bonding with both men and women—we have been bred for that and it is natural—but the experiential base for equal and intimate friendships is in the brotherly bonds of youth.

Brothers

My son has a couple of friends, Butch and Sonny, who are thirtysomething brothers. They are among the healthiest, happiest, spunkiest, friendliest guys I know. I knew their father, Eagleheart. He was a year ahead of me in medical school and he supervised me on several rotations. I admired Eagle for his discipline, his confidence, and his skill, and I learned from him, but I didn't become friends with him.

As long as I've known Eagle, I could never get close to him. Neither could anyone else. He was a martinet. He could never show any vulnerability; he believed he was called upon to be in charge and thus had to maintain an unblemished image, an unchallenged authority. He put on such a show sometimes that it looked as if he thought the world was a testimonial dinner being held in his honor.

Eagle was older than the rest of us. His training had been interrupted when he had to drop out of school to take over the family junk business, which he ran successfully for several years, until he could get his younger brother and sister through college and able to take over the business and the care of their parents.

I knew something of Eagle's family. His mother was a powerful and determined immigrant woman who had kept the family together despite her unreliable, alcoholic husband. Eagle had been battered around a bit, by both parents, and was the man of the house by the time he was eight or ten, running the junkyard, structuring the household, and protecting his younger brother and sister from the parents' abuse. Even now, despite his busy practice and his heavy civic commitments, his grown sons to criticize, and an amazingly tolerant wife he bosses around, he finds time to supervise his middle-aged brother and sister. He is toxically controlling and, like the legendary rooster, believes the sun would not come up without his crowing.

How the hell did Butch and Sonny grow up so healthy despite such a father? Back when they were on my son's cross-country team, cheering one another on and relishing one another's successes, I asked them how they got to be such team players when their father was such a contender. Butch explained lovingly his sympathy for his father, given the position he was put in by his parents. Butch went on to explain that his mother treated his father's autocracy and competitiveness as a slight disability, like a speech defect or facial tic that he couldn't control, but it need not be labored over and must not be emulated. Their mother did not seem to need protecting from Eagle, though the boys clearly identified with her and stood ready to be her champion at any moment. She wisely did not let them go into conflict with their father on her behalf, and she seemed to have her ways of getting Eagle down from his pedestal.

From an early age, Butch knew he must protect Sonny from his father's withering dominance. The two boys bonded tightly as Butch taught Sonny how to play all the games boys and then men must know how to play. In time, Sonny surpassed his older brother in skill and discipline, and could return what he had been given.

They competed fiercely, but only according to the rules of the game, and they never put one another down. They gave one another reassurance and solace through the stormy times. Practicing on one another, they learned to compete and they learned to nurture, but mostly they learned that the relationship is always more important than the game—which they assure me is the secret of brotherhood. They compete now over who can be the best brother rather than who can win the current contest. The other day, Butch was at the house bragging about Sonny's beautiful new daughter and his great finish in a marathon, and Sonny showed up later to brag about Butch's latest promotion and new racing bike.

Butch and Sonny's mother, by patiently staying with her damaged husband, had helped her sons find a way of rejecting their father's macho strutting without turning them against either their father or their own masculinity. Perhaps because they had one another, they were not so dependent upon their father and they weren't hurt by his pathetic need to control, his painful efforts to hide his normal, human vulnerability.

A good brother may be the best protection a boy can have from a bad father.

Pledge Classes

All of us are not blessed with actual brothers, so we have to make the best of our friends. A man may never be as close again to anyone as he was to his friends when he went through puberty carrying a proud, shameful, exciting secret in his pants, a secret he shared only with those who were going through the same wondrous metamorphosis, isolated from the rest of the world as they faced this transformation together.

The boys who go through their puberty rituals together are made Blood Brothers. They have shared the dangers and the humiliations of puberty and they are forever bound to one another. They know each other's shame.

Stephen King's highly personal novella *Stand by Me* is an adventure about four twelve-year-old boys who go forth in search of the body of another twelve-year-old, whom they didn't know, but who had been hit by a train. The quartet are on an adventure to look death in the face, and they encounter various dangers and wonders along the way.

On the trip, two of the boys talk to one another about their loneliness and shame. Chris' father was a thief and Chris has been a social outcast. Gordie's glorious brother has died, and he believes his father wishes it had been him. The boys give each other support, but when their affection gets too sentimental, then one must insult the other.

When they find the body of the dead boy, Gordie has a flashback to his brother's funeral and his father's rejection. He starts crying. Chris hugs the crying Gordie. Gordie says, "I'm no good. It should have been me. My father hates me." Chris keeps telling him, "Your father doesn't hate you. He just doesn't know you." Chris, still hugging him, spells fantasies of Gordie's great success as a writer, and finally says, "Maybe someday, if you're hard up for material, you'll write about us guys." Gordie, wiping his tears, chokes out the insult, "I'd have to be pretty hard up." At that point, older, postpubertal boys who have been tormenting the quartet arrive, find Chris and Gordie sitting there with Chris' arm around Gordie's shoulder, and accuse them of being "homos."

All the themes at the base of male bonding are here in King's story: the pubertal boy as outcast from the world of women; the failure of the father to be there to lead the boy through appropriate puberty rituals; the need to face death to become a man; the hero's journey in which the boy goes forth to face dangers and learn the secrets of the universe; the boy's isolation from those boys who haven't gone through it yet, and from those men who already have achieved the Big Impossible of Manhood; the desperate dependency of boys upon the other males who share this understanding of what they have gone through to be a man; the fear that love between males is a perversity that would forever eradicate hopes of achieving manhood; the insulting, hazing tone men use with one another to express the fear that keeps them forever apart.

Pubertal Outcasts

At the heart of male bonding is this experience of boys in early puberty: they know they must break free from their mothers and the civilized world of women, but they are not ready yet for the world of men, so they are only at home with the other boys, equally outcast, equally frightened, and equally involved in posturing what they believe to be manhood. The less fathering a boy has, the more he needs the other boys in the same boat, but the less likely he is to cross the boundaries of the masculine mystique: "men don't cry," "men don't complain," "men don't show weakness," and above all "men don't need other men."

For better or worse, male bonding is based upon shared risks. Men don't have to talk to one another: what they have in common is the experience of being raised male, of going through masculinity training, and the details aren't the important part of it. What is important is the result of what they risk together: is this man willing to die for the greater glory of masculinity in general? If not, he would not be a reliable friend. But if he would die for you, then you must share everything you have with him.

In *The Three Musketeers*, D'Artagnan, the country boy who has come to Paris, challenges each of the musketeers to a duel. He explains that his father has told him the way to make friends is to fight duels (i.e., if a boy makes a display of masculinity and the willingness to die for it, it will prove that he can be trusted as a comrade at arms). Dumas's "All for one, and one for all" philosophy of 1844 is unchanged from Malory's *Le Morte d'Arthur* four hundred years before and from inner-city street gangs today.

Masculinizing adventures aren't worth having unless a buddy goes along, too. Doc Holliday and Wyatt Earp faced the Clanton Gang together in their *Gunfight at the O.K. Corral*, and survived. *Butch Cassidy and the Sundance Kid* went out together in a blaze of bullets and glory, and they went rather happily after a lifetime of harrowing adventures. In *The Man Who Would Be King*, Kipling's two nineteenth-century-British soldiers, who decided that India "isn't big enough for the likes of such as we," even signed a contract to die for one another before they went off to make themselves kings of Capristan. The bonding between men is based on the hope that either man can rescue the other, but if not, there is the pleasant expectation of dying together in macho glory.

My best high school buddy Charles was a well-muscled weight lifter and a daring adventurer, but like me he didn't play football, the prescribed puberty ritual of the day. Nonetheless, we had seen ourselves as the alpha males in the pack, so we set up other contests to win and made sure we were top wolves in the school. We were both too competitive to be team players back then, but we were too close to compete with one another. (I had, for once, followed my father's advice: "When you find a guy who is so great you can't compete with him, make him your best friend.")

Charles and I were cocky; we felt bulletproof. In fact, at sixteen, we had gotten shot at together. We told Dad about the incident, and he gave me the clearest advice I've ever gotten from him: "Son, never drink homemade whiskey with a tattooed lady hitchhiker." I was a little more cautious after that. Charles wasn't. He had a gambling and entrepreneurial spirit. He's had his share of businesses and his share of adventures. While I was a freshman in college, he was a limousine driver for his father's taxicab company and was driving the car when Hank Williams, the country singer we all knew back then, died in the backseat, perhaps of a heroin overdose. I think of Charles often; I even think of Hank Williams often. But we never talked about that bizarre event that changed his life.

I saw Charles for the only time in decades at the twenty-seventh high school class reunion of our now defunct school. (That may seem like a strange anniversary to celebrate, but it was the first year everyone in the class was out of prison at the same time.) One of our classmates, Ray Scott, had made a fortune as a B.A.S.S. fishing promoter, and reeled us all in for the reunion at his lake house, where he could fish from his bed. I sat all evening with Charles, and it was wonderful to be with him again, but we still didn't talk about Hank Williams. As I look back, we never really talked about anything. Our bonding, like most pubertal male bonding, was based more on shared risks and shared adventures than on shared insights about those experiences.

Brothers love and rescue one another, but they also fight; they learn to contend through their rivalries. Brothers insult one another; the insults are toughening, and the boys can't be friends until they can accept insults without crying to Mama. But the insults are also a compliment to one another's masculinity. To insult a friend implies that you respect his masculinity enough to know he can take it without acting like a crybaby. The swapping of insults, like the fighting between brothers, becomes the seal of the male bonding.

Making Friends

> *A brother may not be a friend, but a friend will always be a brother.*   —Benjamin Franklin

I had no brothers, and no male cousins my age. I had a sister, and she was my best friend always. But I needed male friends, too, and I grew accustomed to having them. They became my alterbrothers. Ebbie lived across the street and was the son of my parents' best friends. He and I were the same age, and our mothers pushed us around in twin perambulators. We were inseparable until the war came and our fathers went to war and separated us. Ebbie grew up to be a small-town lawyer like his father. I haven't seen him in decades.

Bob lived nearby. He was just enough bigger and older and tougher to be a hero to me. At adolescence he blossomed into a startlingly handsome man and a glorious athlete. I envied him, as I found myself courting his friendship—surely he must know the secrets of masculinity that I didn't know. I think Bob was as baffled by the girls trying to get into his pants as I was by the girls who wanted no part of me. What was the secret? Neither of us knew then. I still don't, and I haven't asked Bob lately.

Teddy was the nice, quiet boy who lived next door to my grandmother. Everybody loved Teddy, as they saw an adventurous spirit beneath his calm and civilized exterior. He could even attract the interest of older boys, teenagers who would tease and torment us, even kidnap us and thus make us feel important. Teddy always said he wanted to marry my sister, not just because she's a very special lady but also because he wanted to be my brother. Instead, he went to Annapolis, became a navy pilot, and, thirty-odd years ago, overshot an aircraft carrier and was lost at sea. His mother called me recently. I still miss him.

When I was twelve, my father had returned from the war and we moved to Prattville, Alabama, a new town where I had no friends. I had grown dependent for human companionship on my sister, who always was far better at making friends than I. In Prattville, she immediately found herself in a circle of girls. At first, I was too busy to be concerned with friends. The house was a run-down old ante-bellum mansion with minimal plumbing and holes bored in the floor to spit through. All the big old trees in the yard had been painted white up to eye level. Mother and I spent our first few weeks there painting the tree trunks brown, but as we got everything in order I began to be depressed, and I moped around the house a lot.

Dad came up with a solution: "Don't come home until you've made a friend. I won't pick you up after school unless you call me from some other boy's house." I was panic-stricken. I knew he meant it: I remembered how he taught me to swim by throwing me in the river. So I tried to talk to various guys whose names I thought I knew, but they just walked past me in the hall. I saw one boy my age, who had been nice to me the first day I got there, even though he hadn't talked to me since—nobody had, really. At least I knew his name—Noel—and I knew where he lived because his sister was a friend of my sister.

After school I followed Noel home. He didn't notice me as I walked half a block behind him. He had another friend with him. I stayed behind a tree and, as it got dark, I finally got up the courage to knock on the door and ask him if I could come in to play. He closed the door and talked to his friend about it, and finally let me in. I watched the two guys playing chess for a while before I called Dad and told him where to come to pick me up. By the time Dad got there, Noel and I were playing chess together and making plans to do other things.

Noel had saved my life, and soon afterwards I saved his. He developed bulbar polio and while he escaped paralysis in his legs, he lost his vocal cords and had to relearn to talk. Nobody could hear or understand what he said except over the telephone, so he and I talked every afternoon, and he read things to me over the phone, and sometimes we played telephone chess. We needed one another, in good times as well as bad.

Noel remains a friend who is like family. We've shared forty-five years together. Nobody except perhaps Betsy and my sister Joanna knows me as well.

Blood Brothers

> We few, we happy few, we band of brothers;
> For he today that sheds his blood with me
> Shall be my brother.
>
> —Shakespeare, *Henry V*

Blood Brotherhood develops automatically when boys go through their puberty rituals together, and it can happen easily enough when the boys are young and can play on the same team together, face dangers together, even go to war together. Coming of age is so terrifying and dramatic and unforgettable that we remain forever bonded to our companions in that frightening, exhilarating adventure. But it doesn't happen easily later in life.

At any age, to achieve Blood Brotherhood, the usual male boundaries must be traversed by physically and emotionally stripping and revealing vulnerabilities that men don't usually reveal to one another. And many of us go through life trying to find ways to do this, to create Blood Brothers to ease our loneliness for male intimacy.

In *Women in Love*, Gerald Crich and Rupert Birkin try to get close to one another. Rupert brings up the matter of *Blutbrüderschaft*, the Blood Brotherhood of the old German knights, who made a cut in their arms and rubbed each other's blood into the cut, and "swear to be true to each other, of one blood, all their lives." He agrees that the wounds are obsolete but he proposes that "we will swear to stand by each other—be true to each other—ultimately—infallibly—given to each other, organically—without possibility of taking back." The two men end up not cutting anything or even swearing anything; instead they just wrestle nude before the fire, which serves much the same function. Much of what goes on between older boys and men is an effort to achieve this *Blutbrüderschaft* without having to do anything too painful or too embarrassing. We're trying to recapture the closeness we felt to one another as we went through the pain and embarrassments of puberty together.

But after the intimacy-inducing rituals of puberty, boys who would be men are told we must go it alone, we must achieve our heroism as the Lone Ranger, we must see the other men as threats to our masculine mastery, as objects of competition. So we play games with the men with whom we would bond, we strive against one another in sports, and in that way we make the physical connection we are both seeking and fearing.

We are taught to overcome our yearning for male bonding by clinging ever more tightly to women as the appraisers of our identity as men, and even as our best friends. We are taught that it would be queer of us to feel or to show love for another man.

Homophobia

> The intensity of the fear of sexual contact with boys also makes him withdraw emotionally from boys lest he be "suspect"—like a liberal in the McCarthy era—which makes him dependent on emotional response from females as well. This combination, called homophobia, forces boys to be female-dependent.
>
> —Warren Farrell, *Why Men Are the Way They Are*

The greatest threat boys and men feel to their sense of themselves as men is their fear that they, or someone else, will find "homosexuality" inside them. Whatever "homosexuality" is or isn't, the fear of it is crippling and painfully isolating. Gore Vidal has been quoted as saying, "The average male in the Anglo-American world is hysterical on the subject of homosexuality. It is in the culture, a vestige of Judeo-Christianity, now in its terminal stage. Everyone knows he has homosexual instincts; and since everyone has been told from birth that if he gives way to such instincts he is sick and evil and, in most American states, a criminal, fag-bashing is bound to be very popular for a long time."

When I was growing up, we had few boundaries between us, and we could still share the experience of growing up male together. But boys coming along now are taught before puberty to be fearful of closeness to the other boys, and fearful of dropping their masculine armor around one another. They may grow up without friends, using the other boys only as teammates and competitors, while getting all the love they will ever have from women, who as a result have far too much power over them, disabling them from ever really feeling like men.

Homophobia, the proposed cure for the presumably demasculinizing "condition" of homosexuality, may create serious problems for boys trying to become men. Boys going through puberty keep towels around their waists as they walk through the shower rooms. They wear towels in the steam room or sauna, and sometimes have even been known to wear bathing suits in the shower. Of course, the boys who are most ashamed of their masculine shortcomings don't go to a gym or health club at all. What are these kids afraid of?

Some of the less well developed of them might be fearful that their level of sexual development would not earn them a passing grade into the company of men. They suffer from crippling penis envy.

But others have no doubts about their masculine splendor. Instead they are fearful that other people—boys, girls, parents, strangers—will look at their penis and read their minds. They fear they will get an erection at the wrong moment (and they might), and that observers will then make assumptions about their sexual inclinations or proclivities. And at that age, they have no set sexual preferences—anything that even vaguely reminds them of sex will bring forth a salute.

And, of course, boys don't like to be embarrassed. One fifth-grade swimmer I'm seeing is thinking of dropping off the team because he fears his pubic hair may stick out of his tiny speedo swim suit, and he is sure he will be ridiculed by the boys who haven't yet entered that hormonal maelstrom. As I tried to reassure him, I remember the grief we gave the first pubic boy in our group—we would cover our envy and admiration by dancing around him, acting as if his pubic hair might infect us with something. We pretended to be repulsed; but of course we weren't repulsed at all; we were homophobic—fearful of our attraction to his puberty. By the sixth grade, one boy had grown what seemed to be an enormous penis. I kidded him unmercifully about it, while I went through whatever exercises I could devise to match it.

The boys in the country, where I grew up, spent the summers skinny-dipping, so we always knew the state of one another's development. If there were any doubts, we kept track through frequent measurements. It was another competition between the boys. We worried about one late bloomer, who would never take off his pants around us. I don't know whether he would have gotten ridicule or sympathy if he'd shown us what he was hiding, but his shame was surely sadder than his equipment could ever have been.

Our penile fixations did not lead any of us into a life of homosexuality, and we never thought it would; we knew we were in training for the day when we would expose our delicate masculinity to a female. Even as we kidded and ridiculed one another, we were close enough going through these transitions together that we made each other secure.

Boys must display their masculine shortcomings and doubt, they must seek understanding and solace from other men. Without that their masculinity will be completely in the hands of women, who can't possibly understand it.

Our confused, panicky, and scientifically invalid theories about homosexuality create awful problems both for the men who live a homosexual life and for the great majority of us who live a heterosexual life. Most straight men, whether or not they went through the typical adolescent confusion and anxiety about their sexual identity, live in the fear of either finding homosexuality in themselves or catching it, and so they don't get as close to one another as they desperately need to get.

Male Homosexuality

> We shall not really succeed in discarding the straitjacket of our cultural beliefs about sexual choice if we fail to come to terms with the well-documented, normal human capacity to love members of both sexes.   —Margaret Mead

Perhaps men would fear homosexuality less if they understood it more. Our understanding of it is clouded by homophobia, but also by politics, and it has become a controversial and politically explosive topic. One of the more bizarre political efforts of recent decades has been the crusade to declare homosexual men to be a separate category of people, mutants of some sort who are biologically destined for a life of exclusive homosexuality.

Many people, straight or gay, prefer to see their sexual preference as being biologically determined, and not really under their control. Theories of biological determinism make straight men feel safely different from "queers," while such theories make gay men feel their choice is not their fault.

The latest theory is that gay men may lack some cells straight men have in their hypothalamus, an area of the brain that seems connected with the body's thermostat and perhaps with sexual aggressiveness. It is conceivable—this evidence is quite flimsy—that some gay men weren't as vigorously sexually aggressive at puberty as the rest of us, and ended up feeling different. It would be hard to imagine hypothalamic cells in the shape of sexual objects (though I've had one straight man come in and tell me he thought there was a tall blonde in his hypothalamus while he had a short brunette in his marriage).

Homosexuality is and always has been a normal human capacity, for men and women. The human animal is quite capable of having sex successfully with men, women, children, animals, machines, and certain kinds of plants. Whether one "chooses" to be straight or gay may be simply a matter of taste, though many guys feel they don't have a choice. After working with quite a few gay guys, quite a few straight guys, and quite a few guys who can swing either way, I'm convinced there is no difference between them.

There are undoubtedly countless reasons—biological, psychological, situational—why a man would prefer one to another. And of course, it might be that the guys who prefer homosexuality really are on to something—it may be that other men are more sensitive to a man's needs and more sympathetic to a man's fragile ego.

Homosexuality, in the past, was considered a normal thing for men to do. In ancient Greece, sexual aggressiveness in any homosexual encounter was considered manly, while sexual passivity was seen to be more befitting of a boy or a woman. Foucault, in *The History of Sexuality*, says, "The Greeks did not see love for one's own sex and love for the other sex as opposites, as two exclusive choices, two radically different types of behavior . . . it was common for a male to change to a preference for women after 'boy-loving' inclinations in his youth." They did not recognize homosexuality as a separate kind of love, and certainly they did not recognize homosexuals as different kinds of people. In Greece, a boy became a man at the time of his first beard, and he then was encouraged to stop being the passive sexual partner to an older man, and become the active sexual partner to a younger boy. He could fill his civic responsibility of heterosexual marriage later.

Gilmore, in *The Making of Manhood,* runs down the list of societies that saw no conflict between homosexuality and masculinity: in Greece and Rome, homosexuality "was entirely compatible with, in fact, supportive of, a fully masculine image in the society at large . . . Spartans, like other Greeks of the time, thought that such men made better soldiers because they had their lovers with them on the battlefield . . . in medieval Scandinavia, for instance, a respectable manhood was fully compatible with homosexuality . . . in Japan, as in the case of the novelist Yukio Mishima, homosexuality was not only tolerated but was actually encouraged as a purer form of love." Gilmore describes cultures in which homosexuality is a coming-of-age ritual, a passageway to masculinization. In Sambia of New Guinea, for instance, it is said that "if a boy doesn't eat semen, he remains small and weak."

Vanggaard, in *Phallos,* studies various cultures, including his native Denmark, and concludes: "Any boy, no matter how normal and well adjusted in his family and in society, may be found to be engaged in a pederastic relationship, but if so it is not indicative of future abnormalities in his heterosexual development."

Many boys in my practice fear that the homosexual encounters they have already had would make them unfit for heterosexual life, and would especially make them socially unacceptable to the other guys. I have to remind them that all men are capable of homosexuality: many don't know it; many know it and like it; many know it and don't admit it; many knew it and have carefully repressed it. Knowing the innate bisexuality of all men is helpful whether you want to use it or not, but it is not yet socially acceptable to acknowledge it. It scares people. (Although, as Woody Allen said, "Bisexuality doubles your chances for a date on Saturday night.")

I see gay couples in therapy, and I find they have most of the same problems that the rest of us have, with the added burdens of isolation and double jealousy: men who lead a gay life may be able to get close to one other man, but they may not then be able to have casual friendships on the side. And, of course, gay men, even when they pride themselves otherwise, end up having most of the same limitations from their masculinity training that other men have. Gay men come in bewailing just as loudly as women do at the difficulty of getting close to a man who puts his masculinity ahead of his relationships.

Honestly, despite the prejudices on both sides of the "sexual preference" boundary, we're not really different from one another. We all have the experience of growing up male in a world that expects entirely too much of us as men. And we share the shame of never being man enough.

Chasing Women

> *And, as for women, you make fun of me that I love them.*
> *How can I not love them? They are such poor, weak crea-*
> *tures. It takes so little. A man's hand on their breast, and*
> *they give you all they got.*
> —Anthony Quinn in *Zorba the Greek*

Straight guys, or gay guys who want to pass as straight, may feel the need to reaffirm their straightness to one another. One of the things men do when they get together, to keep them from getting too close to one another and then from going into homophobic panic, is to talk about women. Men chasing women may be a spectator sport men play for one another to keep down the level of homophobia. It is often a bit like dogs chasing cars. It is good exercise and it makes a good show, but there is no effort to actually catch one.

In all the movies about male bonding, there has to be some scene, however brief, to establish the basic heterosexuality of the two guys. After Gerald Crich and Rupert Birkin get through wrestling nude in front of the fire, get through giving one another pain because they can't dare give one another pleasure, they snap on the light, put on their clothes, and start talking about women. The classic triangle has Butch and Sundance, Arthur and Lancelot, both lusting after the same woman—their friendship requires that they not openly lust after one another.

In the 1955 movie *Marty*, best friends Marty (Ernest Borgnine) and Angie (Joe Mantell) are in their mid-thirties and "have been looking for a girl every Saturday night for twenty years." They are careful never to find one. Their mothers keep asking them when they're going to get married. Their conversation is an endless repetition of, "Whadya wanna do tonight, Marty?" "I dunno, Angie, whachu wanna do tonight?" But Marty, finally, accidentally stumbles on a girl, and Angie panics, tells him she's a dog, that he'll ruin his reputation if he goes out with such an ugly girl. Marty stands her up, but after a few more repetitions of the "Whatdya wanna do tonight" conversations he triumphantly calls her. He tells Angie, "I had a good time with her last night. If I keep having a good time with her, I'm going to get down on my knees and beg her to marry me, and then I'll have a date every Saturday night. When are you going to get married, Angie?"

When there are women to be chased, male bonding can be seen as unmanly. Rather than a lifelong *Blutbrüdershaft*, it must be considered merely a slightly embarrassing step along the pathway to *true* masculinity, which can only come when the man grows up enough to take on a wife and family. Male friendships thus serve the same emotional function as homosexuality for the ancient Greeks, but ordinarily without the sex. Men with pride in their masculinity must stand ready to sacrifice their male friends for the love of women and for the sake of their heterosexuality.

Men may try to prevent the loss of their friends in marriage. In *Diner*, Barry Levinson's loving look at boys growing up in Baltimore in the '50s, one of the boys is getting married, but before he does, he and his friends put the prospective bride through a carefully prepared quiz, testing her knowledge of football. He not only makes his friends part of the process, he is determined to choose a wife who will fit into the limited interest spectrum of the men of the Eisenhower era. Women are necessary to affirm heterosexuality, and therefore free the guys to be closer to one another without homophobic panic, but when you start taking them seriously they begin to pull you away from your group of men.

My relationships with guys changed quickly after I married. I was so ecstatic over the level of intimacy with Betsy that I didn't notice my male friends slipping away until they were already gone. At our wedding reception, my groomsmen, led by my med school roommate Barry, a big, burly former college football player, pulled me out of the receiving line and tried to chain me to a chair. The intrepid Betsy, in her peau de soie gown, her veil of Brussels lace, and her long white kid gloves, wrestled the chain from Barry, inflicting whatever damage was required, and fought off the enemy troops to cover my getaway. The lines were clearly drawn.

My father, after a few drinks, might sing the old song, "Those Wedding Bells Are Breaking Up That Old Gang of Mine."

The Loneliness of Men

I know all about loneliness—only I don't whine about it.
—Anthony Quinn as Gauguin walking out on suicidal
Kirk Douglas as Van Gogh in *Lust for Life*

Male friendships are not like female friendships: men are not as likely to have confidants as they are to have playmates. Most of the time male friendships don't need to be like female friendships. Men can silently assume that we have all been through the same ordeals and we all feel pretty much the same about everything. Being together and not having to talk about it is wonderfully comfortable. I sometimes think that if men didn't talk to women, they might not talk to anybody: they might go through life telling dirty jokes and quoting baseball statistics to one another. But sometimes there is something that a man needs to reveal, needs to talk over with another man, and there may be no man available to him. Sometimes, manhood is lonely.

Greta Garbo has a bravura speech in the 1937 film *Conquest*, when she tells off Charles Boyer's Napoleon: "Isn't loneliness a small price to pay for power, Sire? Am I to understand that the master of Europe, who can command a million men to die for him, cannot command one of them to be his friend? Why don't you issue an order, Sire, abolishing your loneliness? You say you're lonely. Where would you receive a friend? In your heart? But it's too full of yourself. In your mind? It's too full of the world—and your desires are unworthy of friendship. You will always be lonely, Sire, but you will bear it. You're pitiless enough, even to yourself."

This is how we are trained. We learn in adolescence that loneliness is a small price to pay for power. Loneliness is what it costs a man to be true to his code of masculinity. Many such men, under the sway of the masculine mystique, lead shockingly lonely lives. Robert S. Weiss, in *Staying the Course*, found the friendship patterns of successful men to be "bizarre": "Imagine having a close friend whom you saw only once every six months, with whom you never had a long phone conversation, and in whom you hardly ever confided."

I know two young men who are best friends. Frost and Glen run together three times a week, and play tennis on the weekends. A couple of years ago, Frost was going through a painful divorce. His wife had tried to get his attention by leaving him and taking the children. She waited for a response. The two wives talked daily about it, sharing every gruesome step. And, of course, Glen's wife told Glen every detail. Yet Frost never mentioned it to Glen, and bristled when Glen brought it up. Instead, Frost began talking to a woman in his office, who was first sympathetic, and then seductive. Soon Frost started an affair with her, filed for divorce, and stopped seeing his kids. And Glen didn't want to risk the friendship by confronting him again.

My father used to talk sadly about his lack of friends. I didn't understand what he meant, because he had a group of men with whom he played poker on Wednesday nights, another for golf each weekend, and others he met for coffee each morning. He was surrounded by men, and they played the games men play, but he was lonely. For a lifetime he had done things with men, had hung out with men, but he'd never really talked to men, and he didn't realize he was missing something until my mother had deteriorated to the point he didn't have her to talk to anymore, and he didn't know how to talk to his friends. He finally declared, "Your friends aren't necessarily the people you do things with, your friends are the people who know you too well and like you anyway." Men may get together for work or play, and make one another feel wonderfully secure, without getting to know each other much at all.

Men who can't find close male friendship may look to their wives or girlfriends to meet all their needs for human contact. This may overload the relationship. And when the marriage goes through troublesome times, as all marriages do, these men are going to have to get close to somebody else. Lucky men have families—sisters, cousins, aunts, sometimes brothers and uncles—or Blood Brothers to talk to about their complicated state of mind. If men don't have family and can't be that close to other men, they may have to find a conveniently available woman to turn into a friend. Some men know so little about intimacy that they confuse it with sexuality, and can't get friendly with a woman without getting sexual with her. Friends should be like brothers and sisters—incest should be clearly out of the question.

Men's post-adolescent confusion about who we can get close to is pathetically sad and utterly unnecessary. Like much of what goes wrong in men's lives, it is a direct result of excessive masculinity training in childhood and adolescence and a shortage of models of men who are doing masculinity right.

Remember how close we felt to the other guys back when we were growing up together, when we found out that the other guys were going through the same scary and exciting things we were experiencing? It hasn't changed. We just stopped talking about it. And if we did open up, whether out in the woods with Robert Bly beating drums, off in a boat drowning worms, or in the parking lot as we leave work, we might feel that familiar closeness, and the world and our place in it would start making sense again.

NINE

Myths of Heroes

There are no great men, buster. There's only men.
—Elaine Stewart in *The Bad and the Beautiful*

The hero is the man of self-achieved submission . . . The mighty hero of extraordinary powers . . . is each of us: not the physical self visible in the mirror, but the king within.
—Joseph Campbell, *The Hero With a Thousand Faces*

We become *male* automatically because of the Y chromosome and the little magic peanut, but if we are to become *men* we need the help of other men—we need our fathers to model for us and then to anoint us, we need our buddies to share the coming-of-age rituals with us and to let us join the team of men, and we need myths of heroes to inspire us and to show us the way.

If we are anointed by our father, then we feel The Force within us, and we step into our father's shoes and apprentice ourselves to him. In time we honor him, give him our benediction, and go off to join our brothers and to search for approachable heroes from whom we can learn more about life as a man.

That would be the easy way. But if we have not been anointed by our fathers, then we might give up and devote ourselves to masculine shame, to hostile competition with the other boys, to hostile dependency on women, and to the search for overwhelming heroes who give us inspiration but deflate us at every turn. And even if we have been well anointed, we may feel the need to be more than just a man.

The unanointed men among us can try to find their lost masculinity, and the anointed ones can try to enhance and focus theirs by taking the path of the hero. Our mythology tells us that heroic masculinity is the Big Impossible; that it is inside us and we must bring it forth; that our mentor must honor it in us after we have passed the requisite tests; and that we must develop it through rigorous and selfless training. Heroism is available to any of us, but it is not easy to come by; it requires much of us, and it is not what we think it is when we start out. We may emulate heroes but decide along the way that we don't need to become a hero in order to become a man. Fortunately, other heroes have gone before us.

Tom Wolfe described heroism in his book about the first astronauts, *The Right Stuff*. He says, "The world was divided between those who had it and those who did not. This quality, this *it*, was never named, however, nor was it talked about in any way. As to just what this ineffable quality was . . . well, it obviously involved bravery. But it was not bravery in the simple sense of being willing to risk your life. The idea seemed to be that any fool could do that, if that was all that was required, just as any fool could throw away his life in the process . . . There was . . . a seemingly infinite series of tests . . . and the idea was to prove at every foot of the way up that pyramid that you were one of the elected and anointed ones who had *the right stuff* and could move higher and higher and even—ultimately, God willing, one day—that you might be able to join that special few at the very top, that elite who had the capacity to bring tears to men's eyes, the very Brotherhood of the Right Stuff itself."

The Hero's Adventure

The man who wishes to be a hero must go on an adventure. Heroes of old got to travel a lot on their adventures; Ulysses went all around the Mediterranean, Orpheus went to the underworld, and Jonah went into the belly of a whale. But in these days of heavy traveling for work, and so much international tourism, the traveling part of the adventure may be passé. The modern arena for our heroic adventures is the "unconscious realm that we tentatively explore in our own dreams . . . , where the monsters inside of us take on terrifyingly real forms, where our deepest wishes sometimes are fulfilled." (David Adams Leeming, *The World of Myth*) Psychotherapy can be such an heroic adventure, as it was for Tom Wingo in *The Prince of Tides*.

Before he is permitted to achieve victory, the hero must renounce his boyish selfishness, his fear of death and of humiliation, and even his desire for glory; he must be willing to give up his life for others. He must go through trials, must be changed in some way, must be tested. Usually he is overseen by a wise mentor, Bly's "male mother" (like King Arthur's Merlin, Luke Skywalker's Obi Wan-Kenobi, or Olympian Harold Abrahams' coach and trainer in *Chariots of Fire*), or perhaps a magical fairy godmother (like Arthur's Lady of the Lake, Siegfried's Forest Bird, or Tom Wingo's psychotherapist). Whatever the gender, the hero's mentor is a source of special wisdom, who is more concerned with developing the pro-

spective hero's soul than with protecting his body from dis-
comfort or danger. This mentor, male mother, or fairy godmother cannot consider the task too difficult, or the would-
be hero too fragile. Above all, the mentor must not declare
the neophyte a victim and offer solace and refuge from the
business at hand, but rather encouragement and inspiration.

The way of the hero is taken alone, but it doesn't have
to be solitary. "We have not even to risk the adventure alone,
for the heroes of all time have gone before us. The labyrinth
is thoroughly known. We have only to follow the thread of
the hero path, and where we thought to find an abomination,
we shall find a god. And where we had thought to slay another,
we shall slay ourselves. Where we had thought to travel out-
ward, we will come to the center of our own existence. And
where we had thought to be alone, we will be with all the
world." (Joseph Campbell, *The Power of Myth*)

That's really what heroes are for: to leave a hero path
through the labyrinth. We use our heroes to model for us what
we have to develop and what we have to renounce in our own
quest for personal heroism. We use our heroes, and our myths
of heroes, to find the potentials within us for something beyond
Father the Provider, something other than lives sacrificed to
"money and death." But what, other than baseball statistics,
dirty pictures, and dreams of glory, is in the souls of men?

Archetypes of Masculinity

The heroes that continue to inspire boys and men are
characterized by aspects of masculine identity that psychoan-
alyst Carl Jung calls "archetypes." These myths and heroes
resonate with something inside us, something of our own,
something universal. They make us aware of what is inside
ourselves. If we choose certain heroes as our heroes, and put

their voices in our male chorus, their voices can encourage and inspire their special aspects of our character.

The four archetypes of the mature masculine, as described by Jungian analysts, mythologists, and Bly colleagues Robert Moore and Douglas Gillette, are *King, Warrior, Magician,* and *Lover.* The King is the energy of just and creative ordering, which makes rules and maintains order, which provides fertility and blessing—I think of the patriarchal father. The Warrior is the energy of self-disciplined, aggressive action, concerned with skill, power, accuracy, and control, with knowing when to take action—I think of the athlete. The Magician is the energy of initiation and transformation, who understands the unseen world and can think through the issues that are not obvious to others, the energy of awareness, insight, and bullshit detection—I think of the psychotherapist or the court jester. The Lover is the energy that connects men to others and the world, the energy of play, of sensual pleasure, and of passion without shame, of aesthetic consciousness and understanding through feeling rather than just through intellect—I think of Mozart.

When these archetypes that are in all of us are not developed into their fullness and are not used to connect with others, when we fear we don't have enough of them so we overdo them, instead of a King we get a Tyrant, instead of a Warrior we get a Bully or a Sadist, instead of a Magician we get a Detached Manipulator, instead of a Lover we get a Love Addict. My practice, my movie screen, and my world are all filled with men who are grotesquely overdoing one or more of these masculine archetypes.

Controllers and homoclites and other domestic tyrants, in their shame, are Shadow Kings, bullying others and trying to display the power and position they don't find inside themselves. Contenders, who never get enough and can't let any other man have a moment of victory, are Shadow Warriors, trying to prove they are winners because inside they feel like losers. Philanderers, sex addicts, and love addicts, who can't love a real partner because they spend all their time getting reassurance or escaping into "in-love" fantasies, who try to define their masculinity through sex, are Shadow Lovers.

I had not thought in terms of masculopathic magicians, since the Magician archetype is not a specifically masculine model these days, but there are certainly destructive therapists, mentors, professors, and experts, who don't serve their clients and students well. Instead of inspiring and nurturing strength and health, they bring others under their control, make them weak and dependent, and even humiliate them. I think of Timothy Leary, who encouraged a generation of young people to "turn on, tune in, drop out." When they became druggie dropouts, it proved Leary's power, but did great damage to his followers.

My Short Life as a Hero

I never saw myself in heroic postures like my father, who starred at sports and fought in the war, or like my Uncle Harry the surgeon, who won medals for operating for days without sleep on a stricken ship in the Pacific, or even like my Uncle Mac the dentist, who fitted Clark Gable for false teeth.

I went to medical school because I thought it would please my mother, and I went into psychiatry because I feared for my health and thought psychiatry was something I could do sitting down. The fact that Betsy's father, grandfather, and great-uncle were psychiatrists certainly made such an unheroic profession seem at least socially acceptable and sane. But once in my psychiatric residency, I chose family therapy out of passion. In my training, I met and worshipped heroes like Erik

Erikson, Margaret Mead, and Abram Kardiner, who came from the social sciences and interested me far more than the psychiatrists I met, until family therapist Al Messer came and inspired me to look past the individual. Messer became both my mentor and my analyst. He introduced me to the founder of family therapy, Nathan Ackerman, a gutsy little man who anointed me by asking me to contribute to books he was writing. I had arrived into professional manhood, but I still needed a dazzling hero to emulate, a hero who could inspire, strengthen, and focus my sense of masculinity.

I read articles by the brilliantly satiric iconoclast of family therapy, Jay Haley, and I had to meet him, but he was all the way out in California. When I finished my residency and was turned down on my navy physical, I took a job in Denver and made the pilgrimage to California and spent two weeks in Palo Alto with Haley and his colleagues, the clinically dazzling golden boy Don Jackson and the love-inspiring earth mother Virginia Satir. I watched in awe as the glamorous, cock-sure Jackson treated families. He walked into the treatment room glowing with confidence, as if he were clad in shining armor. I wanted to be him. I mimicked his gestures and his posture, and his aloof profundities. Jay Haley quickly adopted me and became a mentor, while I fell into hero worship of Don Jackson. I wrote two books with Haley in the '60s and, emulating the model of my glorious hero Don Jackson, I became a psychiatric cowboy who could handle the craziest of patients and the wildest of families outside psychiatric hospitals.

Our project in Denver—family therapy as an alternative to psychiatric hospitalization—was extravagantly successful. I moved back to Atlanta in 1968 to take over the psychiatric services for the big city-county hospital. I was just a kid of thirty-two, and the mental health of Atlanta from 1968 to 1972 would be in my hands. I thought I had to be a hero. I kept Jackson's picture in my mind as I tried to emulate a Jacksonian version of St. George, wrestling people in distress from the dragons of mental illness. Then Virginia Satir came to dinner and told me that Don Jackson had died, perhaps from suicide. I was devastated; I had lost my model for psychiatry as an heroic pursuit.

Soon afterwards, I got a call from the Chief of Police telling me that there was a crazed gunman holding a group of people hostage in a dental office on the twenty-sixth floor of the First National Bank Building. The gunman had stripped these people down to their underwear, and was going to kill them unless someone brought him a shot of morphine. The Police Chief wanted me to find a volunteer to go into the situation. I had no choice but to volunteer, but I knew I would be shot, so I left my brand-new sport coat in my office and switched to a white doctor's coat. A nurse, Suzanne Parks, insisted on going with me. The police escorted us there, carried us through the enormous crowd and the police barriers into the building. At the door, a policeman being held hostage in his underpants let us in and led us to the wild-eyed, shaking gunman, who pointed a gun at my head as he held out his other arm desperately to my syringe filled with entirely too much morphine. He was more frightened than I, so I fumbled for a tourniquet to pump up his vein for the IV injection, and sweetly asked him if I could borrow his belt. As he eagerly dove for his belt, he put down the gun for a second. I quickly picked it up, pointed it at him, and then, not knowing quite what to do next, handed it to Nurse Parks while I went ahead and gave the poor man the shot he had requested. As we were escorted out of the building past the crowd and the TV cameras, I covered my face and urged Suzanne to do so as well. I warned her, "We don't want to get a reputation for doing this sort of thing."

I had had my moment of heroism; I didn't need to do that more than once. I kept thinking of Don Jackson, who tried to be a hero all his short life. F. Scott Fitzgerald once said, "Show me a hero and I will write you a tragedy." I need heroes, but I don't have to be one. I know there is something tragic about the life of the hero. I decided I don't want it. I was to spend the rest of my career working with men who suffered from the longing to be heroic.

The Choice of Our Heroes

Boys and men should be careful in choosing heroes; they give their heroes power to influence their direction as a man and their standards as a human being. Boys and men with anointing fathers aren't as dependent on their heroes, so it won't matter as much if they choose unwisely. Young men and boys who don't have fathers tend to choose superficial and showy role models as guides for display or for victory over their fellows in the games boys play. They have not understood the function of the hero as the model for one's *character*, for the "self-achieved submission" that is at the heart of heroism.

In Australia recently, Betsy and I, with a Swedish couple, chartered a boat for snorkeling and fishing in the Great Barrier Reef. I asked the skipper and the mate of the little fishing boat to tell me of their heroes. The mate promptly chose another boat captain, to whom he had been apprenticed, and who knew the nearby waters exceptionally well. The skipper sang the praises of a legendary fishing-boat captain, who had done well at handling sudden squalls and emergencies on board. Neither of these men had any thought of heroes outside their own field or their own personal acquaintance. They chose the heroes that would be of help to them, but they set the bar low enough to be able to get over it. Their heroes were approachable and they could feel good about themselves and their striving for competence in their field, without much concern over how they fit into the larger world. They, too, had felt anointed by their fathers, and they were unashamed of their lives.

I asked the Swedish man about his heroes. He is a banker who coordinates branch banks throughout the world. Like most men who aspire to greatness as a leader, he admires Winston Churchill most and, as I too had done, made the pilgrimage to Blenheim Palace, where Churchill was born and which might have been his heritage if his uncle had not had a child late in life. If Churchill had become the Duke of Marlborough, he would have inherited his patrimony and might not have taken the hero's journey that gave him the power of language and of will to inspire a resistance that protected the British Empire and the world from Hitler.

My Swedish banker friend had another, more recent, hero, Norman Schwarzkopf, who coordinated Operation Desert Storm, a war that required the coordination of dozens of diverse national forces. Schwarzkopf's feats of organization struck the international banker as an heroic deed. I admired the practicality of the banker's choices of heroes, men with the talents he needed for the job he had taken on. He keeps pictures of Churchill and Schwarzkopf close to him.

I keep icons of many of my heroes: a self portrait of Rembrandt, the man who was not afraid to look deeply into his own face, and a book of Thurber cartoons on my desk. I wear my grandfather's high school ring, and carry a brass Chinese potency coin, showing couples in various sexual positions, that my father brought back to me from World War II when I was eleven. And I have a brass replica of the stick from the plane in which my nephew Pitt was killed.

My own heroes are less likely to be swashbucklers than

to be humorists, like James Thurber, who understood the war between men and women, the secret life of Walter Mitty, and what it felt like for mild little men to walk into a female-dominated house. I have a few stand-up comics in my male chorus, such as Bill Cosby, who understood the helplessness men feel with children, and Woody Allen, who understood the inadequacy men feel with women. The stand-up comic is the modern version of the court jester; therapists and jesters both have the same function of transmitting painful wisdom that would be rejected if it were delivered without either love or self-deprecating humor. As much as we worship our heroes, they lose their usefulness if they get too heroic. I want my male chorus to be a wise and witty comedy routine from humble heroes.

Heroes inspire us, but they are merely oppressive to us unless we can emulate them. Arnold Schwarzenegger, however well disciplined, wouldn't be a helpful hero for me. When men choose the wrong heroes, it makes them feel ashamed. On New Year's Eve, my battery went dead and a young man who worked at a service station came to my rescue. I asked him about his heroes. He mentioned his father, who had recently given up alcohol after eighteen years of abusing his family. He then mentioned Martin Luther King (he himself was white) and the rock group U-2, which supports humanitarian causes, and described his lifelong efforts to become a gentle man quite different from his brutal father. He says his father's heroes are Patton and John Wayne, but lately his father has added "Bill," the co-founder of AA. This boy's father was a man who had spent a lifetime modeling himself after warriors, warriors who weren't always very tolerant of human frailties, while he tortured those around him with his self-abuse, perhaps brought on by his shame over being unable to approach the power and glory of such mighty heroes. All the poor man

had to do to become heroic in his own eyes and in the eyes
of his benevolent, peace-worshipping, helpful son, was to find
another hero, AA's "Bill," that he actually could emulate.

Bigger-Than-Life Heroes

Hollywood is in the business of producing and marketing
heroic images—the well-paid, well-publicized, and widely revered actors are not likely to be actual heroes in the mythic
sense of risking their lives to discover the secrets of the universe
or to enhance the lives of others. Instead, they just have a
look, a style, a manner that serves as a model for what we
think a hero should be. The actors are not really important,
but their idealized images both reflect our culture and influence
it. Those shadows on the screen are telling us what we are
supposed to be and supposed to do if we are to feel heroic, if
we are just to feel manly.

For most of the last century, boys (and girls) have gotten
from the silver screen their images of the ideal for their gender.
There has been a wide range of would-be heroes submitted for
our approval. There have been Great Actors, compelling pres-
ences like Brando, Olivier, Hoffman, and Newman. There
have been Heartthrobs, like Valentino, Grant, Hudson, and
Redford, who fuel women's romantic fantasies and give men
in heat helpful hints on seductive style. And there have been
Tough Guys, like Cagney, Bogart, McQueen, and De Niro,
who understand and accept the rottenness of the human heart
and the world we live in. Men without domestic models may
need all of those images in order to be complete as men, but
what we may find most compelling is the image of the Bigger-
Than-Life Hero, the embodiment of ideal masculinity.

Bigger-Than-Life Movie Heroes seem to come in at least
three varieties: Hero machismus, Hero domesticus, and Hero

juvenilius. There has been a steady succession of heroes of each variety, and an examination of these heroes, chosen by audiences to include in our cultural mythology, tells us how the culture defines masculinity.

There are disturbing trends in our choices of heroes. Domestic heroes have grown older and died off, without being replaced. The adolescent rebellion of our juvenile heroes grows more destructive and extends well into adulthood. Our macho heroes have become increasingly detached from real life; they are fantastically exaggerated characters acting out a child's version of masculinity. Clearly, the boys who choose these heroes do not know what men and masculinity are really like. They are modeling themselves after cartoonish action heroes and perennially alienated kids, without thinking to admire and emulate the heroism of men in family life.

HERO MACHISMUS

Back in the '20s, acrobat Douglas Fairbanks jumped around a lot as he played action heroes. Errol Flynn inherited his tights. But Clark Gable was heroic with both feet planted firmly on the ground. Gable was a romantic heartthrob, with a pencil moustache and a wicked grin. He was a rogue. But mostly he was a man's man, an action hero who was the symbol of masculine action and macho derring-do, a tough and boisterous outdoorsman, leading mutinies (*Mutiny on the Bounty*) and coralling horses (*The Misfits*). With women, he acted bossy and impatient: he slapped those women who carried on, and put a grin on Scarlett O'Hara's face by carrying her up the stairs and raping her. From the beginning of his heroic days, dancing with and slapping around Joan Crawford, to the end, lassooing Marilyn Monroe, Gable's model of masculinity was always to control women.

By the '40s, macho heroes had gotten less civilized and bigger than life. John Wayne could barely drawl out a word of dialogue. He looked disgusted at the thought of having to resort to something as unmasculine as words rather than actions. His most famous line, to Harry Carey, Jr., in *She Wore a Yellow Ribbon* was, "Never apologize, Mister, it's a sign of weakness." He never did. He shot first and asked questions later. On screen and off, Wayne was the idealized American warrior, an alcoholic, misogynist rabid right wing warmonger. On screen he rescued a little girl from the Indians in *The Searchers*, but more typically he brawled with his adopted son Montgomery Clift in *Red River*, and he brawled with every woman who tried to tame him, especially with his spirited redheaded screen wife, Maureen O'Hara, in *The Quiet Man*. Wayne's model of masculinity was at home on the range, but clearly unfit for domestic life.

In the '50s we got an image even bigger and more heroic than John Wayne. Charlton Heston had a face and body that seemed carved in granite, and was not just legendary. He was downright biblical. He parted the Red Sea and led us out of bondage. He then helped Jesus make his way to the cross. (He was far too macho to merely play Jesus—Heston was godlike.) He never quite played God on screen, but he did paint him on the ceiling of the Sistine Chapel. Heston's images of what it takes to be a man just kept getting bigger and bigger and closer to our image of God.

In the '60s, the British had given us Sean Connery as James Bond, a hairy-chested, tattooed muscleman with impeccable taste and manners. He had a license to kill. The American counterpart in the '70s was the far less suave but just as resolutely implacable Clint Eastwood, a hired killer and a man with no name. He rarely spoke, just went around killing people, either on the range, or in the cities. He enjoyed it, and even asked bad guys who might be tempted to fight back, to "make my day." The screen Clint Eastwood was a man without an emotional life, just masculine rage. He had an ugly little counterpart, Charles Bronson, who was just as ruthlessly bloodless in his war against anyone who got in his way. Our '70s heroes were all passionless killers.

By the '80s, heroes needed not only an iron will but also an iron body. Our tastes turned to muscle heroes, and to Sylvester Stallone. In the '70s and interminably since, he played *Rocky*, a dimwitted boxer, loyal husband, and all-around good guy, but in the '80s he became Rambo, a wordless terrorist who refought the Vietnamese War and won. Rambo was an even more alienated, isolated, silent, and bloodthirsty model of manhood than Eastwood or Bronson.

By the '90s, even Stallone was not enough. Instead, our hero was Arnold Schwarzenegger, a man mountain who was in actuality Mr. Universe and Mr. Olympia. He is, ostensibly, not really a human being, so he plays comic-strip characters like *Conan the Barbarian*, and invulnerable robots like *The Terminator*. However overblown and steroidal he is, he has one characteristic no screen incarnation of Hero machismus has displayed since Gable: he knows he's ridiculous, and he has proved a deftly comic commentator on the nature of masculinity. Nonetheless, the image of Arnold Schwarzenegger is our current model of what it takes to be man enough. We keep raising the ante on ourselves.

HERO JUVENILIUS

The Hero machismus reflects what we think we need to be to be man enough for heroism, but there are also coming-of-age heroes, boys showing us how a boy becomes a man. The Hero juvenilius has often been as popular as the big guy.

In the '30s, when we needed masculine energy to pull us out of the Depression, the juvenile hero and the top box-office star was pint-sized Mickey Rooney, a kid who was always getting into trouble for being too energetic and resourceful. He was Puck, Huckleberry Finn, and a teenaged tough guy in *Boy's Town,* and as Andy Hardy he was the brash and bouncy kid who could solve any problem by putting on a show. Rooney may have invented adolescence. His image was always a nice guy who never wanted to hurt anyone and who loved and honored his family—he was just too energetic to be contained in civilized domesticity.

In the '40s, Hero juvenilius was freckle-faced Van Johnson, whose function seemed to be to get himself killed heroically in the war. He was so blandly, uncomplainingly loveable, he was the perfect sacrifice to war, destined to live on only in June Allyson's dreams.

In the '50s the juveniles began to rebel. Marlon Brando became the Hero as Rebel (perhaps a revulsion against the deadly patriotism of John Wayne). Brando played Zapata, Marc Antony, Napoleon, gangsters with songs and gangsters with motorcycles. He beat up and raped Blanche Dubois, and when asked, in *The Wild One,* what he was rebelling against, queried, "What you got?" James Dean followed shortly. Before he killed himself in his brand-new Porsche in 1955 and moved into legend, Dean made three memorable movies in which he was the original mixed-up, misunderstood, unloved kid. All three films are about boys trying to become men when they were not getting anointed by their fathers. In *Rebel Without a Cause,* his father is wimp who can't teach him how to be a man, so he goes drag racing to prove himself. In *East of Eden,* his father disapproves of him, and rejects his gift, so he turns bad and smites his brother. In *Giant,* he is an orphan on Rock Hudson's ranch and is rejected by the man he would emulate, so he gets filthy rich, appallingly powerful, and rude. Dean was the boy who got no respect.

In the '60s, boys who wanted to grow up gave up on grown men and turned first to sex, then to rock and roll, and finally to drugs in an effort to overcome their shame. Punkish Elvis Presley wiggled his way into our pantheon of heroes by shocking the stodgy old grown-ups with the sexiness of his music and makeup. He made a series of dreadful movies about a simple country boy who is just too sexy and too musical to fit in. Presley wasn't really a rebel. He went to war when called, and in the army was the very model of the clean-cut American kid, but despite or because of his legendary hero status, this simple country boy gradually killed himself with drugs. He was the model of musical sexuality as protest against patriarchal efforts to turn boys into human sacrifices.

In the late '70s briefly, we had a slimmer and more urban version of Presley in John Travolta, a sexy dancer with a petulant face who found a kind of simple-minded heroism in narcissism. In his signature film, *Saturday Night Fever*, he has to protect the flashy white suit that will bring him status from his family's sloppy spaghetti dinner. Travolta, in *Grease*, demonstrated that his roots were in the punk rebellion of the fifties rather than the political revolts of the '60s. Boyish heroism in the '70s was simply a matter of flashy, narcissistic style.

For the '80s, we had a brat pack of petulant boys starring in movies. One of them, Matt Dillon, was reminiscent of James Dean. Another, Sean Penn, looked like a punk angel. Still another, Eddie Murphy, covered his sweetness with ghetto bravado. But the least talented and the least angry of the group, Tom Cruise, became the big star. He was pretty, but more than that he had an eagerness to please that we hadn't seen since Mickey Rooney. He costarred with the big male stars like Newman, Duvall, and Hoffman, and was more likely to be battling with his mentor or his brother than with his father (the typical Hero juvenilius of the '80s had already lost that battle). His big film was *Top Gun*, in which he played a highly disciplined hotshot pilot trying to recover from the loss of his father by being better than the old man. In several popular movies Cruise represented the power of youth to develop the skills to take hold of the machinery of the society. The adolescent rebellion was over by the '80s—there were no fathers to rebel against—and boys had to conquer the real world if they were to become men.

So far in the '90s, the coming-of-age star is Mike Myers of *Wayne's World*. Wayne lives at home with his mom, jobless and directionless. He is not rebelling, he is not struggling, and he is not expecting to ever grow up. Instead he worships heavy metal music, dreams of babes, and talks of vomiting. His function in his minimalist life is to invent slang that will distinguish his purposeless generation from the world in which they find no place.

HERO DOMESTICUS

The third species of hero on the big screen is Hero domesticus, the father and husband figure of the man who fulfills his domestic responsibilities. This is the heroic model of ordinary manhood, rather than the stuff of myths, the role model for men's lives rather than for their fantasies. This species of homey hero used to be just as popular as the splashier variety.

Back in the '20s our Hero domesticus was Will Rogers, who never met a man he didn't like. By the '30s, the solid, homely Spencer Tracy was the model for the good man. He played priests a lot, sometimes paired against the sexier, more volatile, Clark Gable. In his back-to-back Oscar-winning films, *Captains Courageous* in '37 and *Boy's Town* in '38, he was the mentor to young boys. From the '40s on, he was often paired with real-life lover Katharine Hepburn as the regular guy learning to deal with a strong, liberated woman. His magic was in his ability to make gentle, frustrated, loving men seem strong even as they realized they weren't the boss.

James Stewart was a more boyish and even more ordinary version of Tracy. He could be a homespun hero like Lindbergh or Stratton or Glenn Miller, or one of Hitchcock's ordinary men caught up in danger and mystery. His innocent heroism showed when he straightened out the government in *Mr. Smith Goes to Washington*. Most memorably he was a family man. In *It's a Wonderful Life*, an angel talked him out of suicide when he thought he had failed his family. In *Shenandoah* he was the father losing his children in the Civil War and discussing the horrors of war, in his halting, shaky voice, at the grave of his dead wife. For decades afterwards he played fathers who had to be educated by their children.

Gregory Peck was the next great Hero domesticus. He was quite handsome, but never seemed tough enough for an action hero. He was at his best looking earnest and doing good, fighting anti-Semitism (*Gentleman's Agreement*) or rescuing lost princesses (*Roman Holiday*). In 1956, he was the symbol of the postwar removal of men from their families in *The Man in the Gray Flannel Suit*. And in 1963 he was the last of the great movie fathers as civil rights lawyer Atticus Finch in *To Kill a Mockingbird*. A soft actor with a warm, gentle voice, he was what everyone wanted from a post-patriarchal father—just soft gentle words and no action.

In the '60s, Tracy, Stewart, and Peck were still holding on, as fathers just got older. But there were few images of young men dedicating themselves to family life and family virtues. Sidney Poitier, the first black movie hero, comes closest. His only real family film was *A Raisin in the Sun*, but he displayed all the domestic virtues. He built churches for nuns (*Lilies of the Field*), taught deprived kids (*To Sir, With Love*), rescued blind girls from evil mothers (*A Patch of Blue*), manned a suicide hot line (*The Slender Thread*), was the perfect son-in-law for white liberals (*Guess Who's Coming to Dinner*), and even helped out racist redneck sheriffs (*In the Heat of the Night*). Poitier was too good to believe, but was number-one box office star in 1968.

There were no further sightings of Hero domesticus on the big screen after that. Husbands were all being unfaithful and running away from home, and fathers (like Dustin Hoffman of *Kramer vs. Kramer*, who didn't know what grade his son was in, or Henry Fonda of *On Golden Pond*, who had never said a kind word to his daughter) definitely did not know best. The only nice guy in the movies seemed to be the decidedly nonheroic Woody Allen, who was afraid of babies and who rarely got the girl. (In retrospect, Allen was most comfortable in *Manhattan* with seventeen-year-old Mariel Hemingway. Grown women were too much for him.)

Men were now a problem, and no longer a solution to family dilemmas. The fathers on the little screen were wimps, nerds, and chumps, like Ward Cleaver on "Leave It to Beaver," or jerks like Archie Bunker. The smaller-than-life fathers on television might make fatherhood look comfortable, but they did not make it look heroic. Only Bill Cosby in the '80s put some life into TV fathering, managing to make fatherhood look worthy of a man's efforts. Cosby seems a reincarnation of Spencer Tracy.

In the '90s, the big screen has finally found a model of Homo domesticus in Kevin Costner, a Jimmy Stewart reincarnation who was squeaky clean as an FBI agent in *The Untouchables* and comfortably at home with his family when he decided to conjure up the ghost of his dead father in his *Field of Dreams.* He showed all the domestic virtues in *Dances With Wolves* and *JFK*, and even carried them back to medieval times in the politically correct *Robin Hood: The Prince of Thieves*, but he didn't seem to be enjoying himself. Does his great popularity mean that there is a longing for men to go back home and do something domestically useful? Perhaps, but it's been hard to make fathering and husbanding heroic when there are so few models of domestic heroism, either at home or on the mythic screen, and when Costner makes it so grimly serious.

Heroism, Men, and Marriage

Family therapist Gus Napier, in his paper *Heroism, Men and Marriage* in JMFT, 1989, looks at the absence of men in modern family life and says, "I believe that the modern hero's journey needs to be an internal one, into that often frightening world of the unconscious where the character of every person takes its definitive shape; and where the reformation of that person's life must ultimately occur . . . Those of us who are the therapists to men know the formidable power of male denial of awareness of the inner self; often this denial must be forcefully confronted, or it can block the entire journey . . . There is a common thread in these men's problems: a pervasive self-focus, a narcissism of imperious habit (condoned by the culture), or of need (unmet in childhood), which makes it as difficult for these men to be emotionally giving and nurturing as it has been for women to learn self-assertion and self-enhancement. Overcoming our narcissism may be the primary challenge for the new male ideal; and indeed, Campbell finds that a willingness to transcend self-interest—in what he calls 'self-achieved submission'—is a marker of the hero."

To me, the men who can't live in families, who can't be husbands and fathers, are men who have incorporated the images of Homo machismus and/or Homo juvenilius, but have not found Homo domesticus in themselves because they didn't see it in their fathers, and so they didn't notice or respect it when they saw it in other men's heroes.

Men who don't feel anointed yet are likely to use the central relationships of their life as opportunities to increase their sense of manliness. Such an immature man will run from brotherhood with his friends, as he envies them and tries to feel man enough by competitive victories over them. He will run from equality and intimacy in his marriage, betraying his wife and trying to dominate her in hopes of feeling man enough through victories over her. He will avoid the true expression of masculinity—fatherhood—and run from children who expect him to nurture them and anoint them; he can't share his masculinity while he doesn't yet feel *man enough* for himself. These men need mentors of family life, preferably real-life Heroes domesticus, before they can dedicate themselves to something larger than themselves, like their family or community. Otherwise, their masculinity is not grounded in what Campbell calls "self-achieved submission," i.e., some larger sense of themselves as existing not in their own narcissism but in the relationships of their lives.

The self-achieved submission of his masculinity would call upon him to abandon his struggle to enhance his masculinity through pubertal displays and adolescent contests, and instead to bestow the boons of his masculinity upon others. Even if he was not anointed by his father, and did not achieve macho heroism through sacrifice and derring-do, he can become a man and a Hero domesticus by brothering his friends, partnering his wife, and fathering his children.

III

BEING A MAN

TEN

A Man Among Men

The mystic bond of brotherhood makes all men one.
—Thomas Carlyle

You and I have been in feminine society, and very nice we found it; but to leave society like that is as pleasant as a dip in cold water on a hot day. A man hasn't time to attend to such trifles; a man must be savage . . .
—Turgenev, *Fathers and Sons*

Joining the Team

My father tried to teach me both the value and the art of male friendship. He tried to tell me how to be a man among men, and I didn't hear him back then. I was trying to win my masculinity. On the sidelines, my father would merely look disgusted with me, which would make me compete even harder. While I was busy trying to defeat all the guys I admired and envied, and to avoid any contest that would expose my shame, my father kept telling me to "join the team." He was trying to teach me to turn competition into brotherhood.

Dad was trying to teach me to be a masculine hero rather than a masculopathic contender. He wanted me to move past my pubertal need to prove I was man enough by winning contests and competitions. (Of course, Mother wanted me to compete ever harder for her glory.) Dad wanted me to move to a more heroic level of male bonding in which I submitted myself and my talents to the brotherhood of the team. He wanted me to realize that the pursuit of personal glory, however self-fulfilling, merely creates envy and distance from the other guys and that truly masculine heroes submit their strivings into the enhancement of something larger than themselves.

My son Frank's favorite sports-page picture of himself shows him joyously and vigorously hugging the teammate who had just beat him for the regional college cross-country championships. His grandfather would be prouder of that than of his room full of trophies. Like his grandfather, Frank realized that life is a team sport.

I finally learned, from my crippling adolescent envy of the gracefully athletic, calmly masculine boys around me, that one of the secrets of happiness is to convert envy into emulation, not necessarily emulation of the specific talents and skills of the more comfortable masculine guys, but emulation of the substance and the internal source of the power that gives them their grace and mastery. It can't be taken away from them, any more than stealing a champion's medals would make a champ out of a thief, but it can be absorbed and it can even be shared. When men bond, they absorb one another's strengths.

Men may or may not need other men for stimulation, but all men need other men for acceptance. It is the acceptance of the other guys, the silent, unquestioning, unchallenged acceptance of shared masculinity that keeps us grounded, that keeps us sane.

The Accepting Silence of Men

> *Friendship needs no words—it is a loneliness relieved of the anguish of loneliness.*
> —Dag Hammarskjöld, *Markings*

> *To communicate through silence is a link between the thoughts of man.*
> —Marcel Marceau

When men feel assured that they are all men among men, a great emotional calm comes over the assemblage. However strenuous the task at hand, even if there is a competition going on, the men who know they are men don't need to strive beyond the competition itself. They don't need to struggle for acceptance: that is extended automatically. The anxiety level drops. Nothing more needs to be explained, nothing more needs to be said.

My Uncle Harry was a man's man. He was a surgeon and had won medals during the war for operating for days without sleep after his ship was hit. He could be counted on to do the manly thing: he always did his duty and he never concerned himself with his feelings. I went to see him once while he was in the hospital himself, in traction for a ruptured disc, and found that he was not in his bed. Instead, he was in the operating room, doing surgery while suspended from the ceiling in a harness that would keep him from putting pressure on his back.

Uncle Harry was the doctor for the Atlanta Braves, and for the Atlanta Crackers for decades before that, and he loved going to baseball games. His other great loves were golf and gin rummy. He spent his life in the men's lounge at the doctor's building. And when he retired, he would spend his days at the country club, playing golf all morning and then playing cards all afternoon, until it was time to go home to watch the ball game on TV with Aunt Emily. Uncle Harry regretted that they had not had children, but otherwise his was just the life he wanted. He got to do heroic deeds, he got to play father to young athletes, he got to hang out all day with other guys playing games, he had a wife who was totally pleased with him, and he never had to talk very much.

Uncle Harry was eighty-two when he heard of his great-nephew Pitt's death. He had a stroke that left him totally paralyzed on one side, and completely incontinent. Aunt Emily had a stroke at the same time, and sank into a pleasant reverie in which she was reunited with her mother and all the dogs she'd raised through the years. We tried keeping them at home, but finally had to put them in the nursing home next to our office.

At least once a week for the next five years, I took Uncle Harry to the club to be with his friends. His friends tried to take him out in the golf carts, but he fell out. They tried to eat with him, but he couldn't keep the food from drooling out of his mouth. They tried to play cards, but he couldn't hold them. He would sometimes try to talk, but no one could understand him. So he ended up just sitting with his buddies while they planned the golfing foursomes, or played gin or bridge, or watched the game on television. His silence was not out of place in this company. The words were irrelevant and the activities merely an excuse for just being together. He was completely content.

I would sit with him in the men's lounge for hours, and began to find it addictively comfortable. There was no intellectual stimulation, and certainly no emotional interaction.

One man's wife had been in surgery for cancer, and the other men had worried over her condition. He walked in and someone asked how his wife was. He reported that she had died. Another man came to the rescue; before the shell-shocked new widower could slip and display an emotion, his thoughtful friend interrupted and asked for the score of the game on the ever-present TV.

Men, in such sanctuary, do not give offense or take it, they do not talk about relationships, and above all men don't cry, even if their wife just died. These men talked about sports, of course, but they didn't listen to one another. The most spirited conversations I heard during my years of sitting there with Uncle Harry had to do with trips into the country to buy especially spicy sausage. And yet when I catch a guy alone, or in a familiar group, and I ask him about his life, his pain, even his masturbatory fantasies, he seems eager to tell me. Men are silent, not because there is only a test pattern going through their brains, or because they have nothing to say, but because the talk between them is not required. Men, unlike women, don't feel loved because somebody talks to them. In a way, silence implies a higher level of acceptance. Love between men means never having to say anything.

I've seen men with their wives; they go on duty, stand up, open doors, bow and scrape, and watch their language, and never for a moment take their attention away from this dangerous intruder into their midst. They certainly love their wives, and will open any door for them, but then they escape to the sanctuary of male silence, away from the anxious world of emotions, from female-imposed sensitivity to the state of people's minds and the nature of people's relationships.

Uncle Harry needed this sanctuary, this escape from the world of women, and it was therapeutic for him. I found it strangely peaceful. I had mostly worked and talked for a life-time, and when I played it was usually because I needed to win, but here the camaraderie was far more important. Here was a world to which men came just to be together, in the quiet, accepting company of men.

Male Depression

> Most men lead lives of quiet desperation. I can't take quiet
> desperation.
> —Alcoholic Ray Milland in *The Lost Weekend*

Men who can't relax in the company of other men have no quick and easy access to emotional security. They tend to get depressed, and then to hide that depression from those around them.

If the quiet company of men does not feel reassuring enough, men who feel imperfectly masculine, who feel terribly ashamed, may have to actually open up and talk to another man about their perceived failure. It can be terrifying for a man—especially a depressed one—to reveal his masculine shortcomings to another man and ask for a bit of anointing and a gesture of acceptance. For many men, it seems easier to keep up the show of male bravado.

Depression is not just sadness. It is a chemical condition in the brain that makes it difficult for people to anticipate things working out well. Depression can occur because of chronic pain or daily alcohol use, or because of a devastating loss, or because of an inherited tendency toward it. But the most likely cause of a man's depression is his failure to be the man he thinks he should be, a situation that leaves him beating up on himself and distrusting the love and other goodies he gets, so his brain chemistry is always registering more pain than pleasure.

I keep telling men that the brain chemicals that can repair a depression are produced by exercise, sex, joy, and triumph, but it only works if the exercise is free of competition, the sex free of guilt, the joy free of danger, and the triumph free of shame.

I also have to warn men that alcohol is especially dangerous for depression: it's a brutal chemical assault on the brain that may offer brief relief from the pain, but can ultimately deepen it to the point of suicide. Still, what depressed men are most likely to be missing in life is acceptance by the other guys, and many men think of drinking alcohol as the requisite ritual for male bonding, since it oils the conversation and may permit some emotions to flow. Some men have never had a conversation with another man stone cold sober. The time of depression is a good time to start.

Men are four or five times more likely to commit suicide than women, far more likely to get themselves killed accidentally, and notoriously more likely to do self-destructive things. Women may appear to have more depression than men, but they are merely more likely to *feel* depression, to tell other people about it, to seek out therapy for it, and to recover. Men are raised to deny feelings and take action instead, to try to act tough and manly, no matter what the circumstances, and to show the world how well they can transcend any misfortune, overcome any obstacle.

Since men are trained to feel defeated if they acknowledge emotional pain or a need for someone else, they try to fake what they feel, while they desperately increase the intensity of their activities. Exercise does help depression more than whining about it, but faking feelings full-time deepens the shame and leads to deeper loneliness and isolation.

A lot of lives would be saved if men could just learn to tell other people, men and women, when they're having a bad day or a bad lifetime, instead of sacrificing their lives and relationships in their effort to show how tough they can be and how little they need. And while much of what we need must come from the women in our lives, we need men, too.

Barriers to Male Bonding

Bonds with other males not only save men's lives but they are part of what makes life worth living. And yet, just as masculinity training builds in barriers against partnerships with women and nurturing relationships with children, it sets up barriers even to our bonding with the other guys. Most of us knew how to bond in the games of childhood and the shared rituals of puberty. But we find out that these bonds are not so easy to establish later in life. It isn't just that men get set in their ways as they grow older. Men get caught up in their relationships with women and drift away from the other guys. Men may be so homophobic they dread intimacy with other men, and can't relax into that comforting camaraderie. They may shrink back from other men because they feel shame over their own male deficiencies. They may not enjoy being around other men because they feel envy for the guys who are doing better than they.

MALE BONDING IN A WOMAN'S WORLD

> *Woman was always so horrible and clutching, she had such a lust for possession, a greed for self-importance in love. She wanted to have, to own, to control, to be dominant. Everything must be referred back to her, to Woman, the Great Mother of everything, out of whom proceeded everything and to whom everything must finally be rendered up.*
> —D. H. Lawrence, *Women in Love*

While male bonding is essentially generic and impersonal, rooted as it is in the universal experiences of manhood, pair bonding with a woman is, above all, exclusive and personal. Women offer a level of intimacy that is far more intense than the camaraderie of the other guys. When men grow up, the fullest expression of their mature masculinity is mating with a woman. They've come full circle: they gained their masculinity by escaping a woman to join the company of men, and now they dedicate their masculinity to an exclusive, engulfing bonding with another woman. Once again, as in childhood, men are letting their masculinity be defined by a woman. But unless the male bonds continue, too, the relationship with the new woman can be devouring.

I know I have never had the male friendships since marriage that I had before—I have something far better in my marriage, but there are times when I miss the camaraderie of my youth. Like most men, I can't easily recapture it as an adult: our energy goes to our families, or our careers, or just maintaining our masculine armor. It seems strange to say that I'm lonely because I'm so happily married. But I long for bonding with men, and that takes time, most of it time spent in emotional silence, talking, if at all, about inanities like sports. I leave my friends with the sense of much left unsaid, and of the boredom of the things that are said. Just hanging out together is affirming. I definitely get that at the health club, and I want more. I'm lucky: my son, my son-in-law, and my nephews can be my masculine playmates and still be part of my family. I can be close to guys without betraying my family.

But to women who draw their identity from the love of their man, friendships between men can feel like a betrayal of their monogamous intimacy. Male bonding seems dangerous to women who fear the other guys dislike women and distrust marriage, and delight in keeping men late at work or play, or pulling them away from home, or pushing them into strange beds. There are special curses for men who try to put asunder another man's marriage. They are not his friends. He'll have to choose friends who'll bolster his marriage rather than compete with it or undercut it.

For a man to love another man, and to freely savor the accepting emotional silence of the company of men, he may have to do a lot of talking to his skeptical wife, who may want to be everything to him, and may not understand that a man's manhood requires that there be men in his life, too.

HOMOPHOBIA

All men know, however loudly they protest it, that they are capable of homosexuality, and most men don't know that every other man knows that, too, so they live in the fear of having it revealed.

When a man, straight, gay, or somewhere in between, feels homophobic or senses a question of his masculinity, he is likely to act macho. He "does gender," as Carol Tarvis describes it in *The Mismeasure of Woman*. He may give up his usual qualities of compassion, sensitivity and warmth, and instead get dominating like a controller, or flirtatious and sexist like a philanderer, or competitive like a contender. He may switch the topic to sports or war or business or cars, or whatever he considers the thing a real man would do right now.

Lionel Tiger, in *Men in Groups,* attributes much that is wrong in our world to our homophobic fear of softness between men. He says: "There are important inhibitions in much of Euro-American culture—if not elsewhere too—against expressing affection between men, and one result of this inhibition of tenderness and warmth is an insistence on corporate hardness and forcefulness which has contributed to a variety of 'tough-minded' military, economic, political, and police enterprises and engagements."

The most personal result of homophobia is that these men can't get close to one another, can't get vulnerable, or loving, or warm. There are men who can't hug their best friends, or even their fathers or sons. And they then try to impose the hardness of their lives on other men, declaring that this hardness, this amputation of warmth, sensitivity, compassion, and nurturance, is true masculinity.

Avery, the masseur at my health club, tells me that homophobic men prefer massages that hurt, while more comfortable men enjoy the pleasure they feel with the passing of male energy from the masseur to the client. Massage is sensual without being sexual, but many men are afraid to let themselves feel good with another man, and see relationships between men only in terms of pain and struggle. Homophobia is not just gay bashing and excessive displays of heterosexuality. This fear of feeling good with another man is homophobia, too. Men must be able to love one another in order to love themselves as men, and anything that lets them feel good with one another is good.

MASCULINE SHAME

> *Avoid shame, but do not seek glory—nothing so expensive as glory.*
> —Sydney Smith, *Lady Holland's Memoir*

Webster defines *shame* as: "a painful feeling excited by a consciousness of guilt, shortcoming or impropriety, or of having done something unworthy, or of the exposure of that which modesty prompts to conceal." There is a strangely toxic form of shame in which men who have done nothing at all wrong feel such unworthiness about their masculinity that they try to conceal their very being from other men. They may feel safe with women, sometimes their wife, sometimes any woman who is not their wife, but they assume they are not man enough to be acceptable in the company of men. With awful loneliness, they fake their life.

Toxically masculopathic contenders, men who compete on the field and off with equally fierce determination to best the other guys, probably got that way by experiencing shame in childhood. Men who have been shamed to such a degree that they are at war with the world around them are likely to grab for power quite ruthlessly, but they're not likely to achieve it or hold it.

Men who find this need for glory are trying to hide their shame. Somewhere in their male chorus is a shaming voice, and the voice that is likely to have been most anxious about a boy's successes is probably his father's. It's hard for a man to kick his father out of his chorus, but if he can't find something his father has given him to make him feel good about himself as a man, he can't afford to keep his father there. A shame-driven man may have to declare himself illegitimate and find himself a new father, i.e., a mentor in masculinity. Our chorus must be led by a man who loves us and wants us to feel good, not a man who is so ashamed of himself that he wants to sacrifice his son for his own glory.

The father might not be the shaming voice in a man's chorus. Boys who have been molested by men, or even by older boys, have been degraded by more powerful males, and they may end up feeling much the same sense of being unworthy of male respect. Boys report getting molested and raped almost as often as girls do, and my observations through the years would convince me that boys are even less likely to report it. If it's reported, it may not be a tragedy, but if it is kept secret, it has the same devastating effect on a man's sense of wholeness and security that it has on a woman's.

A boy in my practice, Richard, was nineteen and anxiously piss proud. He had been in therapy for two years, trying to sort out his sexual identity and come to grips with his sense that his tiny penis would prevent him from ever making it with women. His female therapist was sympathetic and encouraging, but just couldn't get him over the hump, so she asked me to consult.

Richard was straightforward and organized as he told me the story he had been wanting to discuss with a man. He said his penis was only one and a half inches long and a source of ridicule. His mother had gotten him excused from gym class so no one would have to see him naked and make fun of him. I asked him who made fun of him, and he told me that while his father was off living with another woman for a few years, the family had moved to a rough neighborhood in which he had gotten close to Pete, the boy next door, who was about fourteen when Richard was eight. Richard would go over to play with Pete, and the games Pete wanted to play were sexual. Pete would have Richard give him blow jobs, which Richard found unpleasant since Pete's penis was very large, "over a foot long and as big around as a Coke can," according to Richard's estimates. Pete would ridicule Richard's little prepubertal peanut. Once Pete painted Richard's genitals with red fingernail polish and tossed him naked out of the house, yelling out the window, "Come see the world's littlest dick, come see Little Dickie the freak."

I asked the sobbing Richard who else had seen his penis, and he assured me that no one had ever seen it, certainly not his father who was so preoccupied with displaying his own around the neighborhood, and not even the two girls with whom he had tried sex, in the dark, and without orgasms. As I pressed the issue, he recalled masturbating with friends when he was fourteen or thereabouts. He had forgotten those experiences, but now he remembered that his penis didn't seem much smaller than those of his buddies. I suggested that he might have been mistaken about the measurements in such an emotionally charged area, and asked him to take more accurate measurements when he got home.

The next time I saw Richard he confessed that he couldn't bring himself to measure his penis, that he couldn't even bear to go through the humiliation of looking at it. I asked him if he'd mind showing it to me. He jumped at the chance and promptly dropped his pants to reveal a perfectly respectable-looking organ. I looked in the closet and found a yardstick, which Richard held up to his penis. I announced it was three and a half inches long. He seemed flabbergasted and assured me it was a lot bigger when it was hard. We decided it must be normal after all, and that Pete must have been a freak. Richard decided he would go out with the girl who had been pursuing him.

Richard was a happy man when he strutted out of my office. It doesn't really take much to be man enough.

I constantly see men who can't stop competing because of lifelong shame over a physical abnormality, a speech defect, a learning disability, short stature, delayed puberty. One young man blamed his shyness, his alcoholism, and his obesity on his efforts to avoid letting anyone know he had webbed toes; he could take his pants off to shower with the other boys, as long as he kept his shoes on. Men, no less than women, can find physical imperfection to obsess over. But the greatest physical source of masculine shame is, hands down, an inadequate penis. And usually the concern is over penis size.

One full-time contender suffered from hypospadias, a congenital deformity of the penis that made him urinate all over himself if he weren't careful. He has become a cleaning freak and won't let anyone come into his spotless house. One Jewish boy who grew up in Europe felt he had to hide his circumcised penis from his uncut Gentile playmates. And another angry young man attributed his misspent life to his father's anti-Semitic refusal to let him be circumcised and look like all the other guys.

Men such as these did not get reassurance from their fathers; sometimes they didn't have fathers; usually they didn't feel secure enough with their fathers to bring the matter up. If their parents were worried about them because of their defects, they had prepared their little boys for the world's rejection. Since then these men have spent their lives carefully shielding their defects from the other guys, believing that other males would tear them apart emotionally if a vulnerable opening were revealed. They could not take the crucial step necessary for men to feel safe in the world of men: they didn't reveal their greatest shortcoming to the other guys.

ENVY

> *Envy is a drive which lies at the core of man's life as a social being, and which occurs as soon as two individuals become capable of mutual comparison.*
>
> —Helmut Schoek, *Envy*

Men can envy many things about other men. Most men envy the wealth of their rivals. Some men get the idea early in life that wealth is the source of human happiness. They see life as a contest, and they believe wealth is the way in which the score is being kept. I treat rich people and I have rich friends and I know that money isn't likely to make anybody happy, but it doesn't have to make anybody miserable, either. Inherited or married wealth, of course, is a ball breaker. But money that comes from the man's own talents still does awful things to his life and work; too much money takes away the necessary pressure, it erases the goal, it trivializes the man's achievements.

But most devastatingly, wealth does what it is intended to do: it separates men from the common struggle that unites men.

Several of my best friends got rich. They had none of the toxic envy men have when they *need* to be rich to prove their masculinity. But somehow, while they were doing what they liked to do, they made money and retired by the time they were forty or fifty, in the bloom of youth. It was not a pretty sight. My Blood Brother Noel, who had been a race car driver and an artist before he got into the carpet business, sold out early and sat around for three years buying and selling French impressionist paintings, doing just what he'd always dreamed of doing. In time he got bored from sitting around looking at all those Renoirs and Monets. He felt he'd lost his weekends: they were just like his weeks. So he went back to school and started a new career as a stockbroker, which keeps him fully employed again. (He kept the paintings.)

Murray, my intellectually energetic and emotionally stimulating best friend from college, is still trying to make retirement work for him. He lives in a fabulous resort with an amazing view and an amazing wife, who cooks little things for him every few hours. He sits there and tries to enjoy the luxury, but he really has nothing to do but take his scruffy little dog Dexter outside to take a leak. He takes the dog out whenever either of them gets restless. Murray is holding up fairly well, but Dexter has developed a nervous bladder condition.

Other men envy my friends who are so rich they don't have to work. One of the secrets of happiness for men is: the ability to turn their competitive and hostile envy of men who have bested them in some real or imaginary contest into a warm and loving friendship. But it takes a lot of self-confidence, and it isn't always easy.

Many men are so fearful of the potential hostile competitiveness of new friends that they play it safe: they don't get close to anyone new, but they try to hold on to the Blood Brothers of their youth, the boys with whom they shared the coming-of-age rituals of puberty, school, and war; the boys who played by the same set of rules.

If men past the age of puberty are to achieve affirmation from male bonding, the competitive striving for status must be cautiously fraternal and collegial. It is not friendly for men to try to be better than one another; their efforts must be directed toward being more or less as good. Sure, there is competition between men always and everywhere, but it cannot be hostile and desperate. The bonding must take priority over any urge toward competitive victory.

I keep urging envious men, such as myself: if you envy someone, try to emulate him instead, try to incorporate the inherent worth of whatever you envy and develop it in yourself.

It is easier to develop emulation than it is to overcome envy. But first the two guys have to engage in some interaction on a more or less level playing field. If the object of the envy deigns to join a competition, that in itself may be sufficient affirmation to create a friendly atmosphere in which emulation can take place. The willingness to compete is a compliment, an acknowledgment of worthiness. Even when a man challenges another to a duel to the death, it is a sign of respect and, essentially, an invitation to play.

But the best way to overcome envy is to join the same team so that everything we do with one another is an affirmation of acceptance. Men can hardly avoid learning one another's skills and absorbing one another's qualities when they work or play together. Work and play, whatever other functions they serve, are opportunities for men to emulate one another. When men strive jointly, they fall into one another's rhythms and emulate one another's very being. The movement toward equality becomes automatic.

Men Play

> There is no such thing as pure pleasure; some anxiety always goes with it.   —Ovid

Men play games with one another because people look at them funny when they dance together. As they sweat and pant and even bleed together, they affirm their friendship and love and respect for one another, and they relive that golden time when boys ganged together to escape the power of mothers, that brief period in men's lives when they defined themselves in terms of one another, in terms of their shared maleness and the wonders of their shared puberty.

The bonding is the real point of the game. I watch my son Frank IV with my son-in-law Ken, or with his best friend Doug or his cousins Harrison, Paul, and Jimmy. Frank is the great runner and cyclist; Idahoan Ken grew up in vertical spaces and is at home skiing down mountains and climbing up rocky cliffs; Doug has grown gills and fins as a swimmer; Harrison is a former professional golfer; Paul is a spunky guy who will play anybody's game, from golf to marathons. Jimmy is an intellectual and academician, but when he wants to get close to Frank or the others, he does so by skiing, not by talking. These men (they're all grown now) delight in learning other men's sports and teaching their own. Their competitions are legitimate—on the court, by the rules. These men are confident and proud, so they delight in teaching what they know and they delight just as much in learning what they don't know. There's no apparent envy to distort the genuine emulation, and they seem prouder when they teach their buddy enough to beat them than when they beat their buddy. The requisite male kidding and friendly insults fill the soundtrack, but just beneath the words, closer to the heart of the matter, there is intense affection. As these men go through their friendly, confident competitions, they draw closer.

My nephew Pitt, as he always did, led the way. Whenever he saw anyone doing anything he didn't know how to do, he would stop whatever he was doing and pick up a new game and make a new friend. Then when he learned a bit about this new skill, from chess to pole-vaulting to musical farting, he would excitedly rush home to teach it to his brothers and cousin and friends. And if one of them could do it better than he, he felt all the more satisfaction. Pitt had no concept of talent or natural bent at anything; it never occurred to him that he would be unable to do well whatever he set his mind to doing, and while he was state pole-vaulting champion, valedictorian, and president of the class, top gun in flight school, and at 130 pounds quarterback and captain of the championship football team, he wasn't really competitive, just excited at the opportunities to learn things, to do things, and then to teach things.

These guys are healthy men, far healthier than I was. I had no athletic skills with which to compete, so I had to use more verbal talents, which tended toward hostility and sarcasm, and produced distance instead of closeness. Rather than admiring the skills of my friends and enemies, I was so overwhelmed with my masculine shame and envy of those less ashamed of themselves, that I imperiously pretended that the only skills that counted were my own. I think often how different my life would have been had I had the security to emulate the other guys and learn their skills rather than enviously putting them down for not having the skills I had. Competition is quite different for healthy, secure men. I keep noticing how much less competitive professional or amateur athletes are, off the playing field, than academics are with one another.

The game itself may not be very important, but the relationships are, and the men who fret over winning and losing like spoiled, insecure children are missing the point of the game. The game is not a competition to see who is the better man; the better man is the one who holds the team together while the boys compete.

Men Work

> *No other technique for the conduct of life attaches the individual so firmly to reality as laying emphasis on work; for his work at least gives him a secure place in a portion of reality, in the human community.*
> —Sigmund Freud

> *I go on working for the same reason that a hen goes on laying eggs.*
> —H. L. Mencken

Men work because work connects them to reality. Men work because they have lost their sense of being alive and purposeful when they are at home, their connection to their family. For many men, their work is all there is. That is what men do, even how they identify themseles. Above all, it is a man's work that makes him a man among men, that defines his worth in what we might persist in thinking of as the world of men. But work isn't just bonding with males. The women at work become fellow players; they are on the same team. Most men have the same comfort with women at work that they have with the other guys, a task-based camaraderie that is quite different from the emotional tension a man feels around women who are trying to take him away from the work that defines his belonging in the world.

Work really is not drudgery: one of the joys of working is earning the right to complain about it, so we try to make it seem as awful as we can. I had loved doing farm work as a boy, and I cherished the bleeding fingers from picking cotton, the sticky hands from picking figs, the scratches from raising rabbits, the pecks from breeding fighting chickens. I was proud of the mud and cow shit between my toes. Men faced the rigors of work, so if I was bruised, bloody, and filthy, I had worked and, ergo, I was a man.

My first real job was at the cotton mill. I was fifteen, and

Dad, who managed the mills, gave me the safest but most unpleasant job of all. I carried carts of yarn from the spinning room into the conditioning room, a room in which both the temperature and the humidity topped 100. I spent each day wet and filthy, and I was enormously proud of surviving my daily ordeals of fire and water. I'd go home at the end of the day and proudly strip off my disgusting clothes in the front hall so Mother could play up to my manly endeavors by showing appropriate disgust.

Years later, when I was engaged to Betsy, I'd leave the hospital emergency room to join her family for dinner, and if my whites were not sufficiently disgusting after my day of wrestling with life and death, I would smear some body fluids on them to make sure they all knew what a bloody, gory life I could stand. A man's work is his pride.

Work gives meaning to men's lives. I like Joseph Conrad's view of work in *Heart of Darkness*: "I don't like work—no man does—but I like what is in work—the chance to find yourself. Your own reality—for yourself, not for others—what no man can ever know." Work keeps us busy, it gives us structure, it defines us as functioning, contributing, worthwhile citizens. It makes us part of a team, a community of fellow workers— even if we do our work in isolation. If we feel work bringing us closer to our fellow workers or to the human community, we can feel pride and joy in our work, feel mutual emulation with all other workers, and feel ourselves the equal of any man. The mutual emulation men feel as they strive at work together may be far more affirming than any less competitive, less male-bonding activity that is supposed to be fun. But if we see our work only in competitive terms, we expose ourselves to envy and hostile competitiveness and we are emotionally drained by the end of the day.

For most of us, though, work is not only our identity and our connection to the larger world, it is the center of our immediate social life. Lawrence describes it in *Kangaroo*: "That's where I put my manhood—into my work. There I had my mates—my fellow workers. I've had playmates as well. Wife, children, friends—playmates all of them. My fellow-workers were my mates."

When we lose our work, we lose our dignity, our network, our purpose, our structure, and we live in a state of shame. It's nice if our family loves us anyway, but we know we haven't earned it and don't deserve it. How different everyone's lives would be if men drew as much of our identity from our family, from our function as Father, as we do from our work!

Work is not in itself unhealthy. The man who loves his work is likely to be whole and happy, whatever else is going on in his life. And whether we love our work has very little to do with the work itself, but with our attitude toward the process of working. I worry much more about men who don't identify with their work, who don't feel thrills and satisfaction and fraternity from it, than I do about those who can't bear to leave it. Abraham Lincoln reported: "My father taught me to work, but not to love it. I never did like to work, and I don't deny it. I'd rather read, tell stories, crack jokes, talk, laugh, anything but work." Lincoln was famous for his wit and for his unhappiness. Why would a witty man be unhappy? I can only think it is because he didn't get off on just the physical, mental, emotional exercise of work. I've long thought that happiness, like sweat, was a by-product of hard work.

Our work turns into workaholism when we begin to sacrifice our health or our family for it. I see men who travel five days a week, and then play golf with business associates on weekends. They believe they are doing it all for their family, and they believe their only function in the family is economic. In reality, men who live for work are doing it for themselves, despite the sacrifices it requires from their children.

If men want their kids to learn to love work, then they'll have to fit their work into their family life, and make sure everyone in the family understands its selfish but glorious nature.

Friends and Blood Brothers

A friend is, as it were, a second self.

—Cicero

To be accepted by the other guys, a man has to:

1. Play the game;
2. Do the work;
3. Don't threaten the other guys' masculinity;
4. Don't stir up any uncomfortable emotions;
5. Don't overdo the masculine act; and, of course,
6. Have all the Boy Scout virtues.

It really should not be that difficult for a grown man to be "trustworthy, loyal, helpful, friendly, courteous, kind, obedient, cheerful, thrifty, brave, clean, and reverent." Any average twelve-year-old boy can do that. It is not necessary for a man to be big or rich or witty or good looking, or for that matter to be sensitive and romantic, or brilliant and preeminent, or even particularly thoughtful. A man who wants to be accepted by the other guys doesn't even have to risk his life for his fellows; if he has all those other characteristics, it is just assumed that he will do so at the appointed time.

Penn and Tillman are the manliest of men, the funniest of companions, and the best of friends. Contrary to the advice of musketeer d'Artagnan's father, who urged him to make friends by fighting duels, Penn and Tilly have bonded over not fighting, but running away. They were friends in high school back in the '60s, at least they were as good friends as such a mismatched, unlikely-looking pair could be, since Penn is six foot eight and Tilly has to stretch to reach five foot eight. They were both dedicated athletes, but they weren't cut out for the same sports. They hadn't kept in touch through college but, as they waited in line for their induction physicals to go to Vietnam in 1970, Tilly recognized the giant Penn towering over all the others. Tilly was feeling quite vulnerable, and as Tilly so lovably does, he was saying whatever he thought, and at that moment he felt scared. The always-calm Penn felt safe; he felt sure he was too tall for the army. If Tilly could have done so by expenditure of energy and act of will, he would have made himself at least seven feet tall at that moment.

But when they measured Penn, he seemed to have shrunk slightly. He was only six foot seven and three-quarters and ripe for active duty. Momentarily Penn was shaken. But there are advantages to being tall. Very tall men, like very beautiful women, get noticed, and they get offers the rest of us don't. Someone immediately stepped up to the near-giant Penn and told him of a new reserve unit in which there were a couple of openings. Penn signed up and pulled Tilly in with him, and neither had to go to war.

Penn had saved Tilly's life. Tilly knew the code of male bonding required that he save Penn's life in return. So he dragged Penn out onto the street and introduced him to running. Twenty years later, three times a week, the two best friends still run six to twelve miles together, with the wiry little Tilly taking two strides for each one of Penn's, and feeling proudly secure that he is saving the life of his friend.

But Tilly did more than save Penn's life from the wreck his body would have become over forty years of unexercised neglect and abuse. Tilly provided the brotherless Penn with a Blood Brother. Penn and Tilly have no shortage of women in their lives. But men also need a brother or two, and sometimes they have to adopt them.

I admire the friendship I see between many of the men and boys who work out with me. I watch them emulating one another, teaching things and learning things and encouraging one another's successes. They radiate in mutually reflective glories. Bolstered by their relationships, they are serenely confident of their masculinity. They aren't afraid of closeness to other men. And yet they still observe some of the male-to-male boundaries against physical contact that are observed by American, but not European men. Like Gerald Crich and Rupert Birkin in *Women in Love*, they're more likely to wrestle than to hug.

How do men turn their unspoken love and admiration for one another into something that feels as secure as the Blood Brotherhood of our adolescence? That intense a level of interdependency and commitment hinges on shared risk, and shared sacrifices. And it requires enormous respect, protection of the equality of the relationship, and determination that both men can feel fully male.

Perhaps my friends George and Doc have it. George had a heart attack recently and Doc, his workout buddy, is a thoracic surgeon who cracked his chest, cleared the goop out of his arteries, and saved his life. Now George, an exercise physiologist, has taken over Doc's physical regimen and is looking for ways he can save Doc's life. My work isn't as heroically macho as Doc's, but I feel the same sort of thing with friends who have gotten depressed and let me save their lives. A dramatic rescue will bring guys together, but it takes desperate ceremonies to create that ached-for level of male bonding.

Adopting Brothers

Be my brother, or I will kill you.
—Thomas Carlyle, 1837

The most enduring of my life's brotherhoods, enduring at least in spirit, have involved magical discoveries of fraternity, something between the out-of-body experience of falling in love and the relief Robinson Crusoe must have felt when he saw the footsteps in the sand and realized he was no longer alone.

I feel it when I am with my old buddies like Noel and Murray, with whom I've shared my journey into manhood.

I felt it when I first met Rich Simon and we began talking about movies we'd shared in different places in different decades and thus shared a whole emotional history.

I feel it with any man who is afraid like I am and is saying so, like my conscientious buddy Marc Winer, who didn't hide his fear as he headed off to the still communist Moscow to open the world's largest McDonald's restaurant in Pushkin Square.

I feel it with my patients, ordinary or powerful men (there's no real difference), who are feeling vulnerable enough to open themselves up to another man and let me in to share their lives.

I feel it with men who don't have to be macho anymore,

men like John Cleese, who can appear in an American Express ad in red miniskirt, red floppy hat, red high heel shoes, carrying those yappie little dogs from *A Fish Called Wanda.*

I feel it with many of my fellow family therapists, who spend their days and their careers hearing and feeling the same masculine pain that fills my days. Without their saying so, I know they understand what I understand.

I feel it with my son, my son-in-law, and my nephews. I feel it when my impressively masculine nephew-in-law Jim realizes I am not the grown-up I appear to be, comes up and hugs me, and says, "I want to party with you, Big Guy."

This male bonding is an awareness deep in our bones of the shared experience of the struggle of masculinity, and our secure acceptance as a man in the company of men. It requires that another man know you, but also that he know himself enough to stop the macho posturing and competing. When you know a man, when you come to realize that by knowing yourself you know all men, you don't need the envy anymore. You can join the company of men and begin mutual emulation. Guys who go through the self-achieved submission of dropping the macho act, the homophobia, the envy, and the competition are ripe for heroism, and are able to uncover life-enhancing insights about the nature of existence, even the nature of masculinity and heroism itself. And it doesn't have to be talked about.

But it is even better when men do talk about it. I feel most heroic, and most intimately a member of the fraternity of men, when I am exposing and exploring with other men what we have learned, what we all know but have been trained not to say, about the common journey of manhood.

ELEVEN

Mating with a Woman

The average man spends a lifetime denying, defending against, trying to control, and reacting to the power of WOMAN.   —Sam Keen, *Fire in the Belly*

For many a man, the most terrifying thing he can imagine is making a commitment to an equal, honest, intimate relationship with a woman. Clearly the self-achieved submission of his masculinity to such a partnership with a woman is an act of male heroism, and is the process through which a man recaptures the half of himself that was lost through his gender training. But to men who are still running from the engulfing power of Mama, commitment to a woman seems like the loss of their masculine freedom.

Marriage gets a bad rap lately as unanointed boys of every

age work up ever greater fears of female control. And, of course, as fathers run from the power of women, so in turn will their sons. Life is hard and life is lonely for the man who is scared to death of joining forces with a woman. A man can't become a hero if half the human race makes him shake in his boots.

I don't mean to imply that it is men all by ourselves who maintain the absurdities of gender stereotypes. Women doing their gender dance can be just as absurd as men doing theirs. Many of the more absurd things women do are efforts to hide their power and keep from scaring men. It is pitiful to watch competent women acting incompetent out of fear of male panic. Of course, the real horror comes when women believe they actually are powerless and that men really are omnipotent. A woman who sees a man as godlike can then overlook his needs completely while she prays for him to bestow favors and meaning to her life. Such a woman can overlook everything about a man except the degree to which he makes her feel loved.

Hester, a woman I was seeing with her depressed and financially beset husband, called in a panic to tell me: "Hap has locked himself in his library. He won't come to the door and he won't answer the telephone. I just went out in the bushes and climbed up and looked in the window. He's sitting there at his desk with all those papers, and he's holding a gun to his head. How could he do this to me? Does this mean he doesn't love me?"

Irene was explaining to me why she left her first husband. "Ira is a good man. He's very handsome, I carry a picture of him even now. He was good at sex; he was loving of me all the time. We started out poor and Ira made a fortune for us. But he was a terrible dancer. He just didn't have any rhythm in his feet. So I took up with Rudy. I loved the way he danced.

The kids never forgave me, and I ran out of money supporting Rudy—he drank a lot and never liked to work much. And now Rudy has gone and Ira wants me back. But after all these years, he still hasn't learned to dance. You'd think if he really loved me he'd get some rhythm."

A woman may define herself by whether a man loves her or not. And she may define a man by whether he makes her feel loved—by whether he has rhythm, by whether he reads her mind, by whatever cockeyed measures she chooses. At the same time, his masculinity requires that he satisfy her need to feel totally loved. It can look hopeless.

Because men have been raised by women, they go through life letting themselves be defined by women. Consequently, when a man feels powerless, he might assume the woman in his life has taken his power from him. That peculiar notion has been heard in the Men's Movement from men who blame their unanointed state and their shame on Women's Lib. There are men who don't understand the battle over women's rights because to them women have all the power that matters: the power to define a man's worth as a man.

On the other hand, when women feel powerless, they might assume the men they encounter have somehow taken their power from them; and that peculiar logic creeps into the Women's Movement.

The male fear of what Sam Keen calls WOMAN, and the corresponding female anger at male privilege and patriarchy, make anything that goes on between men and women adversarial. Marriage becomes a battleground.

Fear of Female Anger

> *Do you think God knew what He was doing when he created*
> *women? I ask you . . . women? A mistake, or did he do it*
> *to us on purpose?*
> —Jack Nicholson, as "your average horny little devil"
> in John Updike's *Witches of Eastwick*

Women will never be able to understand men until they realize that the most frightening thing in life for men is the anger of women. Men walk around feeling like Charlie Browns in a world of Lucy Van Pelts. Here is a typical example of what goes on between men and women in my practice:

JUDY: "Why didn't you call me and tell me you weren't coming home for dinner?"

PUNCH: "I didn't want you to fuss at me."

JUDY: (calmly) "I would never have fussed about your calling or about your not coming home. I get tied up at work sometimes, too. What would I have fussed about? But by not calling, you made me go through a lot of trouble for nothing."

PUNCH: (agitatedly) "There you go, just like my mother, bitching and nagging, and trying to make me feel guilty. It's no wonder I can't tell you anything."

For many men, Hell seems to have no fury like a woman who is even slightly disgruntled. I started my day with Punch and Judy, but before the day was through I'd seen a man who sneaked outside to smoke cigarettes while telling his wife that the smell of smoke was in her imagination; another man who was hiding a dented car in the bushes; and several who were keeping strange women under the bed. Mixed in with the liars and cheats were men who had temper tantrums if their women ever complained, and others who were crying pathetically because their woman didn't see them as perfect anymore. The men who aren't thinking up lies to keep the women in their lives calm are complaining to one another that their women don't love them enough.

It shouldn't be surprising that big, strong men become frightened children in the face of a woman's anger. We start life as helpless babies, fragile and dependent on our mother's willingness to stay with us and care for us even when we are selfish and give little in return. We fear she'll give up on us and leave us to die. Once we're grown, we know we aren't worth all the care and feeding we've been getting from women all along, and we fear that our "better half" will discover that we are not the omnipotent heroes we pretend to be. The heroes of country songs go off to prison or out to get drunk, and come home to discover their woman has left them for a better man. It could happen to us.

In early adolescence, as we exposed ourselves to absurd risks in the hope of looking and feeling more manly, our mothers tried to keep us safe and reasonably civilized, but it felt to us as if she were trying to keep us from growing up. Now when a woman disapproves of us for being loud or crude or dirty, we suddenly feel like naughty little boys, and we can't obey her or defy her without feeling foolish. "Mama" threatens to take our manhood away from us. This is the feeling Dennis the Menace has around the impeccably parental Margaret.

Somewhere in our coming of age we had to establish ourselves sexually, testing our callow masculinity against women, who had the power to determine our potency as men. Our mythology personifies this fearful female as a witch, a woman who has the power to make men impotent, or in John Cleese's famous line from *Monty Python and the Holy Grail*, "She turned me into a newt."

Even a grown man is likely to suffer from the fear that WOMAN will measure him and find him wanting, judge him and disdain him, test him and flunk him, and then not only will he lose that woman and all her sisters, but because he has struck out in the masculinity contest the woman is refereeing, he will lose the respect of men as well, and be subject to universal ridicule and rejection. A man who fears the power of women to assess his worth may handle it by trying to hide his weakness, and by keeping women distant in various ways.

A philanderer may take up with other women he hasn't hurt yet, damsels in distress who are hard up and unchoosy about the heroes they will accept. A contender may devote himself to work or play in hopes of making enough money or winning enough praise to finally get the woman to accept him as a master of the universe. A controller may try to stop her from bitching. He can get bombastic, and carry on long and loud to prove he's right, or that whatever happened wasn't his fault. The more foolish he feels, the louder he gets. A controller who is truly terrified of the power of a woman may even hit her.

Most of us don't get violent, but we go through this same strange panic in the face of female anger. We feel called upon to be the boss, accused of having all the power, and yet we know we are at the mercy of women, who measure our worth as men. It's scary.

No Warning

"You Picked a Fine Time to Leave Me, Lucille"
—Kenny Rogers song

Knox came to tell me that his wife Lucille had just walked out, hired a divorce attorney, and left a note that said simply, "I can't take living alone anymore." Knox had no idea what that note meant. Fortunately, I did. I'd seen the two of them a few times a couple of years before. Knox remembered only that "Lucille was upset back then, having some sort of nervous breakdown," but he didn't remember any of her complaints about his personal hygiene, his failure to work, his obscene language, his financial irresponsibility, his outbursts of violence, and his infidelity. On prodding, he did recall that she'd been criticizing him a lot, but he decided she was just saying those things because she was upset. As Knox said, "You know how women are." He pondered whether it might help his marriage if he got a job and took a bath. I agreed that those things might be helpful, but pointed out that it was less important for him to make himself perfect once and for all, than for him to pay enough attention to her day to day to know how she was feeling and what she might want.

I've seen men like Knox whose wives and girlfriends scream, yell, jump up and down, throw things, threaten suicide and homicide, and even, in one notable case, drive the car into the living room and right through the TV set, yet the men still don't hear the warning that she is at the end of her tether and may be just about to bolt and run. This seems crazy. Why can't the men hear the message?

Men are easily satisfied in marriage (until another woman comes along) and not likely to feel the situation is bad until their wife leaves and they find themselves at home alone. They think, "I'm not miserable so she shouldn't be miserable. I get my needs met around here so she should, too. I have orgasms so she should as well. If she's unhappy, it can't be me and the marriage; it must be her hormones or her childhood, or maybe that's the way women are."

Men hear anything a woman says with strong emotion as just hysterical carrying-on. And while a woman's anger is as terrifying to a man as the wrath of an angry god, we don't hear what a woman says when she's angry; we only hear that she is angry and we strap ourselves in, turn off our receivers, and wait in terror for the storm to pass. When we men have any important message to deliver, we deliver it as logically and unemotionally as possible. We know that what we say when we're angry should be ignored, and our friends do us the favor of ignoring it. We often wish women would do the same.

A woman may try to tell the man what she would like for him to "be" rather than what she would like for him to "do." Lucille kept telling Knox to "be a higher-class person," rather than asking him to "stop talking dirty and take a bath." She even told him to "be the man of the house," rather than asking him to "get a job." Worst of all, she asked him to "be romantic," when she wanted him to "leave off the television, and let sex last longer than a TV commercial." Women who believe a man will know what a woman wants if he loves her are in for terrible disappointments. Men like Knox (and most of the rest of us) tend to be as dense as concrete in such matters, and are in desperate need of a clearly written instruction book from each woman about what she wants.

Men have gotten so confused over Sigmund Freud's classic question of "What does a woman want?" that some have actually taken the cow by the horns and straight-out asked.

Equality in Marriage

Once made equal to man, woman becomes his superior.
—Socrates

A man's belief in gender inequality and male superiority is going to make him look like an idiot, is going to wreck his marriage, may cost him his career (the workplace is no longer a boy's club), is going to leave him lonely and unhappy, and is going to do great damage to his children (some of whom might be female and others of whom might want to live and work around females). And even while he's going around spouting off about men's superiority to women, we know that underneath the bluster and machismo is the sense of his own inferiority and his fear of women's power to measure him and find him wanting. And we know, conversely, that women can feel men have robbed them of *their* power. The assault is an adversarial standoff that frustrates everybody.

Men and women can live together as adversaries, or one can make the other a slave, but the partnership of marriage can't work unless both the man and the woman dedicate themselves to making the relationship equal.

Marriage is not a contest: there isn't a winner and a loser. Either both win or both lose. Both win when the relationship reflects marital equality—which means, simply, that the two people will have an equal voice in deciding who does what.

I watch our kids struggle to maintain the equality of their marriages.

My thirty-three-year-old nephew, Paul, is surely the sweetest man on earth (six years in a submarine made him tolerant of anything). Paul is married to Anne Hoag, a strong and independent young woman who runs cable companies. Paul had managed a branch bank, but it didn't work out well for him. Some of the women thought they should have gotten the promotion instead of Paul. A woman sued for gender discrimination and was given Paul's job. Paul was crushed. He was happy when Hoag's job brought about a transfer from Augusta to Asheville. But in Asheville he couldn't get a job, and he was getting depressed about it. He went to a male therapist, who saw the problem as Hoag's power. The therapist suggested that Hoag had "castrated" him in the move. Paul wisely walked out, as he realized this therapist was trying to make him feel like a victim of powerful women; he knew that accepting such a definition of the problem would damage both his character and his marriage, and make it impossible for him to deal with a world in which men can't expect to be always on top. Paul found another therapist, who wasn't afraid of women, and he worked temporarily as a salesman. He developed his skills at pleasing people and getting them the things they wanted. By the time he became a bank manager again, he was a far more accommodating boss, measuring his success by his ability to please rather than control.

FINDING THE POINT OF EQUALITY

> *All animals are equal, but some animals are more equal than others.*
>
> —George Orwell, *Animal Farm*

Even when couples want an equal marriage, they may not know how to find the point of equality.

Lou had an oppressive first husband, who wanted to be Head of the Household. She left and married Marty, whom she calls a "sensitive new age guy." When he's not apologizing for the terrible things men do, he's teaching good values to the kids and cooking nice meals for Lou. Marty bends over backward not to be oppressive to her, and he carefully leaves all the decision making to her. But Lou wishes Marty would worry more about finances, would come up with ideas about vacations, would have a plan sometimes, instead of admiring her and telling her she's great, and assuming she'll handle it. "He's beautiful, loving, and thoughtful, and he'll do whatever I ask. But I'm tired of having all the responsibility. I want him to have an opinion, too, and then we can discuss and negotiate things. I want a partner."

Marty tried to make things "fair" through *affirmative gender action*. Men like Marty try to avoid the gender inequities of the male-dominated past, but they may get so carefully unoppressive they end up being merely squishy.

On the other hand, I see less trusting people who try to achieve equality by *keeping score*. They insist that each partner contribute the exact same amount of money to the household, and they may keep separate accounts and careful financial records to make sure neither puts in more than half. They may be similarly rigid about washing the same number of dishes as their partner or getting up the same number of times with the baby. This "compulsive equality" makes the partnership hostile and impersonal.

Norma and Norman, for example, tried to measure out equality. Both had been married before and both marriages had run aground when one partner tried to be captain of the ship. Norma and Norman were determinedly equal, so they kept tight schedules on car pools and washing dishes; they even kept careful records on who chose the movies they watched.

Norma and Norman started having problems when Norma's mother got sick, and they needed to visit her more often than they visited Norman's mother. When Norman's teenaged children began to visit on an irregular schedule, it interfered with Norma's night for choosing TV shows. They couldn't keep the finances precisely equal when Norma's daughter needed braces on her teeth. When Norman's paycheck was cut back, Norma had to make his car payment out of her savings. They got panicky and forgot about the relationship while they fought about the equality of the charts.

I've seen couples who try to create equality by *doing everything together*. However inefficiently, they shop together, cook together, wash together. They become a set of Siamese twins, immobilized by the togetherness. Osgood and Opal, for example, tried that. They only needed one car. Opal would drop Osgood off at his office and go on to her shop, where they met after work to eat and work out together, before they went home to clean up together.

Osgood and Opal's togetherness worked fine until they started talking about having a child, and there were aspects of that which only one of them could do. How could they maintain equality when they weren't doing the same things?

Equality comes from two people being flexible enough to do whatever needs to be done. It's stultifyingly rigid to be so phobic about inequality that couples keep score, or restrict independent functioning, or even refuse to perform any job traditional for your gender. Equality is not in the schedule or the job assignments. Equality is not in affirmative gender action, in efforts on the part of men to make up to a woman for what some ancestor or neighbor did to his wife in the name of holy patriarchy. Equality is in the attitude that makes sure that both partners get a voice in making the decisions, and in the mutual determination that the partnership is more important than any job or any decision. Two people won't get equal by cutting each other down to size; they'll do it by learning how to make one another feel more powerful.

Equality requires an appreciation, on both sides of this artificial gender boundary, of what both men and women have sacrificed on behalf of their gender training. Gender is not just a female complaint.

Barriers to Equality

> You can sort of be married, you can sort of be divorced, you can sort of be living together, but you can't sort of have a baby.   —David Shire

BABIES

When babies come, biology intervenes and temporarily threatens to screw up the equality of the marriage. Gender equality is most threatened at childbirth, when women get to be heroic and men feel useless. Birthing babies is indeed woman's work, the moment at which women are most miraculously powerful. When a baby comes, a man is likely to feel useless and to step back into his separate life. But if the father lets the baby be the mother's baby, he may lose them both as they bond with one another and share their resentment of his absence and neglect.

The biological distinction between a mother and a father ends completely at the point of weaning. After that, there is nothing a woman can do for a child that a father can't. And even before that, fathers can do a lot more than they usually do. The more involved the father is, the better he will bond to both his wife and his child. The heroic father submits himself totally to his family, to his partner, and to his child, and finds it the most exultant leg of the hero's journey toward unravelling the mysteries of the human condition.

Our nieces and nephews on Betsy's side of the family are in a reproductive mode right now. Each of Betsy's nieces had a couple of babies in the past two years. Annie is an obstetrical fellow in Baltimore and her husband Jim a plastic surgery resident. Annie had Spencer when she was on a delivery rotation that tied her down at all hours, but Jim was on a lab rotation and able to take time off to be with the baby. Jim is the cook in their family, so he provided much of the nurturance. He'd stay home with Spencer, and while Annie delivered babies at the hospital, the guys would watch John Wayne festivals on the tube. It worked fine. But then Addie was born when Spencer was terribly two, and Jim was doing surgery day and night.

Jim and Annie are both totally committed and totally absorbed by these two babies. They've stopped talking about equality. They've stopped talking about the unspeakable but immutable gender issues. They've even stopped talking about who is exhausted. They are in a survivalist mode with each doing whatever needs to be done until he or she collapses. Annie nurses Addie and feels connected, but Jim can't feel like a nurturer until Addie can eat the food he cooks, and meanwhile biology dictates that Jim wrestle with his toddling son and leave his suckling daughter to her mother. The Renaissance Man Jim has discovered the secret of parenting: "You don't have to do it right; you just have to do it."

Jennifer, a physical therapist in New Jersey, can work part time, but her environmental protection lawyer husband John is on a new job and can't take time off easily. Maggie and Drew are fourteen months apart (as Tina and Frank IV were, and as we remember with horror). Jennifer makes sure she works one day a week while John wrestles with them; John can thus both appreciate what Jennifer does and can bond with his children. Jennifer is determined to go back to work soon, and John will have to figure out a way to be home at five for the witching hour, rather than at seven to kiss his little angels good night. John says he's getting better: "When she comes home from work or from the store, I don't meet her at the end of the driveway holding a wet, screaming baby anymore."

Now Jimmy and Aubrey, math teachers in New York City, are expecting their first baby. Jimmy, teaching in college, can arrange to teach only two days a week. Aubrey, teaching in high school, can take a month's leave, but then has to teach every day. Jimmy may end up getting to be with the baby more than Aubrey does. The two of them spend less time than we did talking about nurseries, bassinettes, and baby clothes, or even the name for the kids, and more time struggling with how to divide the labor in a way that keeps them both equal and both parents.

SEX

An orgasm is just a reflex like a sneeze.
—Dr. Ruth Westheimer

There should be nothing two people could do that would be more equal and more equalizing than getting naked, getting their things together, and giving and receiving pleasure. Sex can be nice. But for some people sex is so monumentally meaningful that the potential pleasure gets buried beneath a struggle for power or status or reassurance or identity. When sex gets too important it stops being fun.

Gender keeps screwing up sex. A man who sees sex as power may feel devastated if he can't make his partner have an orgasm, or a dozen orgasms, every time he wants her to, whether she wants to or not. A man who sees sex as reassurance may bemoan his wife's failure to make sexual overtures to him, while another man who sees sex as authority may be unable to perform unless the woman is totally passive. And a man who hasn't been trained as a rapist will do a quick penile shrink at the first hint of a woman's anger.

Women have their own special sexual hang-ups. Some women have been trained to see sex as something men are taking away from them. So they have to test out the perfection of the love for a while before they give it. They use sex *if* everything is nice, rather than using sex *to make* everything nice. There are women who have been inadvertently trained to be prostitutes, to see sex as something to trade for something else, perhaps for love, perhaps money, perhaps reassurance or even adoration.

Many men don't have much feeling for the difference between having your genitals inside you, right next to your soul, and having them safely on the outside, where they can be observed dispassionately in all their phases. For men it is the sexual performance that is on the outside, to be observed and assessed, while the ego that is at stake is hidden beneath the male bravado. For a woman, though, her actual sexual response can be hidden, but the effect she is having on a man sticks out like a sore thumb. While she's testing the relationship, he is watching her grading his performance, and both of them are so anxious it is a wonder it ever works at all.

Couples who want to make it possible (but not required) for both people to enjoy sex have got to discuss all these gender and ego matters out of bed, before they do the part that comes naturally: getting naked, getting friendly, and forgetting about gender.

INFIDELITY

> *If you wonder whether certain behavior constitutes infidelity,*
> *I recommend that you ask your spouse.*
> —Frank Pittman, *Private Lies*

Insecure men who fear that marital equality would enslave them and rob them of their fragile masculinity set up their own barriers to equality. One of the most popular is infidelity. Infidelity is more than just sex with another person, more than just breaking the sexual agreement of the marriage. It is a power play, an effort to get something or know something your partner doesn't know. The secrecy of the affair destroys the equality of the marriage, and thus does more damage than the sex. The longer it is kept secret, the more damage it will do.

Men are more likely to screw around than women, but most men are faithful most of the time. Having an affair doesn't mean a man doesn't love his wife. Men don't sleep around because they have imperfect marriages—they may, but that is no reason to be unfaithful—men sleep around because they don't feel man enough. The roots of infidelity are in the defective relationship between a man and his father, not a defective marriage. I can not imagine any problem in marriage that would be solved by sneaking next door, popping into bed with his neighbor's wife, sneaking back home, and lying about where he'd been. That isn't an effort to solve a marital problem, it's an effort to protect himself from marital equality to someone he fears will see that he's not the hero he wants her to think he is.

Men don't have affairs with women who are more perfect than their wives—perfect women don't mess around with married men anyway. A man who is feeling a bit of a failure at the moment is likely to seek out a woman he hasn't hurt yet, a damsel in distress to whom he seems to be a conquering hero. The issue is not that his wife doesn't understand him; the problem is that she does, and he wants the sanctuary of someone who still thinks he's wonderful. In the film of Clare Boothe Luce's play, *The Women,* Lucile Watson consoled cuckolded Norma Shearer by explaining, "A man has only one escape from his old self—to see a different self in the mirror of some woman's eyes."

A man may enter an affair rather blindly, usually reassuring himself that he is appropriately committed to his wife, and that this little dalliance is really quite meaningless. He may assure himself that he deserves this, either as a trophy or as a solace. "It's a guy thing," he says. "What a woman doesn't know won't hurt her. She'd just get stirred up." He may not be prepared for the alarming changes that take place in him and in his marriage as he tries to keep his dirty little secret.

A woman having an affair is likely to think it through quite differently. She knows very well what she is risking, what the dangers might be. And she justifies each step along the way by collecting her husband's offenses against her and his disgusting failures to live up to her fantasy of the ideal husband. She works it out in her head until she is sure that he has earned her betrayal, and that whatever she does, he made her do it. Clearly, her affair is his fault.

Women don't always take responsibility for what they do sexually, but every woman has been trained to take responsibility for what men do sexually, and when he has an affair, she is likely to blame herself, feel terribly threatened, and assume the other woman is the winner of a contest she herself has lost. Her errant husband may even encourage her to believe that. She may have trouble understanding how stupid and innocent it all was at the beginning when he merely slept with another woman and hadn't started the adversarial process of violating the equality of the marriage by lying to his wife, keeping secrets from her, and trying to mess with her mind so she won't understand him.

Traditionally, men were told that they should always lie to women, since women don't like reality and are uncomfortable knowing the truth about unpleasant things. I saw one man who went jogging each evening. When his running clothes ceased to stink, his wife followed him to his secretary's apartment, where she found him standing naked in the other woman's closet. He told her, "You do not see me here. You have gone crazy and are imagining this." She had been lied to for so long that she almost believed him.

Short of AIDS, the worst thing that could happen to a man in the course of his carousing would be to "fall in love" and leave his wife and children for this desperate woman who sleeps around with married men. When a man does that, he just erases his wife and sometimes his children from his emotional awareness. He knows he's made a mess of his life, and he only feels safe around the new woman. Five years after such an idiotic caper, more men in my practice are back in their original marriage than are still married to the distressed damsel for whom they and all their family were expected to lay down their lives.

After watching thousands of men mess up their lives with infidelity, I urge them to find some other way to meet their adolescent needs of feeling man enough. But if a man slips up, then he should tell the truth about it.

Infidelity will eat at him and destroy the intimacy of his marriage, but telling the truth can clear the confusion and enable the couple to get close again. An equal marriage can hold up under just about anything the world throws at it, even infidelity, but it can't survive much dishonesty.

MONEY

> *The Golden Rule: Whoever has the gold makes the rules.*
> —Folk saying

Men may protect or preclude themselves from marital equality by laying claim to the family money. Couples often make the mistake of assuming that the person who brings in more money should have a larger voice in deciding where it goes. That doesn't work. It not only unbalances the relationship; it plays hell with the budget. When two people are a couple, they are either both in the black or both in the red. They are either both rich or poor. Otherwise, they are in a war between the haves and the have-nots.

I've seen a lot of poor women who are married to rich men. Pierpont was a rich man who convinced his wife that they had become poor because he had given all their money to charity. She wasn't much interested in money, but she did manage to save enough from her grocery allowance to go to sales from time to time with her friends. When Pierpont died after she had lived fifty years in tight straits with him, she inherited $50,000,000 and didn't have the foggiest notion how to handle it, so she gave it to the children to play with. Their lives have been disasters as a result.

Quarterman was a young doctor who had grown up poor with a mother who put his father down for not making more money. Quarterman scrimped through all those years of training, until he entered practice and had money for the first time. He wouldn't let his wife, Queenie, who had grown up rich, have access to any of it—cash, checking account, or credit cards. He was afraid that she would spend *his* money foolishly if she got hold of it. Queenie and the babies, without transportation, stayed home all day. Once a week, Quarterman would leave his office early, in his new Mercedes, to do the grocery shopping and to pay the gas and water bills in cash.

I saw them after she began threatening homicide. Quarterman didn't understand what Queenie was upset about, since it was *his* money and she had no right to it. He pointed out that she was spoiled and he was taking good care of her. With much difficulty, I convinced him that it would free him up to make more money if he let her do the household shopping. A first step would be to let her have a weekly household allowance. He finally agreed to give it a try.

The first day of this new arrangement, Quarterman came home from work to find that there was no dinner since Queenie hadn't gotten any groceries. Instead, she had stepped into a little boutique on the way to the grocery store and found a perfect black velvet cape with red satin lining that would look wonderful on their daughter if she grew up and became a ballerina. Quarterman's refusal to include her in the financial decisions up until then left her unprepared for taking over the money now. It would take a little practice before she got the hang of it. But Quarterman was too panicky about the power of a woman to wipe him out, and jeopardize this financial symbol of his manhood. I couldn't talk him into giving Queenie any more money to practice with.

Maintaining such control not only ruins the equality of the marriage, and makes domestic life unpleasant, it also makes for false economy. One common arrangement is for a man to divide the money into the part he saves and the part his wife spends. He may give her an allowance, however "generous," while he gets to play with the investments. Any money that is saved is money he has taken away from his wife and any money that is spent is money that his wife has taken away from him. This setup encourages his wife to feel an equal partner only if she can undercut his savings plan and spend as much of the money as she can. But if she is an equal party in deciding what gets spent and what gets saved, she feels she is enhancing her power by saving money rather than spending it.

The real inequality is that the partner who has the grandest career and the most impressive income has already won the game and gotten the major goodies one gets from work and money: the pat on the back of a job well done, the aura of success. Spending the money is a minor pleasure compared to making it, yet that is the main financial pleasure left to many women and some men who have set aside their own careers for the sake of the family. For the one who gets the glory to also expect to hoard the spoils seems greedy. The least a guy can do to pay back a gal who has downpedaled her own career and tended him and their kids, while letting him have all the fun of devoting himself to the selfish pleasures of work, is to make sure she gets to blow the money. If he can make her feel it is her money as much as his, she'll feel more nearly equal and will probably take better care of the money and better care of him.

Of course there are people who don't want fiscal equality in marriage. There are women who believe that the money a husband makes or inherits belongs to the marriage while money a wife makes or inherits belongs to the wife. And we all know of married men who believe that the paycheck that comes in their name belongs to them! They may not understand who owns what until they hear it in court.

CHORES

> *A woman's place is in the home.*   —Anonymous

> *A woman's work is never done.*   —Anonymous

Another way men have protected themselves from the power of women is to keep them too busy to stir up much trouble. Raising the children, feeding the family, cleaning the house, running the errands, caring for the possessions, feeding the chickens, churning the butter, fending off Indian attacks, tending to all that needs tending—these were traditionally known as "women's work." As Horace Vandergelder told Dolly Levi, "It takes a woman, all pretty and pink, to clean out the drain in the kitchen sink."

But, never fear, if women really beg, and don't mind putting up with some grumbling, men will "help out"—as long as all the work remains the woman's responsibility.

Men's expectations of women can be outrageous. Some men expect women to come home after a day's work, or after wrestling with children all day, and begin her second job of waiting on him. It's not just unequal, it's unfriendly.

Why do otherwise sane, competent, strong men, men who can wrestle bears or raid corporations, shrink away in horror at the thought of washing a dish or changing a diaper?

Some men really do believe that men and men's work are all-important, and that women exist only to tend the care and feeding of men. One of the few acts of violence that ever occurred in my office concerned an arrogant and impatient man who had stepped in a mess left on the lawn by the family dog. He told his wife he wanted her henceforth, each day when she got home from work, to patrol the lawn with a little shovel and bucket to collect anything unpleasant left by dogs. That way, he would not have to look down as he took his afternoon stroll across his property. His wife, upon hearing this insistent and unyielding request, threw a cup of coffee into his face. He didn't understand her reaction, since to him the request was a reasonable expectation of someone whose function in life was to attend to his comfort. He really believed his wife was his servant, and she had not, until that moment, realized that was his belief.

Few men are insensitive enough to express such a belief, but many men act as if they believe it. Such a man might "inspect" the house and even supervise the work that's done there, as if he were the boss and his wife were his employee. He might even explain to his wife how well his mother had served him, and expect his wife to model herself after his mother. Such men are in desperate need of gender retraining; they are disoriented to the nature of the relationship.

Not all the men who are uncomfortable with true domestic partnerships are sexist monsters. Some are merely insecure. They believe that truly masculine men should appear competent at all times. Since they don't know quite how to perform the chores in question, they fear they would look foolish if they tried it. They believe their wives, presumably expert at the activity in question, might lose respect for them if they looked clumsy or unsure, might even ridicule them, or try to supervise them, and then, of course, their balls would fall off. But if he is only "helping out," then the task remains clearly his wife's job, his amateurish efforts are not his fault, and his wife has to be grateful even if he makes a mess she is expected to clean up. The logic is convoluted, but I've heard it many, many times.

In recent years, I find more men willing to take on the creative and showy jobs around the house, such as the fancy cooking for company. And we men who pride ourselves on our cooking can put on quite a show with it. Of course, we do expect applause when we fire a steak, and a standing ovation for every paté or soufflé. There are few men who will pass up a chance to show off a skill, particularly a skill his wife has not developed. But the really good guys also clean up the kitchen when they're through showing off.

My rock-climbing dare-devil son-in-law, Ken, inherited his great aunt's antique sewing machine. My daughter Tina, busy with work and graduate school, could not be bothered with sewing, so the daring Ken gave it a try. When their cousins Annie and Jim produced Timothy Spencer Namnoum, the first member of his generation, Ken celebrated by sewing something for his newly born cousin—a sailor suit, which I'm sure made both the guys feel more masculine. But what turned Tina on was that, after Ken sewed the sailor suit, he wrapped it and mailed it himself, and then he cleaned up from it. Now, there's a man!

The Secret of Marriage

> Swimming instructors who teach drown-proofing have learned that drowning occurs when people are afraid of the water and struggle to stay above it. If they could go ahead and immerse themselves in the water, they would find they could float securely, breathe comfortably, and relax totally. The effort while in the water to keep from being engulfed by it is exhausting and potentially fatal.
> —Frank Pittman, *Turning Points*

Marriage, like swimming, is all or nothing. It certainly isn't heroic to be partially married, but it may not even be safe. The effort can drive everybody crazy.

The whole point of marriage is its inherent equality. Any effort to protect oneself from it by undercutting the equality will turn the marriage into a battleground.

Men, no matter how much they fear the power of WOMAN, need to relax and tread water until they feel the safety and the warmth of being fully and completely married, however imperfect their partner, however imperfect themselves.

A man's commitment is to the marriage and to himself as a marriage partner as well as to his wife. His commitment to something greater than himself and his overweening masculinity enhances his masculine heroism. He must keep reminding himself that this is not only her marriage but HIS marriage, which empowers and expands and enhances HIM; it is not some evil female plot to rob him of his precious masculinity.

My Life as a Husband

> Marriage isn't a 50-50 proposition very often. It's more like 100-0 one moment and 0-100 the next.
> —Billie Jean King, Billie Jean

I'm a "happily married" man. That doesn't mean that I'm *happy* all the time; one of the secrets of happiness is to let yourself go through the full range of human emotions on a daily basis, and I do. What it means is that I'm *married* all the time; I'm not fighting against it, or blaming the ups and downs in my mood on my marriage.

I might well have been a happy man even if I'd married someone other than Betsy, but the only people I ever considered marrying, back in the days when I liked being seen with beauty queens on my arms, have ended up being miserable, so I assume they would have made me miserable, too. Most likely Betsy and I have been happy together because we would have been happy anyway, or maybe Betsy and I have been happy because we don't require that we be happy all the time. We're just totally and completely married, and that immediately does away with the usual things that make men unhappy: the guilt and anxiety of infidelity, the concern with whether he has married the right person, the question of whether he is deserving of his mate, the question of whether his wife really loves him. Betsy and I know we're together for better or for worse, so if we want to be happy we'd better figure out a way to be happy together. I'm going to have a hell of a time being happy if I'm making her miserable.

Betsy and I have been married for thirty-two years. When I met her, I was a poor, pressured medical student. We were all so exhausted we didn't even have time to be friends to each other. We certainly didn't have time to go through the usual bullshit of dating girls. I didn't need a date; I needed somebody in my life. I told Aunt Emily, who stood in loco parentis, and she introduced me to the daughter of friends. Betsy was home for the summer before her senior year at Sweet Briar. As I rang her doorbell, the parking brakes failed in the '49 Dodge I'd inherited from Uncle Walter. It rolled back down the vertical driveway at her parents' house. I glimpsed the stunningly beautiful Betsy at the front door as she watched me trying to catch a runaway car. She gave out a liver-shaking guffaw. She wasn't afraid of herself or of me. I knew I was going to marry her.

Betsy worked as a hospital administrator and supported us through my internship, but Tina was born on the first day of my psychiatric residency. While I was in academia in Atlanta and then in Denver, Betsy stayed home raising babies. I didn't work very hard and we didn't have much money. I bicycled home for lunch each day, played with the kids, refinished furniture, built things. Betsy did things for fun. She sang in an opera. She helped with Head Start programs at a local school. I wanted to save the world, and I was doing important research, but I didn't want that to interfere with my life, which was at home with Betsy and the kids. We were happy.

But back in Atlanta in the '60s, I was running an enormous mental health service. I was a big deal, and I was working myself to death. I neglected my kids and dumped everything on Betsy. She tried to get my attention, but I was overwhelmed by duty and my sense of my own importance.

By the time I burned out on my job of saving the world, Betsy had a bad case of cabin fever. She wanted to work, as the women in her family had always done. But more than that, she wanted our life to change. She was not going to raise the children alone while I dropped by to collapse. I realized I had two full-time careers going, one practicing psychiatry and one writing. I agreed to shelve the writing until the kids were grown. Betsy thought of going back to graduate school but decided we needed to work together rather than separately. We hired the calm, steady Susie to be at home with the kids, while Betsy and I opened a psychotherapy office near the house. We've worked together every day for the past twenty plus years.

I took over the jobs that could be scheduled: I did the cooking at home, and drove the morning carpool. Betsy handled the money, at home and at the office. A division of labor emerged. I'm the gardener, Betsy is the yardman. I build rose beds, plant roses, and spray them. Betsy fertilizes and prunes them, and brings me a vase of them each morning. I paint walls, Betsy does windows. I do plumbing and wiring, Betsy hangs wallpaper.

There's no gender basis for our division of labor. We both get to do what we like, and then we fight over what's left. The equality isn't in the schedule but in the attitude that the relationship takes top priority. It has been a highly communicative relationship, in fact a noisy one—we fight daily but neither of us tries very hard to win.

Ours is an equal relationship; we don't do much of anything unless we come to agreement about it. When I teach around the world, Betsy and I go together. I need her structure; I'm lost without her. She doesn't often get bored with hearing me talk, but she's good at entertaining herself when she does. The attention I get is sometimes hard on her; she fears I'll take myself seriously again. Mostly, she lives in the fear that I will say the wrong thing and bring shame and degradation on all of us. I do say the wrong thing often, and I embarrass myself, but no disasters have happened so far. I feel more bulletproof than she does.

I couldn't do what I do without her, and I can't imagine what would have become of me if I'd married a less secure woman, who expected to get her identity from me and saw me as the enemy anytime she was having a bad day.

Betsy is confident, outrageously sane, and raucously funny, and you always know exactly what she's thinking and what she's feeling. She laughs at my jokes and eats my cooking. I got bald right after we were married, and my little bow legs get scrawnier by the year, no matter how hard I exercise, so I'm no romantic hero. I'm no romantic anything. I'm sexy as hell, but I can't dance. Fortunately, she knows that I love her. And she does the amazing trick of reminding me I'm a fool while she makes me feel like a man.

TWELVE

Life as Father

Any fool with a dick can make a baby, but it takes a real man to raise a child.
　　　　　　　　—Larry Fishburne in *Boyz N the Hood*

In 1897, my great-grandmother died in childbirth, leaving behind five small children and a bewildered husband. Her family sent over a young woman to help with the kids, but my poor great-grandfather was so terrified of being a single parent that he married the selfish, ill-tempered woman, disastrously for all concerned. He took a job traveling and left the children with their despised new stepmother. My eight-year-old grandmother vowed she'd never be stuck with children to raise alone. She was determined to have her own career. At eighteen she broke off her engagement to a young doctor, and married my farmboy grandfather, who had promised her that if she would marry him, he would do all the cooking and would take primary responsibility for raising the children. He did, quite happily, and both my father and my aunt grew up to be enthusiastic parents, as have all their children.

A tradition of happy parenting can run in families, unless there is some curmudgeon like my great-grandfather who runs from the joys of creating and nurturing life. My great-grandfather had made four enormous errors: First, he thought that child raising was "women's work." Second, he thought it came naturally to women, so any woman could automatically do it better than any man could. Third, he thought that children who had mothers or stepmothers didn't need fathers. Fourth, he didn't realize that raising children is the greatest pleasure, challenge, and revelation life can offer. Fortunately for my family, my grandfather corrected his father-in-law's errors. Unfortunately, though, most men in our society never learn what my grandfather came to know:

Once a baby is weaned, there is absolutely nothing that needs to be done that can't be done just as well by a man as by a woman.

A man doesn't have to have all the answers—children will teach him how to parent them, and in the process will teach him everything he needs to know about life.

Fathering makes a man, whatever his standing in the eyes of the world, feel strong and good and important, just as he makes his child feel loved and valued.

Mercifully, parenting is not an efficient process—the old concept of "quality time" is a cruel cop-out. As a parent, he gets to hang out with his children, reliving the joys of his childhood. The play is the thing.

Becoming Father the Nurturer rather than just Father the Provider enables a man to fully feel and express his humanity and his masculinity. Fathering is the most masculine thing a man can do.

Fear of Fathering

There is a strangely pervasive fear of being a father. We might call it "patriphobia." Patriphobia takes a variety of forms. Adam left his wife and two small sons, giving them up for adoption. Benjamin is a bachelor, i.e., "a thing of beauty and a boy forever." He'll date a woman as long as she doesn't push him to actually marry her, settle down, and have children. Caleb started having affairs as soon as his wife was pregnant with their first child. Daniel went into an agitated depression and threatened to check himself into a psychiatric hospital unless his fiancée would have a abortion. Ephraim ran off with another woman while his wife was in the delivery room. When Francis's children were small, he got a job traveling and is rarely at home. Gabriel watches ballgames on television all night and plays golf all weekend while he leaves his children to be raised by their mother. Hosea had a vasectomy while still in his twenties. He married a woman with children, but treated them in such a way they opted to go live with their father. Isaac has children by each of his wives, and he's proud of them, but he doesn't attempt to live with them.

These men want to be their own pampered child, or that of some woman, but they don't want to grow up. They think they will have a happier life if they refuse to develop any further. A real child would be competition for him, and would expect him to become an adult. It isn't that these patriphobic guys are doing something so important, like finding a cure for AIDS or stopping the erosion of the ozone layer, that they can't be distracted by children; they have a full-time job not growing up.

The women and children from whom these men run may think they are at fault somehow, that men break their commitments to them because they aren't worthy of being part of the man's life. Actually, the problem with patriphobic men lies not with the women he escapes or the children he abandons but with his relationship with his own father, who left him with the feeling that being a father is a burden.

Those of us who raise children, our own children or other people's children, perfect children or badly damaged ones, are baffled by this. We know that raising children is the central experience of life, the greatest source of wisdom and self-awareness, the true fountain of pride and joy, the most eternal bond with a woman. We know that being a father is life's fullest expression of masculinity. Why would any man forgo all of this? I keep asking, and the answers I get are really quite sad.

Some men tell me that they sat around with the other guys back in their twenties and, over a few beers or joints, thought how much more fun they were having than their fathers, and how they didn't want to ever spoil it by becoming fathers themselves. They had no way of knowing that their fathers, at that very moment, were having an even better time thinking of their sons off somewhere, over a few beers or joints, philosophizing about the nature of life and feeling that familiar camaraderie of youth with the other guys.

These boys, at that age, somehow didn't understand what gave their fathers' lives meaning. The fathers had struggled to support a family and give their children advantages they themselves didn't have; the fathers had worried through sleepless nights trying to think of prayers or curses or charms that would protect their children from the dangers of life; the fathers had pumped hopes and dreams into children who willfully and expectably persisted in being who they were rather than who the fathers hoped they would be. But the fathers had failed to inspire the sons with an awareness of the rewards that returned to them from these emotional investments.

Other patriphobic men tell me how guilty they felt for

being so much trouble to their parents. They felt they put their parents through hell. (Do we all assume that in adolescence we were wilder than we really were?) Those who still identify with their adolescent rebelliousness may forget what a small, predictable, and actually rather funny blip that was in the flow of their lives. Yet these guys see themselves as destructive and unlovable, with nothing of value to pass on to their own children.

Still others remain angry with fathers who blew up, stayed away, or demanded too much. They fear they aren't perfect, either, and that they'll do the same thing their fathers did: raise children who feel toward them as they feel toward their abusive or neglecting fathers.

And, of course, the largest number of patriphobic men had fathers who ran away from fathering, too, leaving a family tradition of men too overwhelmed and ashamed to hang in there and learn what fathers get to learn.

These guys who fear becoming fathers don't understand that fathering is not something perfect men do, but something that perfects the man. The end product of childraising is not the child but the parent; the child on whom the parent has been practicing and learning how to be a human being must then go on and learn it for himself by practicing on his own children. That is the way it works. As parents, we must remember to be grateful to children for letting us practice peoplemaking skills on them. If we don't make our children aware of what the process was, and how it felt, and what we got out of it, they may opt to skip it themselves. They would deprive themselves of the most productive stage of their development, when in the process of childraising we examine and question everything we thought we knew about human development, about masculinity and femininity, and about the nature of the human condition.

Being a father, to our own children or to someone else's, or being something like a father—an uncle, a mentor, a coach, a teacher, a therapist—is the real way to become a man. We gain our masculinity not by waving it from flagpoles or measuring and testing it before cheering crowds but by teaching it to boys and girls, and to men and women who haven't known a man up close and don't know what men and masculinity are all about. If men would raise children, it would not only save the world in a generation or two, it would save them their lives.

Will this generation discover the healing power of fatherhood? As I look at the young men coming into manhood now, I see many patriphobic guys running from fathering, but I also see the ones who are willing to risk equality with a woman. They end up being hands-on fathers in a way that was rare in my generation and even rare among the baby boomers, who have seemed so patriphobically determined not to grow up and not to take on any experience that might lead them toward adulthood. My son and son-in-law and nephews are yearning for children, not just children to have but children to raise. They are not alone. I feel optimistic about the sort of fathering these guys will do. The trend is clear: the boys who got fathered want to be fathers, and the boys who didn't get it fear it.

Boys and Girls

> *You can have fun with a son, but you've got to be a father to a girl.*
> —Rodgers and Hammerstein, *Carousel*

What are children? Much of our attitude toward our child depends on what we consider to be their basic nature. We might see them as first blood-sucking and then milk-sucking parasites who draw their lives from us and give nothing in return. We might see them as repulsive: babies leak, and for a while everything that comes out of them is disgusting. But once babies begin to smile at us, to talk to us, to run to us, they become the sun and the moon and the stars—unless of course we believe they are "women's work," none of our affair until they are older, and meanwhile just our rival for a woman's affection.

Many men feel comfortable raising a son, but frightened of raising a daughter. In the Rodgers and Hammerstein musical *Carousel*, Billy Bigelow discovers his wife is pregnant, and sings about the joys of raising his son, but when he realizes he may have a daughter, he panics.

I have read that fathers of sons are less likely to divorce than fathers of daughters. Men may know they are emotionally important to their sons, yet not know that they are just as important to their daughters.

If a man is going to raise a daughter to be a strong, secure woman, he must both like and respect women. His daughter's self-esteem depends upon his attitude. If the father believes that women are limited in what they can do in life, that women are weak and need to be protected by men, that "girls' stuff" is foolish, then his daughter is likely to grow up feeling limited, weak, and foolish. To a large degree, her successes in life and in love are in his hands. As he raises his daughter a father may have to question everything he thought he knew about gender, about the differences between men and women.

Of course, there is no better way for a man to understand women than by raising his daughter, and then letting her teach him some things about gender as she goes through puberty. My daughters and nieces continue to do a thorough teaching job with me. If a father can overcome his need to control and protect women who don't need it, if he can hope that she enjoys her sexuality and her gender as much as he enjoys his own, and if he can grant her an equal right to conquer (or not conquer) the world as she sees fit, then he and his daughter can remain buddies for a lifetime, and he will finally understand the mysteries of womanhood.

Divorced Dads

> *Am I still Chelsea's father when she is not here?*
> —Kip Eastman, "Just Visiting," in *The Father's Book*,
> edited by Carol Kort and Ronnie Friedland

In our divorce orgy of the past few decades, men ran from home, believing they had nothing to give, believing they would find their heroism somewhere else. I wonder if all those men would have danced away from their marriages if they had known what effect it would have on their children. I wonder how many of them would have danced away if they had known what effect it would have on them.

We tried for a couple of decades to believe that children were too mature to need parents, that children were the real grown-ups. During those years of spiraling divorce rates, we believed firmly in the invulnerability of children. Children in the movies were exposed as demons from hell, like *Rosemary's Baby* (1968), *The Exorcist* (1973), and *The Omen* (1976). We distrusted them, thinking of them as willful adults parading as helpless children just to trap grown-ups and make them feel guilty. We tried to believe children could take care of themselves better than we could take care of them.

In 1975, in Martin Scorcese's *Alice Doesn't Live Here Anymore*, Ellen Burstyn's truckdriver husband dies, leaving her not only penniless but set free from a life in which she has never before made decisions for herself. She and her twelve-year-old son pull up stakes and head west, where Alice ends up working as a waitress, and having a series of awful encounters with awful men. At each turn, the little boy is wiser and more practical than the mother, and he's certainly far more mature and reliable than the men she meets along the way. She returns from work, flops on the couch, and tells her son her troubles as he massages her sore feet. They even swap confidences about their sex lives. And finally the perfect man appears and rescues them both.

There was a series of divorce pictures in those days, most of them silly comedies or teary melodramas, but a few tried to give us some insights on what we were doing to ourselves—notably Paul Mazursky's *An Unmarried Woman* in 1978 and Allan Parker-Bo Goldman's *Shoot the Moon* in 1982. In these topical films, the fathers would get into affairs and leave home, while their wives collapsed and their children would have to become the grown-ups in the household. As Michael Murphy walks out on Jill Clayburgh in *An Unmarried Woman*, he actually turns to her for sympathy. She angrily tells him that it is his job to tell his daughter what he intends to do, and then she leans against a street pole and vomits. The daughter takes over as the adult. After Murphy's affair runs its course, he tries to return home, but Clayburgh has grown stronger and no longer needs him. The daughter makes a few faces, but gets on with life quite maturely.

In *Shoot the Moon*, Diane Keaton discovers that her writer husband Albert Finney is having an affair. She confronts him, and they break a lot of dishes, but we know she has given up and lost the battle when she leans over and starts picking up the broken china. He walks out and she collapses, smoking a joint in the bathtub. Their twelve-year-old daughter takes over the household and the care of her three younger sisters. The girl refuses to speak to her father or accept his gift of a typewriter, and is furious with her mother for engaging in a one night reconciliation, and with her sisters for making peace with him. She is the voice of wisdom and maturity in this family in crisis, the one who sees clearly that the father is acting unacceptably.

Back then, we believed that divorce was temporarily disruptive but ultimately liberating for housebound wives, but was no sweat for children. After Judith Wallerstein's book, *Second Chances,* told us what we really knew all along but didn't want to admit—that divorce is a disaster for children—we could no longer pretend that the kids could breeze through a divorce and merely have a few bad years and then recover. We know now that the scars are permanent, and even if the child returns to functioning after a while, the divorce rate among children of divorce is several times higher than normal. We know better than to see the child as the adult in families that are dissolving.

UNCLE DAD

An article that shocked a lot of men (several patients tearfully brought me copies) was C. W. Smith's "Uncle Dad" in *Esquire,* March 1985: "Years ago I called a college buddy I hadn't heard from in a while. He had divorced his first wife but had remarried. I asked him how many kids he had now.

'Just the one.'

'One? I thought you had two.'

'Ah hell!' he snorted. 'You're thinking of the ones I had with Judy. They don't count.' "

Smith continues: "Maybe 'They don't count' meant that since he had botched that job, he could hope for a better grade on a new project, offer 'the one' as evidence of his reformation . . . When we feel our efforts produce only the frustration of impotence, then we cease trying . . . Most of the divorced fathers I know still hang on in some way despite the trouble and pain. We form a legion of what novelist Bryan Woolley has termed the Uncle Dads. Unlike travelling dads, we never will come 'home' to any welcome or to settle a quarrel or to hear an appeal, and our children gnaw on the suspicion that we've rejected them; unlike stepdads, we live in another house, or even in another city, perhaps with other children whom our 'real' children suspect are getting the best of our attention . . . we who have let our children live with the burden of guilt that makes judgment more difficult. When something goes wrong, we immediately go for our own jugular."

King is a big bruiser of a mechanic who intimidates everyone else but is putty in the hands of his children. His father was an alcoholic, who slept around behind his mother's back and finally left her. She committed suicide. King lived for a while with an aunt, but lived out most of his childhood in an orphanage. His father's new wife wouldn't let him live with them, since there was suicide in the family, and she didn't want him blowing his brains out, upsetting her children, and messing up the carpets. He swore he would never get a divorce.

King grew up, married Wilma, and had three children. He wasn't home much: he mostly bowled. But then his wife decided she was a lesbian, and he was an asshole, and she wanted him out. He panicked. Admittedly, he hadn't paid much attention to his children. But he'd done the thing he thought was most important: he hadn't gotten a divorce as his father had done. Wilma didn't care whether he got a divorce or not, as long as he left her alone.

Now King lives in a little apartment, and spends most of his time and energy with his kids. He won't divorce Wilma, so he can't marry his wonderfully nurturing girlfriend. He has anxiety attacks every time he gets close to getting a divorce, although his children beg him to face the reality, accept it, and move on for all of their sakes. They tell him that the marriage is dead, and the divorce is merely a legal, economic formality. But King knows firsthand the horrors of divorce, and he doesn't want his children feeling about him the way he still feels about his father.

I try to convince him that the disaster of divorce for children is not in the legal formalities, but in the conflict leading up to it, in the loss of security and stability, in the loss of the sense of the family, and above all in the loss of the father, who goes away, as his father did, and sets up a new life without his children, leaving the childraising to the beleaguered mother. So far, in the breakup of King's family, his children had gained, not lost, a father, and he, rather than losing a family, had actually gained one.

What King does understand is that his rediscovery of his children and of himself as a father had given him more security, more grounding, more sense of belonging in the world than any of his relationships with women, with friends, or with fun and games and work. He has caught on to the meaning of life, and now must figure out a way to still be a father, even after he is divorced.

The Fatherless Father

> "On my father's wedding day,
> no one was there
> to hold him. Noble loneliness
> held him. Since he never asked for pity
> his friends thought he
> was whole. Walking alone, he could carry it."
> —Robert Bly, "My Father's Wedding, 1924"
> from *The Man in the Black Coat Turns*

Men who didn't see their father's joy in fatherhood can only see fathering as an operation in which a child sucks the father's blood as surely as it sucks the mother's milk, requiring the father to work and save and come home at the end of the day to an exhausted woman, who has given all she's got to that bottomless pit of a baby, who uses up the life of the parents and gives nothing back.

Men whose fathers ran out on them—literally or emotionally—are likely to approach fatherhood with trepidation. In the movie version of Robert Anderson's play, *I Never Sang for My Father*, an aging father (Melvyn Douglas) and his middle-aged son (Gene Hackman) confront one another on the day of the mother's funeral. The son is staying with the old man, helping him get ready for bed. They talk about the old man's life. He was the son of a violent alcoholic, who ran out on the family. He has raised his younger siblings, and has gone through life feeling proud of himself for being a solid citizen, a good provider, and a stable family man, for being everything his father was not. Unfortunately, the old man offers no warmth, no vulnerability. He doesn't notice what his son senses so painfully: that he has gotten no joy from raising his children.

The son tells the father that he is planning to marry again and move away. The father feels betrayed and tries to make the younger man feel guilty for leaving him. The son confesses that he had never felt loved by the older man, and had never felt love for him, only admiration and respect, but he feels hope now that they will finally be able to sit in a room together and talk. With sympathy, affection, and great trepidation, the son invites the father to come live with him. The father refuses any help, announcing his credo: "I don't need anybody. I can take care of myself. I've always had to take care of myself. Who needs you? Out! I've lived my whole life so that I can look any man in the eye and tell him to go to hell!" That night, the son leaves the father's house forever.

The tragedy of the fatherless father is that no matter how hard and how successfully he tries to be unlike his own father, he has no models of how to be a man and a father, only how not to be, and he is not likely to guess correctly. In *I Never Sang for My Father*, the old man didn't know that his restrained dignity and state of invulnerable moral superiority—shields he had adorned in his battle with his own father—would also keep his son from getting close to him. By leading his life so that he could look "any man in the eye and tell him to go to hell," he might have bolstered his pride and his independence, but he took on a model of masculinity that did not let him give and receive love with his father or even with his own son. He had achieved the respectability and the stability his father could not achieve, but he couldn't let his son do something for him in return; he couldn't show his son that he needed and valued him.

We can feel love for the proud father's own pathetically alcoholic father, dying alone after a shamefully misspent life, and we can certainly feel love for the gentle grandson of this three-generational tragedy of fathering, but it is hard to love the father who is prepared to look us in the eye and tell us to go to hell—he cannot show us enough vulnerability to let us connect with the pain we see so clearly, but which he doesn't acknowledge at all. The father was quite happy being needed; but he couldn't need anything from another man, even from his son. There could be no give and take. Being fatherless himself, he didn't know that fathering gives as much to the father as to the child.

At the end, the son was thus left unanointed by his father, unable to be the man in the relationship, the one who has the strength and the wisdom to protect and comfort the father. There was a healing that could not take place, and both father and son lived out the rest of their lives in loneliness.

Healing Fathers

> "I am that father whom your boyhood lacked
> and suffered pain for lack of. I am he."
> Held back too long, the tears ran down his cheeks
> as he embraced his son . . . Then throwing
> his arms around this marvel of a father
> Telemakhos began to weep. Salt tears
> rose from the walls of longing in both men,
> and cries burst from both as keen and fluttering
> as those of the great taloned hawk.
>
> —Homer, *The Odyssey*,
> (Robert Fitzgerald translation)

The wells of longing in both fathers and son fill with tears and may drown the emotional life of any man who can't connect with his father or his son, who can't breach the generation gap, or the fear, or the anger, or just the determination to be able to tell any man to go to hell. But unless the connection is made, the man is left stranded, detached from the flow of history and from his own past or his own future, and dependent upon women for the love and intimacy of his life.

I spend my day with men like the Melvyn Douglas character in *I Never Sang For My Father*, who can't be fathers because they couldn't be sons. And I find men who have lost their fathers and men who have lost their sons who still find ways to become whole. Rather than go through life unanointed and unanointing, hiding their masculine shame behind women, trying to feel good by making other men feel bad, trying to hide the pain and loneliness they feel, they have found men to be their mentors, and they have found boys to father and to mentor. Men learn humanity from raising children. It is through fathering that men become fully men, able to give something back to others, rather than wasting their lives still trying to win the contests, seduce the women, control the situations that will make them feel man enough.

The most popular movie of 1991 was *Terminator II*, a noisy sci-fi hardware epic with Arnold Schwarzenegger as an android from the future, who comes back in time to blow up buildings, kill bad guys, and rescue a feisty little boy and his tough mother. The boy admonishes him not to use his power to kill people, and then gradually teaches this muscle machine about human love. When the machine must finally self-destruct, it is sad: it has gained from the child some sense of a life. It has become almost human. That happens to men who father children, their own or someone else's.

Here are the stories of some men I admire. They found in themselves the need to father, so they devoted themselves to it, in one way or another, and fathering gave their lives meaning.

Chris

One friend of mine, Chris, had a busy father who saw his function as economic. He lost everything in business, went into a depression, and committed suicide when Chris was not quite grown. Chris inherited his mother, his sister, and his father's debts. He found mentors among his uncles and bosses and in time had recouped the family fortunes and made himself quite rich. He was hard-nosed, unhappy, drinking too much, working on an ulcer, but doing what a man's supposed to do . . . even if it killed him.

He had married a loving but unstable woman. The couple had a houseful of children, but Chris had neglected them and exhausted himself in his struggle to recover what his father had lost. He was also failing to make his fragile wife feel loved. She was smoking marijuana constantly, and getting stranger and stranger; the older children were complaining about her bizarre and frightening behavior, and the youngest child was getting silent and withdrawn. Chris made the hard decision: he cashed in his business and retired, before he was forty, so he could spend more time with his family. His wife, who had blamed her weirdness on his absence, now blamed it on his presence. She deteriorated further and gradually drifted away from the family; first she joined a motorcycle gang and then a religious community. Gradually, they divorced. Chris devoted himself to raising his children, and as they grew older, to coaching their teams. When they no longer needed him full-time, he volunteered to coach sports teams where he could oversee the lives of other young men.

After all but the youngest of the children had finished school and gone off to spectacular successes in various fields, Chris remarried. His new wife had some difficulty understanding his closeness to his now grown children, who called him many times a day from various parts of the world, and still liked to sit in his lap. The gentle and beautiful youngest son, after years of anxious silence, showed talent as a writer, and a lifetime of emotion flowed out unashamed. Chris goes around finding lost boys and lost girls who need a little fathering, and can always recommend orthopedic surgeons for my accident-prone son. I call him St. Christopher, whom my mother considered the patron saint of fools, drunks, and travelers, always there to point the direction. He's a very happy man with a very well-spent life.

Doc

Doc is a thoracic surgeon, and he's also the strongest man in my health club. His father was a nice man with absolutely no interest in anything physical, and Doc was destined to be physical. He grew up in awe of my slightly older brother-in-law, Jimmy, a powerful athlete in his youth who became the gentlest of internists and the most noble of characters. Doc is a gentle giant, who loved having a mentor, and loves being one. Mostly he loved his children. His oldest son was eighteen and a senior in prep school when he was killed in a car wreck by a drunk young woman running a red light at midnight on New Year's Eve.

I described to Doc the last scene from *Tender Mercies*, in which Robert Duvall is a washed-up alcoholic country singer who has married a woman with a son whose father has been killed, and then he is reunited with his own daughter, and she is killed. Duvall returns from the funeral of his daughter and, while he is hoeing his cabbages, he tells his wife: "I don't know why I wandered out to this part of Texas, drunk, and you took me in and pitied me and helped me to straighten out, marry me . . . Why? Why did that happen? Is there a reason that happened, and Sonny's daddy died in the war . . . my daughter killed in an automobile accident . . . Why? You see, I don't trust happiness, I never did, I never will." Nothing more is said, but Duvall has noticed the miracle that he has lost his child and Sonny has lost his father and fate has somehow brought them together. He gives Sonny a football, and they go out into the field and start throwing the football back and forth, and the movie ends.

Doc didn't say much for a few months, and was rarely seen at the club, but he finally started working out again. And he began to gather around him young boys who sat at his knee and looked up to him as their mentor in physical fitness, in building the body of an athlete and the heart of a man. They must feel toward him the way he felt toward my brother-in-law. Of course, I feel that way about my brother-in-law too. This year, as usual, Doc and I spent New Year's Eve working out and talking about his son and my nephew.

The students at his son's boarding school contributed to a fund with which they built a pavilion in his son's memory. Doc spoke briefly to the student body assembled in the pavilion: he said, "Bud must be so happy with himself—to influence this many people that they named a building after him! I want you to know that you are loved just as much as Bud. Regardless of what you might feel or what might go on between you and your parents, you are the single most important thing in their lives. They are as proud of you as I am proud of my son Bud."

Doc saves men's lives for a living. His recreational mission is to make every boy feel loved. After my son Frank IV's accident, it was Doc who got him a job.

Roger

Roger was a wiry little fellow, nervous and jumpy, and sweating a lot. He looked as if his blood vessels were full of full-strength coffee—black. His wife Jessie said she'd been with him for fifteen years, and she had never seen him smile except when he was collapsing at the end of a race. The two of them worked together, traveling around the world selling toys. They could do just as well without the travel, but he couldn't imagine what he would do with all that time.

Roger's father was a joyless man who worked at a hardware store, and thought his son's interest in sports and games was frivolous. The old man had refused to leave the store to go to any of Roger's track meets in high school, and hadn't come to either of Roger's weddings. He didn't like parties or celebrations. Roger got out of there as quick as he could. But when his high school sweetheart showed up pregnant, he quit college, married her, and went to work for his father. They had a son, Jerry. Then one day he had the feeling of being trapped in a life like his father's. There were things he hadn't done, places he hadn't been, women he hadn't had. He left his complacent wife, gave up Jerry, had a vasectomy, and was off to see the world, to experience all the things his father had missed.

Fifteen years later, he thought of Jerry constantly, but he

thought he had done enough damage and Jerry would be better off without him. His friends, his father, and even a therapist told him that. I didn't know whether Jerry needed him or not, but Roger was disgusted with his pointless life of narcissism. He was tired of running, and he needed to be a father to someone. His steady wife Jessie understood, and they cried about it. They called Jerry.

Jerry, now seventeen and at odds with his stepfather, jumped at the chance to meet the father he had never known. They had a lot to talk about, a lot of explaining to do, but by the end of the first meeting, they were in each other's arms. Jerry is now living with his father, going to college, appreciating his father for coming to his rescue. Roger doesn't travel much anymore. Instead, he plays games and sports with Jerry. He smiles, and he doesn't shake anymore.

For the first time since he ran away from home to find a life different from his father's life, he is a happy man. The difference between his happy life and his father's unhappy one is that he puts his energy into fathering his son, rather than into pouting over the burden of a child.

My Life as a Father

> *I have heard more than one man describe the surging joy, the love beyond all anticipation, that came with his first sight of his offspring; and even for the most constitutionally blasé among us, such a memory calls up the word "miracle" with surprising regularity . . . But, in general, miracles need to be helped along.* —Harry Stein, *One of the Guys*

My life as a man began on July 5, 1961. That morning, I began my psychiatric residency, and that afternoon, Betsy gave birth to Tina, our first child. It was not only the happiest day of my life, but the most stabilizing. I was a father; I now existed as part of the succession of the generations. I was now a link in the biological and historical chain of human history. I was now connected not just to the past but to the future of the human race. On that day, at last, I was a man—even if I didn't yet know how to act like one.

Since that day, my most important job has been child raising. My raw material has been our three children, plus seven nieces and nephews who volunteered to varying degrees to let us take a hand in their raising. All ten have been more important to me than I have been to them.

Tina was my oldest, and I accepted her as the standard of perfection. I worshipped her, in much the way my Mother worshipped me. I never punished, or even criticized her. Tina says now that it scared her that I didn't find more faults in her to correct. She remembers how frightening it was for her when I sat back in awe of her, and assured her she was practically perfect in every way. She thinks she was eight at the time. Tina is now—to no one's surprise—a ringer for her mother, a comfortably competent person with amazingly good sense—and a husband to match. Appropriately she is a family therapist, and will have received her doctorate by the time you read this. Tina writes, too, and she and I write articles together.

I don't remember raising our youngest child, Ginger. She was born in Denver, when I was in academics and had plenty of time to hang out with my children. But by the time she was two, I was running the mental health services for Atlanta and was overwhelmed by my highly public position. I was in my early thirties, and was pretending to be strong and sure and masculine enough for the power I was wielding, but I was in an establishment position still working out some of my rebellious attitudes. I was still working out some conflict with my father, who hadn't gotten my mother the help she needed. I managed to be too aggressive, too abrasive, and I got into too many unnecessary political battles. Within a few years, I had changed the mental health delivery system, and had offended everyone who had authority over me. I was still the son, and not yet the father. I was neglecting my children, and the development of myself as a father, and therefore as a man.

I went into private practice. Betsy was working with me, but leaving the office in mid-afternoon to be there for Ginger. By the time I got home at night, Ginger had had all the parenting she could handle. In our neighborhood, by chance, all the children were just Ginger's age, and she went up the street to play and I don't think she came back until she was twelve.

I was just distracted for a little while, but Ginger had grown up horribly fast, and I missed it. So I tried to get to know her, and found it wasn't that easy. I knew then what my father had gone through when he got back from the war and couldn't make contact with me. I'm still working on it. I admire her enormously. She has my mother's startling beauty, but little of her grandmother's insecurity. She is a highly talented actress and singer, and I am her most eager audience. She's at home now, starring in local plays and going to graduate school to become a family therapist.

Frank, a year younger than Tina and four years older than Ginger, was the most challenging for me to raise. I'm sure most of the problem was my unsureness about my own masculinity, and my fear I wouldn't be man enough to raise a son. I thought I was supposed to *do* something to raise him into a man; whatever it was my father had failed to do for me, so I kept criticizing and driving him, looking for problems in him that I could then fix.

But also, Tina was my standard of perfection, and Frank wasn't just like Tina. I suppose I hoped that Frank would have my talents as automatically as he had my name. Instead he seemed more like my father, a great athlete and an omnicompetent person without my verbal preoccupations and my intellectual restlessness. He could memorize anything, and make good grades when he had to, but he wasn't a scholar like his cousin Jimmy in the same grade. Why not? I asked.

Frank looked much like my father. He was nothing that I was, but everything that I would have loved to have been. He had some inate ability to fix things and he always knew where everything in the house could be found. Girls were chasing him, and catching him, from the day he hit puberty. Mostly, he was an athlete. He was all-everything in running sports. He organized a team that won the state championship. He founded and coached a girls' running team. His name and his picture were in the paper every week for years. He was written about as a celebrity, and recalled as a legend.

I remember when he was in the eighth grade, and couldn't seem to pass history. I drilled him in it for hours, just on the difference between Vasco da Gama and Cabeza de Vaca. My frustration mounted, and he still couldn't make the distinction. But he got worried about my blood pressure, and talked me into going running with him to loosen up before we started in again. He had cleared a cross-country track that ran for miles along the creek behind our house. I ran with him, but after a mile and a half, I threw up and fell in the creek, and he carried me home.

As Frank grew older we fought, but in time he could overpower me. That scared us both. We went to therapy around one of his adolescent crises, in which I was, as usual, trying to fix someone who wasn't broken. The therapist asked me, "He's wonderful, and this is the way adolescents act. You know that. Why are you trying to perfect this normal, wonderful person, and stop him from growing up?" I realize now that I wasn't worried about whether Frank was OK, as much as I was worried about whether I was OK. The therapist, who knew me well, thought I was a bit much—too aggressive, too energetic, too *masculine*, so to speak. He gave me permission to cool down the show of macho bravado that had made me so obnoxious for so long. I got from him the one thing I had not gotten from my father, i.e., acknowledgment from a man that I was a man and could stop showing off about it.

I stopped trying to fake masculinity, and began to study it, and gradually came to realize that we all have many of the same experiences in our struggles with the masculine mystique, but we have been trained not to talk about it. At that point, I decided to go ahead and give Frank what I had never gotten from a man: I hugged and kissed him and loved him. He liked that, and feeling anointed by me, he explained to me what more he needed.

Frank said, "Dad, you always worry about me, and you try to tell me how to do things better, and it makes me nervous to know you're so worried. I can get good advice from my friends, my coaches and my teachers, and go to a therapist if I need to. What I need from you is just to be there, acting proud—that's important. Watch me, admire me, love me, but don't jump in unless you need to save my life. Otherwise, please don't do anything, just be there. Of course it might help if you would screw up from time to time so I could come to your rescue."

I think that was the secret: "Don't do anything, don't fix anything, just be there." It worked great, for him and for me. Once I stopped trying to fix him, all that I had put in him and all that he had inside himself began to emerge. The first thing we did was to take all that energy I'd directed at perfecting him and he'd directed at resisting me and channel it instead into something useful. We worked together building four rooms on the house.

Frank had been a professional triathlete until he was run over by a pickup truck while bicycling in South Carolina two years ago. He moved back home for more surgery on his mangled arm, his snapped ankle, and his cracked vertebrae. He is recovering. He is an accountant, with a nationwide practice of triathletes. He goes to graduate school, and, after seven operations, is beginning to run, swim, and bicycle competitively again. He is engaged to the bubbly Gaybie, who works with his Aunt Julie in the public relations office of the crippled children's hospital, and who fits right in with the family. She brings me barbecue and spicy sausage from her hometown down in the country.

Frank and I are very close, and work out together regularly. Frank becomes more like me all the time. Or maybe I become more like him. We're proud of one another. He is impressed with how much weight I can bench press. I'm impressed with his wit and diplomacy. He tells me in various ways what my father didn't tell me, and what I did finally tell him, that in his eyes I am a man and he is proud of me. Of course I was proud of my father, too, but I never told him.

After my nephew Pitt was killed, the family went out to a log cabin at the foot of Long's Peak, the highest mountain in Rocky Mountain National Park, a mountain Frank and I had climbed with Pitt. Tina, Frank, and Ginger, Pitt's brothers Paul and Harrison, his sister Virginia, his widow Shannon, and Betsy's niece Annie and her husband Jim climbed Long's Peak, and standing together on the top we told tales of Pitt. I felt physically whole and emotionally connected, and yet I could only think of my dead father. Would he approve of my efforts as a father and an uncle? One of the kids had been lost, but he'd gone down as a hero, and the others were winners, and more importantly were wonderful people. I knew Dad would approve. I knew he would anoint me. Dad has become a hero to me, and since I feel his approval, he is bolstering and good—but he still keeps me on my toes.

As I look back on my experience as both son and father, I see I had exaggerated expectations of my father, my son, and myself. I did better as nephew and as uncle, and as father to my daughters; there was less ego, less vulnerability in those relationships. My sense of myself as a man was not on the line. Without the anxiety, it was easier to make the "self-achieved submission" that is the soul of masculinity, of heroism, and of fathering.

Fearing I didn't have enough of it, I was in awe of masculinity. I thought my father had some magical power he wasn't passing on to me, a secret he hadn't told me. And then when I became the father, I thought I needed to do something or say something powerful and extraordinary as a father to my son, and I was so anxious about any shortcomings I found in him, I made life difficult for both of us. Frank became a man, not because my anxious hovering over him showed him the way but, at least in part, because he knew I loved him. He knew I respected his masculinity. And he made me proud of himself and of myself as men.

Postscript: As I've lived through my life as a man, I've learned the secrets of happiness. I pass them on to my kids, and I pass them on to you: forgive your parents, join the team, find some work and some play to do, get a partner to do it with, keep it equal, and raise children, wherever you find them.

Sources

BOOKS CITED:

Bly, Robert. "Fifty Males Sitting Together." In *The Man in the Black Coat Turns*. New York: Doubleday, 1981.

———. "My Father's Wedding, 1924." In *The Man in the Black Coat Turns*. New York: Doubleday, 1981.

———. *Iron John*. Reading: Addison-Wesley, 1990.

Campbell, Joseph. *The Hero With a Thousand Faces*. Princeton: Princeton, 1949.

———. *The Power of Myth*. New York: Doubleday, 1988.

Chesler, Phyllis. *About Men*. 1978.

Conrad, Joseph. *Lord Jim*. New York: Bantam Classics, 1981.

———. *Heart of Darkness*. New York: W. W. Norton Critical Edition Series, 1972.

Conroy, Pat. *The Great Santini*. Boston: Houghton-Mifflin, 1976.

———. *The Prince of Tides*. Boston: Houghton-Mifflin, 1986.

Cosby, Bill. *Fatherhood*. New York: Dolphin, 1986.

Demos, John. *Past, Present and Personal: The Family and the Life Course in American History*. Oxford: Oxford University Press, 1986.

Dickey, James. *Deliverance*. Boston: Houghton-Mifflin, 1970.

Dinnerstein, Dorothy. *The Mermaid and the Minotaur*. New York: Harper and Row, 1976.

Dumas, Alexandre. *The Three Musketeers*. New York: Bantam Classics, 1984.

Eastman, Kip. "Just Visiting." In *The Father's Book*, edited by Carol Kort and Ronnie Friedland. New York: G.K. Hall, 1986.

Eisler, Riane. *The Chalice and the Blade*. San Francisco: HarperCollins, 1987.

Farrell, Warren. *Why Men Are the Way They Are*. New York: McGraw-Hill, 1986.

Flaubert, Gustave. *Madame Bovary*. 1857. New York: Norton, 1965.

Fleming, Karl, and Anne Taylor. *The First Time*. New York: Simon and Schuster, 1975.

Fromm, Erich. *The Art of Loving*. New York: Harper, 1956.

Foucault, Michel. *The History of Sexuality*. New York: Random House, 1978.

Gilligan, Carol. *In a Different Voice*. Cambridge, Mass.: Harvard University Press, 1982.

Gilmore, David. *Manhood in the Making*. New Haven: Yale, 1990.

Grinker, Roy Sr. "Mentally healthy young men (Homoclites)." *Archives of General Psychiatry* 6, 27–75, 1962.

Hammerskjöld, Dag. *Markings*. New York: Ballantine, 1989.

Homer, *The Odyssey*. Translated by Robert Fitzgerald. New York: Doubleday, 1961.

Jones, Ernest. *The Life and Works of Sigmund Freud,* New York: Basic Books, 1953.

Kann, Mark. *On the Man Question*. Philadelphia: Temple, 1991.

Keen, Sam. *A Fire in the Belly*. New York: Bantam, 1991.

King, Billie Jean. *Billie Jean*. 1974.

Kipling, Rudyard. "Mother O'Mine." 1891.

Kundera, Milan. *The Unbearable Lightness of Being*. New York: Harper and Row, 1984.

Lawrence, D.H. *Sons and Lovers*. New York: Bantam, 1985.

———. *Women in Love*. New York: Penguin, 1976.

———. *Kangaroo*. New York: Penguin, 1980.

Leeming, David Abrams. *The World of Myth*. Oxford: Oxford University Press, 1990.

Lerner, Gerda. *The Creation of Patriarchy*. New York: Oxford University Press, 1986.

Machiavelli, Niccolo. *The Prince*. New York: Oxford University Press, 1984.

Mailer, Norman. *Cannibals and Christians*. 1966.

Malory, Sir Thomas. *Le Morte d'Arthur*. New York: Collier, 1986. Penguin, 1962.

Mead, Margaret. *Male and Female*. Westport, CT: Greenwood, 1977.

Melville, Herman. *Billy Budd*. New York: Penguin, 1986.

Moore, Robert, and Douglas Gillette. *King, Warrior, Magician, and Lover*. San Francisco: HarperCollins, 1990.

Napier, Augustus Y. "Heroism, Men and Marriage." *Journal of Marital and Family Therapy*, 17:1. Jan 1991.

Orwell, George. *Animal Farm*. New York: Signet Classics, 1974.

Paglia, Camille. *Sexual Personae*. New York: Vintage, 1991.

Pittman, Frank. "Bringing Up Father." *The Family Therapy Networker*, 12:3, May–June, 1988.

————. "The Masculine Mystique," *The Family Therapy Networker* 14:3, May–June, 1990.

————. *Private Lies: Infidelity and the Betrayal of Intimacy*. New York: W.W. Norton, 1989.

————. "The Secret Passions of Men." *Journal of Marital and Family Therapy*, 17:1, Jan 1991.

————. *Turning Points: Treating Families in Transition and Crisis*. New York: W. W. Norton, 1987.

Schoeck, Helmut. *Envy*. New York: Harcourt, Brace, and World, 1966.

Schwarzenegger, Arnold, and Douglas Kent Hall. *Arnold: The Education of a Bodybuilder*. New York: Simon and Schuster, 1977.

Shakespeare, William. *Henry V*. New York: Macmillan, 1961.

————. *Hamlet*. New York: Macmillan, 1961.

Smith, C.W. "Uncle Dad." in *Esquire*, March 1985.

Smith, Sydney. *Lady Holland's Memoir*, 1855.

Sophocles, *Phaedra*.

Stein, Harry. *One of the Guys*. New York: Pocket Books, 1988.

Tannen, Deborah. *You Just Don't Understand*. New York: Morrow, 1990.

Tarvis, Carol. *The Mismeasure of Woman*. New York: Simon and Schuster, 1992.

Thurber, James. *The Thurber Carnival*. New York: Harper, 1944.

Tiger, Lionel. *Men in Groups*. New York: Random House, 1969.

Turgenev, Ivan. *Fathers and Sons*, 1862. New York: Norton, 1989.

Twain, Mark. *The Adventures of Tom Sawyer*. New York: Bantam Classics, 1986.

Vanggaard, Thorkil. *Phallos*. New York: International Universities Press, 1972.

Walker, Barbara. *The Crone*. San Francisco: Harper and Row, 1985.

Wallerstein, Judith S., and Sandra Blakeslee. *Second Chances*. New York: Ticknor and Fields, 1989.

Weiss, Robert S. *Staying the Course*. New York: Macmillan, 1990.

Wolfe, Tom. *The Right Stuff*. New York: Farrar, Straus & Giroux, 1979.

————. *Bonfire of the Vanities*. New York: Farrar, Straus & Giroux, 1987.

FILMS CITED:

Alice Doesn't Live Here Anymore, Robert Getchell, 1975.
The Bad and the Beautiful, Charles Schnee, 1952.
Bambi, Walt Disney, from the book by Felix Salten, 1942.
The Best of Times, Ron Shelton, 1985.
Boy's Town, John Meehan and Dore Schary, 1938.
Boyz N the Hood, John Singleton, 1991.
Butch Cassidy and the Sundance Kid, Bo Goldman, 1969.

Captains Courageous, John Lee Mahin, Marc Connolly, Dale Van Every. From the novel by Rudyard Kipling, 1937.

Casablanca, Julius J. Epstein, 1942.

Chariots of Fire, Colin Welland, 1981.

Conan the Barbarian, John Milius and Oliver Stone, 1982.

Conquest, Samuel Hoffenstein, 1937.

Cousin, Cousine, Jean-Charles Tacchella, 1975.

Dances With Wolves, Michael Blake, 1990.

A Delicate Balance, Edward Albee, 1973.

Diner, Barry Levinson, 1982.

East of Eden, Paul Osborn. From the novel by John Steinbeck, 1955.

The Empire Strikes Back, Leigh Brackett and Lawrence Kasdan, 1980.

The Exorcist, William Peter Blatty, 1973.

A Fish Called Wanda, John Cleese and Charles Crichton, 1988.

Field of Dreams, Phil Alden Robinson, 1989.

Gentleman's Agreement, Moss Hart, 1947.

Giant, Fred Guiol and Ivan Moffat. From the novel by Edna Ferber, 1956.

The Godfather Trilogy, Mario Puzo and Francis Ford Coppola, 1972.

Gone With the Wind, Sidney Howard. From the novel by Margaret Mitchell, 1939.

The Graduate, Calder Willingham and Buck Henry, 1967.

The Grapes of Wrath, Nunnally Johnson. From the novel by John Steinbeck, 1940.

Grease, Bronte Woodard, 1978.

The Great Santini, Lewis John Carlino. From the novel by Pat Conroy, 1980.

Guess Who's Coming to Dinner, William Rose, 1967.

Gunfight at the O.K. Corral, Leon Uris, 1957.

The Homecoming, Harold Pinter, 1973.

I Never Sang for My Father, Robert Anderson, 1970.

In the Heat of the Night, Sterling Silliphant, 1967.

Indiana Jones and the Last Crusade, Jeffrey Boam, 1989.

Indiana Jones and the Temple of Doom, Willard Huyck and Gloria Katz, 1984.

Interiors, Woody Allen, 1978.

It's a Wonderful Life, Frances Goodrich, Albert Hackett, and Frank Capra, 1946.

JFK, Oliver Stone, 1991.

Kramer vs. Kramer, Robert Benton, 1979.

Life with Father, Donald Ogden Stewart. From the play by Howard Lindsay and Russel Crouse, 1947.

Lilies of the Field, James Poe, 1963.

The Lost Weekend, Charles Brackett and Billy Wilder, 1945.

Lust for Life, Norman Corwin. From the novel by Irving Stone, 1956.

The Man in the Gray Flannel Suit, Nunnally Johnson. From the novel by Sloan Wilson, 1956.

The Man Who Would Be King, John Huston and Gladys Hill. From the novel by Rudyard Kipling, 1975.

Marty, Paddy Chayevsky, 1955.

The Misfits, Arthur Miller, 1961.

Mr. Smith Goes to Washington, Sidney Buckman, 1939.

Mommie Dearest, Frank Yablans et al. From the book by Christina Crawford, 1981.

Monty Python and the Holy Grail, Graham Chapman, John Cleese, Terry Gilliam, Eric Idle, and Michael Palin, 1975.

Mutiny on the Bounty, Talbot Jennings et al, 1935.

My Life as a Dog, Lasse Hallstrom et al, 1985.

Nothing in Common, Rick Podell and Michael Preminger, 1986.

The Omen, David Seltzer, 1976.

On Golden Pond, Ernest Thompson, 1981.

A Patch of Blue, Elizabeth Kata, 1965.

The Philadelphia Story, Philip Barry, 1940.

Psycho, Joseph Stefano, 1960.

The Quiet Man, Frank S. Nugent, 1952.

Raiders of the Lost Ark, George Lucas and Phillip Kaufman, 1981.

Rambling Rose, Calder Willingham, 1991.

Rambo, Sylvester Stallone and James Cameron, 1985.

Rebel Without a Cause, Stewart Stern, 1955.

Red River, Borden Chase and Charles Schnee, 1948.

Return of the Jedi, Lawrence Kasdan and George Lucas, 1983.

Robin Hood: Prince of Thieves, Pen Densham and John Watson, 1991.

Rocky, Sylvester Stallone, 1976.

Roman Holiday, Ian McLellan Hunter and John Dighton, 1953.

Rosemary's Baby, Roman Polanski, 1968.

Saturday Night Fever, Norman Wexler, 1977.

The Searchers, Frank S. Nugent, 1956.

She Wore a Yellow Ribbon, Frank S. Nugent and Laurence Stallings, 1949.

Shenandoah, James Lee Barrett, 1965.

Shoot the Moon, Bo Goldman, 1982.

Sleeping With the Enemy, Ronald Bass, 1991.

The Slender Thread, Stirling Silliphant, 1965.

Snow White and the Seven Dwarfs, Ted Sears et al, 1937.

Sons and Lovers, Gavin Lambert and T.E.B. Clarke. From the novel by D.H. Lawrence, 1960.

Stand By Me, Raymond Gideon et al. From the novella by Steven King, 1986.

Star Wars, George Lucas, 1977.

Steel Magnolias, Robert Harling, 1989.

Tender Mercies, Horton Foote, 1983.

Terminator II: Judgment Day, James Cameron and William Wisher, 1991.

Terms of Endearment, James L. Brooks. From the novel by Larry McMurtry, 1983.

Thelma and Louise, Callie Khouri, 1991.

To Kill a Mockingbird, Horton Foote. From the novel by Harper Lee, 1962.

Top Gun, Jim Cash and Jack Epps, Jr., 1986.

To Sir, With Love, James Clavell, 1967.

An Unmarried Woman, Paul Mazursky, 1987.

The Untouchables, David Mamet, 1987.

Wayne's World, Michael Myers, Bonnie and Terry Turner, 1992.

When Harry Met Sally, Nora Ephron, 1990.

Who's Afraid of Virginia Woolf? Ernest Lehman. From the play by Edward Albee, 1966.

The Wild One, John Paxton, 1954.

The Witches of Eastwick, Michael Cristofer. From the novel by John Updike, 1987.

Women in Love, Larry Kramer. From the novel by D.H. Lawrence, 1969.

Yentl, Jack Rosenthal and Barbra Streisand. From the story by Isaac Bashevis Singer, 1983.

You Can't Take It with You, Robert Riskin. From the play by George S. Kaufman and Moss Hart, 1938.

Zorba the Greek, Michael Cacoyannis. From the novel by Nikos Kazantzakis, 1964.

INDEX

About the Author

Frank Pittman, M.D., is a psychiatrist and family therapist in Atlanta, Georgia. His revolutionary research on family therapy as an alternative to psychiatric hospitalization, conducted with Langsley and Kaplan in Denver in the mid-1960s, won awards from both the American Psychiatric Association and the American Family Therapy Association. In the late '60s and '70s, Pittman championed community mental health as he directed the public psychiatric services at Atlanta's Grady Hospital.

For the past twenty years, Pittman has been in private practice, teaching in the department of psychiatry at Emory University and in the department of psychology at Georgia State University, and doing workshops around the world.

Since 1983, he has written a regular movie review column for the *Family Therapy Networker*. Since 1991, he has written a monthly advice column for men in *New Woman* magazine.

He works and lives in Atlanta with Betsy, his wife of 33 years, and a steadily changing ménage of their grown children, nieces, and nephews.